# HELTER-SHELTER

## Security, Legality, and an Ethic of Care in an Emergency Shelter

*Helter-Shelter* is an ethnographic account of the manner in which an emergency shelter is governed on a daily basis, from the perspective of the personnel who are employed and tasked with providing care.

Prashan Ranasinghe examines how the founding ethos of the shelter, an ethic of care, is conceptualized and practised by focusing on its successes and failures. Ranasinghe reveals how this logic is diluted and adulterated because of two other important logics, security and legality, which take precedence and trump the import of care. The care that is deployed is heavily legalized and securitized and it is also administered inconsistently and idiosyncratically. As a result, disorder and confusion pervade the shelter.

*Helter-Shelter* offers a unique perspective on the delivery of care, and how this laudable objective is undermined by daunting challenges.

PRASHAN RANASINGHE is an associate professor in the Department of Criminology at the University of Ottawa.

PRASHAN RANASINGHE

# Helter-Shelter

## Security, Legality, and an Ethic of Care in an Emergency Shelter

UNIVERSITY OF TORONTO PRESS
Toronto Buffalo London

© University of Toronto Press 2017
Toronto Buffalo London
www.utppublishing.com

ISBN 978-1-4875-0261-4 (cloth)     ISBN 978-1-4875-2206-3 (paper)

Library and Archives Canada Cataloguing in Publication

Ranasinghe, Prashan, 1977–, author
Helter-shelter : security, legality, and an ethic of care in an
emergency shelter / Prashan Ranasinghe.

Includes bibliographical references and index.
ISBN 978-1-4875-0261-4 (cloth). – ISBN 978-1-4875-2206-3 (softcover)

1. Homeless persons – Care – Moral and ethical aspects.
2. Shelters for the homeless.  I. Title.

HV4493.R36 2017          362.5'92          C2017-903716-1

This book has been published with the help of a grant from the Federation
for the Humanities and Social Sciences, through the Awards to Scholarly
Publications Program, using funds provided by the Social Sciences and
Humanities Research Council of Canada.

University of Toronto Press acknowledges the financial assistance to its
publishing program of the Canada Council for the Arts and the Ontario Arts
Council, an agency of the Government of Ontario.

Canada Council      Conseil des Arts
for the Arts        du Canada

ONTARIO ARTS COUNCIL
CONSEIL DES ARTS DE L'ONTARIO
an Ontario government agency
un organisme du gouvernement de l'Ontario

Funded by the      Financé par le
Government         gouvernement
of Canada          du Canada

Canadä

# Contents

# Figures

# Acknowledgments

Writing this book has been both a challenging and rewarding experience. The journey began some six years ago when I commenced fieldwork – in fact, much long ago when I conceived of the project. Along this journey, many events have (re)shaped my life and strengthened me as a person. This book, in some ways, is representative of this.

This book would not have been possible without the help and generosity of a plethora of people, a few of whom need explicit mentioning. First, I am immensely grateful to the numerous persons in the shelter who freely gave their time and thoughts, both in relation to their professional and personal lives. I hope this book does some justice to the immensely important service emergency shelters serve in everyday life and the personnel who toil for low wages to make this happen. As well, I am grateful to Lisha Di Gioacchino for serving as a research assistant on the project. Many of the ideas developed in the book, I had the good fortune of discussing with others and revising because of these conversations. In particular, I am indebted to Steve Bittle and Randy Lippert who read a part of the manuscript and provided much needed suggestions and reassurances. Some of the ideas developed here borrow from previously published articles: "Discourse, Practice and the Production of the Polysemy of Security," *Theoretical Criminology* 17 (1) (2013): 89–107; "'Undoing' Gender and the Production of Insecurity and Fear," *British Journal of Criminology* 53 (5) (2013): 824–42; and "The Humdrum of Legality and the Ordering of an Ethic of Care," *Law and Society Review* 48 (4) (2014): 709–39. I benefited greatly from the "conversations" I had with editors and reviewers when working on these articles. Indeed, I benefited greatly from the two reviewers who read the manuscript, to whom I am greatly indebted. At the University of

Toronto Press, Douglas Hildebrand shepherded the book with guidance and support: he indeed made this an extremely smooth and pleasant experience. I am also indebted to the Faculty of Social Sciences, University of Ottawa, for financial support through its Publication Assistance Program which has helped defray some of the costs associated with preparing the index for the book.

Finally, and most importantly, I will forever be indebted to my family, an important source of love and support. Thus, to my parents and my brother, I owe very much. To my wife, who had to endure a hectic and largely irregular schedule, I cannot thank you enough.

In the midst of revising the book, I received some fantastic news about my professional career. That day, the first "person" I had the pleasure of "telling" this to was my dog. Sadly, however, within about two-and-one-half-months to that date, he needed to be euthanized, an incident that still haunts me (those who love dogs will understand this; those who do not will think I am "out to lunch"). Time is only too slowly healing these wounds. Most recently, the birth of my son – not yet three weeks old at the time I pen these thoughts – has gone a long way in alleviating this pain. He is indeed a blessing for this and numerous other reasons. As I sit to write these very thoughts, he has already interrupted me thrice, and this free time is only made possible because my wife is comforting him. To me, this book is a personal triumph and represents a victory over many struggles – Romans 8:31 and Psalm 91, indeed! In this vein, then, I dedicate this book to the many significances of November 14.

HELTER-SHELTER

Security, Legality, and an Ethic of Care
in an Emergency Shelter

# 1 Introduction

I had completed more than three-fourths of the time I would spend at the site where I was conducting fieldwork – an emergency shelter – when, one afternoon, an employee entered the front-desk area to speak with another employee. Upon noticing me, she said to me that she had been thinking about my work and had stumbled upon an apt title for it and the book that would emerge from it. This was not the first time I had received such suggestions. An employee whom I will refer to as "Captain Delight," for example, was never shy about offering his thoughts, and the phrases he provided were meant not only to capture the state of the site, but the plight of his life as well. A good example of this is "What a Life," a phrase meant to capture the decay that slowly but surely encompassed the site. Another was "What a JOB," the emphasis just as "Captain Delight" himself insisted on, which was meant to capture a feeling of hopelessness, this time from his perspective as an employee. As he bluntly put it: "I am wasting my life here."

I had always keenly listened to, even deeply thought about, the various phrases, labels, and titles provided to me by numerous employees. However, the one provided by this female employee, on this day, struck me and stuck with me. She suggested "Helter-Shelter," which I eventually chose as the title for this book. In using the phrase helter-shelter, the employee was loosely invoking the well-known and infamous phrase "helter-skelter"[1] to convey what she thought the order in the shelter looked and felt like.

At the very moment this phrase was uttered to me, I thought it succinctly captured everything I wished to convey about the order in, and of, the shelter. The usage of helter-shelter invokes the dictionary definition of helter-skelter, which can be traced to the sixteenth century.

The *Oxford English Dictionary* defines helter-skelter as a sense of chaos, disorder, and confusion, precisely the words I use to describe the feelings of order in the shelter, plainly visible both in the significant and humdrum. This is what I seek to narrate in what follows, and the title *Helter-Shelter* aptly captures this.[2]

This book explores and explicates how an emergency shelter for men is ordered on a daily basis; that is, the myriad strategies, techniques, and types of knowledge that form the basis upon which it is governed, both in thought and practice. My intention, as noted above, is to narrate what this order looks and feels like throughout a typical day in the shelter, and the processes through which this order comes to take hold of it.

The interest for such an inquiry can be traced to a curiosity about, even fascination with, space, in particular how different types of spaces give rise to different strategies and techniques of governing. These strategies and techniques themselves are products of space, one that constitutes people, behaviour, practices, and things – that is, the constitutive nature of space (Lefebvre [1974] 1991; Bachelard [1958] 1994; de Certeau [1980] 1984). More specifically, this work grows out of an interest in the relation between space and the governance of visible poverty and marginalized populations, both in contemporary and historical times (e.g., Ranasinghe, 2010a, 2010b, 2011, 2012a, 2012b, 2015; Ranasinghe and Valverde, 2006).

There currently exists a voluminous – and still heavily growing – literature on marginalized populations and visible poverty, in particular on the homeless and homelessness. It would not be hyperbolic to claim that virtually every conceivable aspect around homelessness has received, if not detailed attention, then at least passing consideration. Attention has been cast, among others, on the definition and quantification of homelessness (e.g., Berry, 2007; Burt, 1995; Rossi, 1989, 45–81); documenting the different types of homelessness, such as youth, family, female, and elderly homelessness (e.g., Karabanow, 2006; Klodawsky, 2006; Klodawsky, Aubry, and Farrell, 2006; Moore, McArthur, and Noble-Carr, 2011; O'Grady and Gaetz, 2004); explaining the causes or otherwise contributing factors to homelessness (e.g., Anderson and Christian, 2003; Dear and Wolch, 1987; Layton, 2000); understanding the effects of homelessness on the lives of the homeless, ranging from health and mortality, psychological well-being, and family relations to drug and alcohol addiction, as well as the myriad ways the homeless survive or negotiate the streets (e.g., Snow and Anderson, 1993; Casey, Goudie, and Reeve, 2008; Gaetz and O'Grady, 2002; Hagan and

McCarthy, 1997; Huey, 2007, 2012; Karabanow et al., 2010; Mitchell and Heynen, 2009; Walby and Lippert, 2012); explicating the relation between homelessness and crime, security, and myriad means of governance and regulation (e.g., Fischer et al., 2008; Gaetz, 2004; Hagan and McCarthy, 1997; Huey, 2007, 2012; Martell, 1991; Tyler and Beal, 2010; Walby and Lippert, 2012); and the relation between homelessness and mental illness (e.g., Benbow, Forchuk, and Ray, 2011; Pearson and Linz, 2011; Ponce et al., 2012). These examples reveal the extant literature as rich, detailed, and virtually exhaustive.

This book focuses on a specific aspect of visible poverty, namely, emergency shelters. Emergency shelters – commonly referred to as homeless shelters, though this label, as will become apparent, is not without serious problems – have received attention in inquiries about visible poverty and homelessness. However, the extant literature has significant lacunae. One pertinent issue is that the inquiry itself is marginalized and largely occupies a peripheral place in visible poverty and homelessness scholarship – in fact, some inquiries focus not specifically on emergency shelters themselves, but on a variety of housing types, including shelters for abused women (e.g., Loseke, 1992). More pressingly, however, these discussions of emergency shelters are narrated through the lens or perspective of the visibly poor, that is, the "clients" of these shelters and how and why they come to these sites and how they perceive and experience them (e.g., Glasser, 1988; Ferrill, 1991; Williams, 2003; Connolly, 2000; Desjarlais, 1997). Despite emanating from a rich ethnographic tradition and offering sophisticated, detailed, and insightful analyses of emergency shelters, unsurprisingly given the above, these inquiries are limited because they are largely one-sided. What they fail to explore and reveal is the life of the emergency shelter from the perspectives of the personnel who work in these sites, that is, the service providers. There are some exceptions. Scott Seider (2010), for example, discusses how undergraduate students at Harvard University run and operate a homeless shelter, the Harvard Square Homeless Shelter, during the academic year. Lisa Ferrill's (1991) discussion of a homeless shelter for women is narrated from the perspective of her tenure as a manager. Similarly, Vincent Lyon-Callo (2004) examines the "interconnections between homelessness and housed people through a focus on the homeless sheltering industry" (20; see also Rae Bridgman's [2003] interesting ethnography). Acknowledging the pressing lacunae at hand, this book is intended as a remedy, even if only as an initial step in this direction.

I claim that to meaningfully understand the ordering of an emergency shelter – what it is, what it stands for, and how it puts its ethos into practice – it is necessary to explore and examine it from the perspective of those who provide services, both those who write its policies and those charged with delivering services. How important this is, is evinced in the extant literature that tends to paint the life of (and in) the shelter as largely harmonious, comprised of unity and mutual accord. For example, although Donileen Loseke (1992) takes pains to explain how the employees at a battered women's shelter reproduce the ethos of the shelter at the expense of the diversity of the battered women and their lived experiences – "workers continued to transform the heterogeneity among clients into the homogeneity of the battered woman type of person and in so doing ... gave themselves a warrant and mandate to act toward these women in particular ways" (94), which, in turn, "was a way for workers to justify their interventions into clients' lives and ... make sense of the *practice* of shelter work" (117; emphasis in original) – it appears as if this practice was performed uniformly and harmoniously. In fact, even in the rare instances where conflicts and tensions are brought to light, these are largely glossed over (e.g., Seider, 2010; Connolly, 2000). Thus, although Seider (2010) mentions disagreements among service providers at the Harvard Square Homeless Shelter – ranging from whether whole or skim milk should be served to the inconsistent application of the rules (196–200, 212) – for the most part, the students are presented as a unified group. Unpacking the conflicts, tensions, and disagreements among service providers, I suggest, provides an important perspective into the make-up and ordering of the shelter.

## Ordering an Ethic of Care

Broadly conceived, an emergency shelter is premised with welfare in mind (e.g., Seider, 2010, Glasser, 1988; Friedman, 1994; Conradson, 2003; Karabanow, 2002). Its ethos, in other words, is an ethic of care. Conceptually, care, as Carol Thomas (1993) explains, can be rather ambiguous, often giving rise to "a partial and fragmented picture ..." (649). Nel Noddings (1984), however, in a clear and definitive attempt to articulate this concept, ties an ethic of care to morality in claiming that citizens are (or, at least, should be) morally disposed to embrace a caring attitude as opposed to an attitude of indifference or, at worst, hostility. Humanity, in other words, is morally obligated to care, an argument made by others as well (e.g., Held, 2006; Robinson, 2011; Slote, 2007). In making sense of care, two important and related elements need consideration. First, the (pre)conditions upon which care is delivered and received, including the relationship between the caregiver and receiver. Thus, with respect to the former, emotions such as "compassion," "sympathy," and "empathy" are precursors that may produce a desire, even a need, *to* care (Clark, 1987; Held, 2006; Slote, 2007), while other issues ranging from financial pressures to mental distress may form the need *for* care. The rules around the "sympathy etiquette" (Clark, 1987) is a good example of the need to account for and make sense of the bases upon which care is provided, and the relationship between the caregiver and receiver. The second element of care is the substance that comprises care, that is, how caring is provided and what it involves. Examples can take the form of material goods, such as money or food, as well as non-material products, such as time spent with someone. Given these two related elements, and drawing and relying upon the word ethics – as an injunction, grounded upon moral principles, to act (see Noddings, 1984; Held, 2006; Robinson, 2011; Slote, 2007) – I utilize the term "ethic of care" to refer to the provision of myriad services, ranging, for example, from the essentials of life (such as food and shelter, clothing, and medical treatment) to miscellaneous services (such as treatment for drug and alcohol addictions or aid in securing employment or welfare, encompassing both material and non-material goods). All this, I claim, is grounded upon and buttressed by a moral commitment, and thus, desire, to serve and help those in need. This desire – in some instances, the lack thereof – emanates from, and is sustained by, a plethora of emotions ranging from pity, compassion, empathy, and sympathy to apathy, anger, and resentment (see Held, 2006, 10, 157).

Particularly germane to what follows is the (supposedly) explicitly and overtly gendered nature of the caregiving relationship. "Caring, however defined," Thomas (1993) writes, "is a *predominantly female activity*" (651; emphasis added). This point is made forcefully by others as well, leading to a reading of an ethic of care as feminist (see Gilligan, 1982; Noddings, 1984; Held, 2006; Robinson, 2011). This is largely because "'femininity,'" as Virginia Held (2006, 16) notes, "constructs women as carers." Although this conclusion (or presumption) is not without debate (see Slote, 2007), it is pertinent given the particular gender dynamic at hand between the employees and clients, namely, an exclusively male clientele served by both male and female employees. In other words, how care is conceptualized and administered is heavily dependent upon the engendering of a gendered relationship in a space that is itself highly gendered. What results is an ethic of care that is, unsurprisingly, gendered, the ramifications of which are profound.

This book explores and explicates the travels and travails of an ethic of care in the daily life of the shelter as it is conceptualized and practised. I argue that despite the laudable, even noble, intention that grounds the mandate of the shelter – the provision of care – the ethic of care is, ultimately, severely adulterated. This is because two other important – and, on paper, supposedly secondary – logics interact with an ethic of care, and take precedence over it. These are the logics of security and legality. Thus, the ethos of the shelter, premised upon an ethic of care, is translated into an ethic of and about security and legality, so that the ethic of care becomes one that is highly, and inherently, securitized and legalized. This adulteration makes the provision of care not simply difficult, but profoundly impossible because of the messiness, ranging from idiosyncrasy to inconsistency, that characterizes – in fact, constitutes – it.

### The Logics of Security and Legality vis-à-vis an Ethic of Care

A contiguous relationship – one of apposition rather than opposition – between security and legality works in tandem to severely adulterate an ethic of care. Conceptually, care is influenced and shaped by the environment of the shelter, which is heavily securitized. The preoccupation with securitizing the shelter is driven by a legal obligation to so do. Thus, an image of security is cast upon the entire shelter. The quest for securitization and its image of security, therefore, tend to trump an ethic of care. The result is that what an ethic of care is, ought to be, and *can be* is inextricably linked to security.

Specifically, what exactly security is – and, by extension, ought to be – is unsettled and disagreed upon among the key actors in charge of conceptualizing and delivering care. In this conflict, one axis of the problem is illuminated. For management, the concept of security is defined narrowly as an issue of physical safety involving violence and bodily harm. This is often referred to as "primary safety" – "the basic physical safety of oneself and one's loved ones" (Valverde, 2001, 84); it is also referred to as the "pure safety conception" (Waldron, 2006, 461), or that which closely parallels what Anthony Giddens (1984, 50) calls "ontological security." The employees, as well, take violence and bodily harm very seriously. However, for the most part, a plethora of other issues, ranging from poor remuneration and a lack of job security to stress and health concerns (relating, for example, to bed bugs and having to deal with other dangerous or unclean materials) are all translated into a discourse of security and treated as such. In this translation, these issues take precedence over violence and bodily harm. Thus, a term such as "human security" – in reference to the "welfare of ordinary people" broadly conceived (Paris, 2001, 87; see also Zedner, 2009, 39–44) – rather than primary safety, best captures the ways the employees conceptualize security and practise it. Thus, a marked and palpable disjuncture – between an overtly narrow and precisely constructed concept of security and a broad notion of it – lays the groundwork for a profound and significant struggle over security, creating the site of struggle that security is. It is in this site – both literally (a physical place and space) and figuratively (a conceptual terrain) – that an ethic of care is rendered problematic.

The preoccupation over primary safety is a product of an overly legalized environment that clearly and unequivocally spells out the tenor of what security ought to look and feel like. Management, clearly "obsessed with security" (Zedner, 2009, 1), draws upon and utilizes a strategy of "governing through security" to achieve its obligations. By "governing through security," I refer to the ways that numerous areas of public life are subsumed under the concerns over security (Valverde, 2001, 89–90; see also Simon, 2007), leading to what is referred to as a "security society" (Zedner, 2003b, 156) or "security state" (Hallsworth and Lea, 2011). Interestingly, it is the very logic of "governing through security" – one legally mandated and facilitated – that permits the employees to translate myriad issues that ostensibly might not necessarily be security concerns into issues of security. This is one aspect of the problem.

The other aspect of the problem, briefly alluded to, is the *place* of legality in the ordering of the shelter, in particular the relation between legality and an ethic of care. By legality I refer to two related things, both crucially important to making sense of the term. First, the official and (often) codified norms – for example, those found in legislation or rules – that clearly state the tenor of the shelter, and are, therefore, paramount to the production of order. Two normative systems order the shelter. Provincial legislation and by-laws of the city constitute one aspect. These norms detail the foundation on which shelters are formed and the provision of care is conceptualized and delivered. The second – the focus of this work – are the myriad in-house rules and regulations, some codified, others not, that are equally, if not more, important to the daily ordering of the shelter. These rules seek to capture, mimic, represent, and deliver an ethic of care, and it is in this attempt that light is shone on the place of legality in the ordering of the shelter and the inherent problems that constitute the conceptualization and provision of care.

The second aspect of legality concerns the ways the rules of the shelter, both formal and informal – codified and un-codified – are thought about, made sense of, and put (or not put) into practice by actors. This is one aspect of what is referred to as legal consciousness. There is a voluminous – in fact, a disparate and rather contentious – literature on legal consciousness that need not occupy focus here (Silbey, 2005; Ewick and Silbey, 2016, provide good overviews, including problems with the concept; see also Ranasinghe, 2010b, 2014, for practical applications). For present purposes, legal consciousness can be understood as a term that "broadly denote[s] thoughts, feelings, and behaviors with respect to the law" (Levine and Mellema, 2001, 173). This includes the ways actors *do not* think about the law, that is, what Laura Nielson (2000) claims concerns "the assumption[s] ... about law that are simply taken for granted" (1059), and the processes by which actors come to so think, be, and act. In sum, legal consciousness can be understood as the way the institutional power of law is sustained over time and space (see Ewick and Silbey, 2016). The ways that actors think about law is a crucial aspect to this.

The manner in which an ethic of care is adulterated by legality unfolds as follows. At least facially, the in-house rules of the shelter are treated reverentially: they are seen as the source upon which order is founded; in fact, the rules themselves are seen as order. In this sense, the shelter functions as many others where law and order takes precedence in everyday life (e.g., Stark, 1994, 555–6; Wharton, 1989, 59; Glasser, 1988, 69; Williams, 2003, 9–11, 67; see also Bridgman, 2003, 4). Yet, and importantly, this reverence is more apparent than real. On the one hand, management wholeheartedly vouches for the import of rules, explicitly and unequivocally stating that rules equal order. On the other hand, the employees wholeheartedly believe that the strict and consistent enforcement of the letter of the law cannot – and *should not* – be practised. This is because of what they see as an important limitation of the law, namely, its constitution. That is, the binary logic upon which the law is founded, constructed, and operates – essentially a reductionism between legal and illegal (see Luhmann, 1989; Teubner,

1989; Bourdieu, 1987, 832) – makes it impossible to meaningfully conceptualize and administer an ethic of care. This is because the ethic of care, as it is conceptualized, made sense of, and practised in the shelter, is not uniform or singular, but polysemic. In other words, different employees conceptualize and make sense of it in different ways. Thus, an ethic of care cannot be reduced to a binary logic as the rules of the shelter are. The two remain fundamentally incompatible and incommensurate, certainly in form and, as a result, in substance as well.

What results, thus, is that the rules are either wholeheartedly disobeyed or circumvented in part by the employees. The order in, and ordering of, the shelter, in other words, operates and exists outside or beyond the rules in the same ways, for example, that the cattle owners whom Robert Ellickson (1991) studied settled disputes extra-legally, or the businessmen whom Stewart Macaulay (1963) observed conducted their businesses outside the formalities and guarantees provided by contracts – the list is vast, perhaps the classic example being a couple who does not invoke the law during separation (Mnookin and Kornhauser, 1979). The ordering of, and order in, the shelter via extra-legal strategies splinters management and employees leading to significant problems in the daily life of the shelter.

Although the extra-legality that governs the shelter is partly responsible for confounding the order in it, what is more pressing is that the tool of extra-legality is itself without consistency. In other words, the rules that are either disobeyed or circumvented are done so in such an inconsistent, ad hoc, and idiosyncratic manner that the result is confusion and disorder not just among the management team, but also among the employees, the very group responsible for rule violation.

In one sense, none of this is, nor should be – indeed, cannot be – surprising. Given that the ethic of care is polysemic, and different employees have different, even competing, views and beliefs about what care is and means, it is only commonsensical that rule violation or circumvention should also – and thus *will* – take place in an eclectic fashion without recourse to consistency. Consistency, in other words, cannot be the norm or expectation and, therefore, rule violation or circumvention will also be multifaceted. Thus, each employee will break or circumvent the rules depending on his/her belief of what ought to be done to ensure that care is effectively deployed. What results, thus, is chaos, one characterized by confusion and disorder, and the care that is administered is, at best, idiosyncratic and inconsistent.

The disorder and confusion that constitute the order in (and of) the shelter I call administrative chaos because these problems are a product of, and further magnified by, legality (in the dual sense that I use the term). The very effort to order the shelter via a system of rules only makes matters worse – evinced, for example, by the paranoia about primary safety and the never ceasing quest to securitize the space of the shelter, itself, it should be recalled, a requirement produced by the law. A system of law, then, in this space and in these circumstances, cannot – and, as I argue, *should not* – serve as a solution to the problem of order because it acts as a significant hindrance to the fundamental ethos of the shelter, that is, an ethic of care. This much the employees appear to understand very well, though, and, ironically, their effort to counteract it through a system of extra-legality only creates further disorder and confusion. This, in turn, leads to even more problems when management seeks to rectify these matters. The problem, as it unfolds daily within the walls of the shelter, then, is a spiral of confusion and disorder, and, administratively so, one that severely adulterates the ethic of care, leaving it substantively idiosyncratic and inconsistent. This is the order in (and of) the shelter, that is, helter-shelter.

The *Oxford English Dictionary* defines "chaos" as complete disorder and confusion. The word "chaos" – and, more broadly, the phrase "administrative chaos" – is employed in a very specific sense for a specific reason. As noted at the outset, it is precisely these sorts of descriptors (i.e., disorder and confusion) that aptly capture what the tenor of the shelter looks, feels, and even sounds like on an everyday basis. In this sense, the word chaos is meant to evoke two distinct yet related feelings, impressions, and imaginations, both germane to the everyday life of the shelter. On the one hand, chaos – and the chaotic – is represented and illuminated in what is easily or plainly visible, that is, palpable. Thus, the spillage of blood, a not so infrequent occurrence, is one example of the palpability of chaos: it is not simply what blood represents, but the fallout of what blood means logistically that underscores the chaos that envelops the shelter. Other examples also abound. One is found in the daily sounds – in fact, noises – of the shelter, where yelling and screaming, often replete with profanity, take hold of everyday life; similarly, threats of physical assault or verbal abuse levelled by clients against other clients or against employees also palpably illuminate the chaos in the shelter. This, as noted above, is one way chaos takes hold of the shelter. There is another as well, a manner that while routine and ubiquitous is far from palpable and vivid. That is, the humdrum and mundane also shines light on the chaos that constitutes the daily life of the shelter. Thus, and to take related examples, in the very silences of (and in) the shelter – epitomized in clients who are sitting quietly or sleeping – the chaotic nature of the shelter, rather ironically, is illuminated. As well, basic and routine questions posed by clients and fielded by employees, far from belligerent or comprised of bellowing and without any pretensions of violence or threats, in fact, being quite amicable in spirit, also brightly shine light on the chaotic nature of the shelter and the interactions between the two parties.

Although it is probably not controversial to claim that blood, belligerent behaviour, or bellowing sounds can be read as evidence of chaos, my intention is to suggest, somewhat polemically, that a similar state of chaos is ever present even when things look orderly on the surface. That is, I contend that on a deeper level, the humdrum and mundane reveal the profound sense of chaos that is part and parcel of the shelter. In fact, it is my contention that it is precisely here that the shelter is severely disordered, and it is this, more than anything else, that jeopardizes the ethic of care. Thus, while it would be remiss to claim that "complete" disorder and confusion envelop the shelter, it is reasonable to claim that the tenor of the shelter is mostly disorderly and constituted by confusion, among other problems. This, as noted above, is evinced not just in the palpable, but also – and more importantly – in the humdrum and mundane. Thus, to pay heed to this and ensure that light is shone upon it, I utilize the word chaos – and, the phrase administrative chaos – to capture the tenor of the shelter.

**The Big Picture**

Although a key subject of this book concerns visible poverty, and although it is most plausible that many (even most) of the clients of the shelter are homeless – an ambiguous term in its own right (see Rossi, 1989, 10–13, 45–81; Rossi, 1994, 344–5; Hopper, 2003, 15–25; Takahashi, 1996, 292–3; Bridgman, 2003, 25) – in the broadest sense, this is not a book about homelessness or the homeless per se and is not intended to be read in such a light (or, at least, not only in this light). To put this differently, the site of study, an emergency shelter for men, might be one that is frequented and occupied by the homeless. However, the primary focus of the book is upon the ethos that constitutes the shelter – an ethic of care – and its travels and travails in the daily ordering of this site; that is, the processes by which it is produced and reproduced, and the effects it has upon other logics and vice versa. In the strict sense – and, as alluded to at the outset when the interest for, and history of, this work was noted, albeit briefly – this is a book about space, in particular about how space, as a discursive construct (see Ranasinghe, 2013c), takes things, subjects, and their behaviours into its purview and about what unfolds from such an appropriation, even expropriation.

To claim that space appropriates, even expropriates, is to state something that has now been repeated *ad nauseam*, namely, that space is constitutive; space, in other words, has constitutive power bringing everything into its ambit. Henri Lefebvre ([1974] 1991), for example, repeatedly states this in *The Production of Space*, perhaps best evinced in the pithy statement, "To change life ... we must change space" (190). Fredric Jameson (1984) ties the birth of postmodernism to a concern about space and writes "that our daily life ... [is] dominated by categories of space" (64). Similarly, Michel de Certeau ([1980] 1984) writes that "spatial practices ... structure the determining conditions of social life" (96). Even Michel Foucault ([1976] 1980), who was admonished for failing to account for space in his work, specifically geography, admitted, though somewhat later, that "space is fundamental in any form of communal life; space is fundamental in any exercise of power" (252; see also Foucault 1984).

Presupposing the constitutive nature of space, this work examines how the space of the shelter produces and reproduces an ethic of care, which, in turn, reproduces the space of the shelter and the ways that different logics, namely, security and legality, play a pivotal role in this (re)production. In so doing, I treat space as "a set of relations between things" (Lefebvre [1974] 1991, 87). That is, and following the distinction carved by de Certeau ([1980] 1984), I subscribe to the view that "space is a practiced place," and by place I refer to a particular site, a site which locates and orders things and people in a particular manner – that is, for something to be in one place means that it cannot simultaneously be in another (117). Thus, while I speak of the site of the shelter (place), I focus upon its discursive and material (re)productions (space) and its relationship to an ethic of care.

As much as this work draws from spatial theory, it also draws from the sociology of law,[3] specifically, the notion of the extra-legal and legal consciousness. This work pays homage and contributes to both literatures, a reflection of the eclecticism within which this inquiry, both in form and substance, is situated (a detailed description of the methodology, including the research site, is found in the appendix).

## Organization of the Book

Chapter 2 begins with a discussion of the *place* of the shelter in relation to its city, locating it in historical and contemporary times. This provides important context for the shelter in relation to the city and the ethic of care. Chapter 2 also discusses the term ethic of care through the words of the personnel working in the shelter in order to paint a picture of what an ethic of care looks and feels like to them. In chapter 3, I examine the materiality of the shelter and explicate how an ethic of care is underwritten into the material structure of the shelter, both the mobile and immobile. This endeavour further illustrates what an ethic of care looks and feels like beyond discursive constructions. In particular, I explore the relation between comfort and an ethic of care, and illustrate the boundaries or limits within which comfort can – and must – exist and operate if a particular conceptualization of order is to be created and maintained. Then, in chapter 4, I examine key personnel in the shelter, namely, the clients, front-line employees, and caseworkers, with the latter two groups occupying the bulk of my discussion. Through an examination of the work lives of front-line employees and caseworkers, I explore how the ethic of care is represented and illuminated in both the significant and humdrum; the ethic of care, I suggest, has a specific look and feel to it that verges on the jocular and ridiculous. What results is that the vision of what an ethic of care is and should be as it is conceptualized by management and written into policy is vastly and palpably different from what it is on the ground level.

Chapters 5 and 6 work in tandem to tackle security. Chapter 5 discusses security as a site of struggle and explicates this struggle in relation to an ethic of care. Chapter 6 discusses the gendered nature of security and the production of fear and illustrates how this gendering contributes to an ethic of care that, itself, is gendered. This, I claim, has profound implications not just for the ordering of the shelter, but for the conceptualization and deployment of care as well. These chapters illuminate how the logic of security – driven because of, and thus sustained by, legality – begins to take precedence over an ethic of care so that the care that is provided is not simply heavily securitized, but securitized in a heavily gendered manner as well.

Chapters 7 and 8 also work in tandem to illustrate how legality, the other important logic that governs the ordering of the shelter, plays an important role in the adulteration of an ethic of care. Chapter 7 examines the place of legality – specifically the rules themselves – in relation to this order, and then explicates why order through a system of rules is bound to be problematic and fail. I also narrate the administrative chaos that constitutes the ordering of (and in) the shelter. Chapter 8 further explores the place of rules by examining the manner in which the mundane and ridiculous also characterize not just the rules, but also knowledge of and about them and their application. The focus of this chapter is to further expound upon the disorder and confusion that is part and parcel of the shelter. In the concluding chapter, I explicate the place of rules in ordering a site that is premised upon care and argue that a system that is built upon rigidity is likely to give rise to chaos.

# 2 Locating the Shelter, Locating an Ethic of Care

## The Shelter: The Past and the Present

The emergency shelter under consideration here is a large municipally run shelter. It receives a substantial portion of its budget from the city and province. In addition, fundraising activities and charitable donations are also part of its operating budget. As noted in the introduction, the shelter offers services solely to men. There is one exception to this rule: each weekday, between 3:00 and 3:30 p.m., the shelter offers a meal to anyone in the "community" who is in need of one. The shelter has about 120 beds: 90 on the second floor and 30 in the basement, in what is referred to as an "overflow" section (this section was being phased out during the twilight of my study).

From the perspective of many senior members of the management team, there is simply one way to make sense of the history of the shelter: it was instrumental in the formation and, later, the development and growth of the city. Originally premised upon a Christian ethic, the shelter was, according to Rob, a senior member of management, who discussed its history at length, "mostly church-based, doing community outreach ..." and providing for the visibly poor and down-and-out, mainly immigrants from England and Ireland.[1] The large number of immigrants was not necessarily a concern about poverty, but about the need to house them, especially those who were brought in as (semi) skilled workers. Thus, while the governors of the shelter admitted, according to Rob, that "there is a need for social programs ..." there was also a recognition for the "need for affordable-type rooms for the migrant workers that were [brought] in to create, to help build, the city ... [because] people that are [sic] [in the] skilled trades were coming to town to work but had nowhere [to live] ... There was no housing capacity for them."

The foregoing should not be read as a history of the shelter or of the city. Rather, its purpose is to introduce how the shelter was (and, as will be apparent, is) conceived of by the personnel working in it, one undergirded by an ethic of care. For these persons, the shelter, both instrumentally and symbolically, was significant to the formation and progress of the city; that is, but for the shelter, the city would not be what (and where) it is today. In this picturing, what is visible is that the function of the shelter, as conceived during its inception and early days, was tied to the provision of services derived directly from an ethic of care: the shelter's "mission *has always* been to be in service to the poor, to the less fortunate" (emphasis added), Rob stated. However, the shelter was premised upon much more than the delivery of care, especially of the charitable kind.[2] In its early days, charitable service did not encompass the key work of the shelter. It was, rather, designed for the growth of the city as a whole: the shelter provided a key plank in the development of the city by housing and feeding workers. In that sense, it was not simply a place for the poor; it was *the site* upon which the development and growth of the city was founded and unfolded.

It is true that these workers were poor. Nels Anderson's (1923) discussion of the American hobos of the early twentieth century, for example, vividly describes how they lived hand to mouth travelling from city to city in search of employment. They were, however, not homeless in the ways homelessness is thought about today – as ambiguous as that term is (see Rossi, 1989, 10–13, 45–81; Hopper, 2003, 15–25). Yet the different manner in which the clientele of the past and present are viewed has important ramifications and implications for the delivery of care. According to Rob, during its early days, close to 90 per cent of the clientele of the shelter paid for their lodgings (similar to the travellers described by Anderson). "Ninety per cent [were] self-payers," Rob noted, "who needed a cheap room to stay while they worked in the city, and some of them maybe even went home on the weekends or couple of times a year ... or, when the construction went down [read: ended], they went home." This narrative not only paints the clientele of the past as different from those of today – they were *not* homeless by any stretch of the imagination, and actually had a place of their own to call home – but the function of the shelter and the means by which it was funded were vastly different as well. The shelter, in its early days, was a self-sufficient, fully functioning place of abode where hard-working men building the city stayed, but, and crucially so, only on a temporary basis. This was also the case well into the mid-twentieth century. Rob continued his narrative as such: "Move forward, then, into the ... First World War [and] Second World War, after each one there was a building spurt that took place here, again in the city, and most of those jobs went to ex-service men ... who were given a first crack at jobs." The result, he stated, was that "again, it was about a 90 to10 per cent split, where 90 per cent [of the clients] were payers and 10 per cent were indigent folks."

There is a palpable change in the perception of the personnel at the shelter concerning what has been unfolding since the early 1980s, especially with respect to the large government cut-backs and the deinstitutionalization movement (see Layton, 2000; Dear and Wolch, 1987). From the standpoint of management, this is not simply pitiful, but, more pertinently, problematic to the daily ordering of the shelter. "One of the biggest changes that moved and shaped our services was when ... mental health went to [a] community-based model, and that was thirty years ago," Rob stated. This deinstitutionalization movement, he continued, created a "paradigm shift" where "folks were moved out of ... mental health institutions and moved back into the community, and [they] immediately gravitated to places like the shelter because they ... had people that they already knew, they were warm and safe versus ... having to deal with landlords and being out on the street ... So we became the *de facto* mental health institutions [*sic*]." This shift created two related problems as well, both still affecting the daily ordering of the shelter. First, it changed the very nature of service. As Rob put it, "We weren't just providing 'three hots and a cot,' as we used to call it. I mean, with a migrant worker ... he wanted three square meals a day and a nice warm bed to be in. Now a mental health person wants that too, but because of the other complications in their lives they also need a whole bunch of other services." To make matters worse, an additional problem emerged. It became increasingly difficult to fund these services because "we started moving from ... self-payers to more and more people becoming indigent or becoming homeless to the point where about the mid-[1980s] ... we had flip-flopped completely the other way. We [now] had 90 per cent [of the] people who couldn't pay and 10 per cent of people who were actually paying their own way."

In commenting about – and, for good measure, underscoring – the current state of things at the shelter, Rob added: "And that's basically the state that we are in now. Only it is even less than 10 per cent. It is only about 1 or 2 per cent right now." Thus, according to him, the concept of the shelter, in about 100 years, has shifted drastically, "from being a cheap place to be able to pay for a stay, to more or less being *the* social safety net" (emphasis added), essentially functioning as the "dumping ground for human refuse," as Kim Hopper (2003) soberly puts it (80; see also Culhane, 1992, 431; Culhane, 1996, for similar descriptions).

As perceived by the personnel working in the shelter, the emergency shelter of today is not what it was in the past, both in concept and practice. This change, however, is not simply a change over time, in the ways, for example, that numerous institutions undergo. Rather, a fundamental shift to its very core has taken place. The shelter of the past was primarily about housing workers – that is, those who were employed and, by extension, employ*able* – and, in so being, paved the way for the building and progression of the city. Accordingly, the city and the shelter went (perhaps go) hand in hand: the history of one cannot be narrated without the other. Today, however, the shelter has become, as Rob claimed, "the social safety net" that every kind of poverty-related issue is funnelled into and through. It is in this sense that an ethic of care that constitutes the mandate of the shelter must be understood, because it is an ethic that is very different from what it was in the past. Thus, the *place* of the shelter, both in relation to the city and an ethic of care, must be understood as such: it is now not about city-building nor its development, but, rather, about its management (cf. Culhane, 1992, 429; Hopper, 2003, 26); in particular, it seeks to maintain a particular aesthetic of order and peace – both within and without – so that the consumptive ethic that constitutes the life of the urban dweller and suburbanite alike can be put into the limelight, cherished, and safeguarded (see Ranasinghe, 2011). An examination of the location of the shelter reveals one important aspect of its place in the contemporary city.

### The Shelter and the Conspicuous Consumption of (and in) the City

At first glance, there is nothing peculiar about the building that houses the shelter, nothing, that is, that particularly stands out. In some ways, it is easy to miss the building that is (almost cosily) nestled among the hustle and bustle and infrastructure of the "Centre Square"[3] (hereinafter, the Square), and largely dwarfed by the high-rise buildings that surround it. A closer look, however, quickly reveals that it is a building that does not belong where it is – it stands out as an eyesore of sorts, something illustrative of the drastically changing times of the city and the place of the shelter in it. It is interesting to underscore that the site of the shelter was handpicked by its governors, in consultation with the city, precisely because it was in a prime location that allowed workers easy access to and from work. Thus, according to Rob, when the city was in consultation with the governors of the shelter, they were told that this is "*our* [the city's] *preferred location* for you to come, and you tell us what it is that you can do [for us]" (emphasis added). A hundred years later, perhaps not surprisingly, the very site where ground was broken to spearhead the development and progression of the city is now the very site that is said to pose myriad concerns to its well-being. In other words, where the shelter was once responsible for the progress of the city, it is now responsible for the management of the very problems that are a product of its own existence. This is an irony not lost on many employees, evinced in the comments of a caseworker: "I think, unfortunately, some of the things the shelter do[es] is hide the elements. Some people we just can't help. So *we just take them in and hide them from everybody else*" (emphasis added; cf. Culhane, 1992, 1996; Hopper, 2003, 26, 80; Snow and Anderson, 1987, 1339).

The shelter, as alluded to, is located amid the hustle and bustle of, and in, the Square. The Square attracts both locals and tourists alike. It is full of restaurants, bars, nightclubs, and residential units, inclusive of condominiums, as well as hotels, and caters to a variety of shopping and other leisurely activities. The Square is the emblem of conspicuous consumption at its best, paraded to see and enjoy, feeding the incessant desires, even addictions, of an unquenchable and unimaginable consumptive ethic (cf. Bauman, 2007; Featherstone, 2007; Hannigan, 1998; Zukin, 2004). Among, and commingling with, the diversity of these activities and people, is a palpable desperation and despair visibly manifested in the poverty in – though not necessarily *of* – the area. This is largely because in close proximity to the Square are several large shelters serving the visibly poor, inclusive of the one under consideration here. Thus, it is not surprising that the Square attracts a large number of indigent persons seeking any sort of assistance they can receive from the generosity – perhaps naivety – of passersby. These shelters, as can be appreciated, play an important role in the everyday ordering of life in the city. In this sense, however, part of the problem is the shelter system itself, in particular, the locations of these shelters. Thus, the shelter and its daily operations must be understood from this vantage. While, on the one hand, the shelter is purposed to care for and serve the needs of the visible poor, on the other, it is most mindful that part of this task entails a careful shielding, both aesthetically and auditorily, of visible poverty and the poor – what David Snow and Leon Anderson (1987, 1339) call a "superfluous population" who have become the "collateral casualties of consumerism" or the "flawed consumers," to use two of Zygmunt Bauman's (2007) phrases (122–5, 56, 99) – from a public on the go, eager to spend and consume, sit and relax. As I explicate below, however, this is a task the shelter drastically fails at, largely because the order of its internal space requires at least some dysfunction and disorder to be cast upon the outside world, aptly evinced in the visible poverty that permeates the Square.

Daily, the personnel in the shelter are called to justify not simply the *siting* of the shelter, but its very *place* in the ordering of the city as well. "So that's why ...," Rob stated, "when people go on to us about, 'well you're in the ... [Square] [and], therefore, you're *drawing* the homeless,'" he will often respond emphatically with a "No!" and for good measure highlight the history of the shelter, as he did when we spoke: "The homeless, or the prerequisite [read, precursor] to the homeless ... was ... the working class ... the transient worker ... [who] was here because ... this was the area of the city [that] was being built and established" – in the same ways that Hopper (2003, 16) notes that "one period's 'vagrant' ... may be another's 'Tramp,' only to show up later as 'migrant worker.'" Rob's intentions are clear: he wants to carve out a space for the place of the shelter, one which requires a historicization of its constitution. Yet his emphatic "No!," for all the vigour with which it is uttered, cannot mask the fact that, if not directly, then at least indirectly, shelters "draw" the visibly poor given their location – if they did not, they would lack their ontological essence and cease to exist. This conundrum, along with many others, he and his colleagues are forced to attend to daily. Thus, despite its rather inconspicuous look at first glance, the shelter stands out vividly and glaringly.

## A Look at the Shelter

The shelter is housed in a three-storey brick building, and is, for the most part, in good condition. However, in relation to the surrounding buildings, that is, the new(er) high-rise condominiums, the building looks severely dilapidated. This is the first sign that the building does not belong in the area. The entrance to the shelter is situated on a major arterial road directly opposite a condominium. Walking along this street in the vicinity of the shelter, the visual gaze of the passerby is immediately confronted by the heavy concourse of men hovering around the entrance of the shelter and its nearby surroundings, including the opposite side of the shelter where the condominium is sited (the magnitude of this concourse is more palpable during the summer when the weather is more conducive to such gatherings). Often, on Friday and Saturday nights, many clients, both young and old alike, would, while smoking cigarettes, watch bar and club patrons as they move to and from their sites of consumption. This is an especially keen exercise in the late hours of the night and into the early hours of the morning when revellers walk – or stagger – past these men, providing the men with a modicum of respite from their otherwise dreary lives. These young revellers, however, more interested in getting to their cars, hailing taxis, or looking for something to eat, appear to take very little notice of the clients and their gawking eyes – yet another sign of the palpable divide between the world of the shelter and its clientele, and everything and everyone else on the outside.

This, however, and somewhat unfortunately for the ordering of the shelter, is not always the case: the shelter, its clients, and their activities pose numerous concerns to many residents and visitors alike. The summer is particularly problematic or, at least gives such a feeling, where an aura of chaos seems to take hold of the front entrance and its surrounding vicinity. In many ways, the scene is quite vivid and glaring. Often, one finds anywhere from about 30 to 50 (sometimes more) men of all ages, dishevelled, raggedly attired – the bare chest is a commonality – usually drunk, sometimes on crack cocaine, loudly conversing with, even berating, each other with incessant profanities and other vulgarities. The air is often filled with a thick layer of smoke from the voluminous cigarette consumption that makes even standing around a sickening experience. Very early in my study, while observing what was unfolding in the area, I listened to what can only be labelled as an outcry from a security guard who told me that the smoke was making it very difficult for him to perform his job of standing outside on guard for eight hours per shift – within a week or so he was no longer on such duty, possibly after requesting a transfer.

If these sights and sounds are not enough to raise the ire of residents and visitors, the nearby drug transactions (the buying, selling, and consumption mostly of marijuana or crack cocaine), unfolding daily and somewhat incessantly, give the impression that the area lacks even a modicum of order – in the vein of the predictions of "broken windows" (Wilson and Kelling, 1982, 1989), it was believed that things would only get worse. This was particularly distressing to the residents in the nearby condominium complex, one sharing the same arterial road the shelter is located on. What was particularly disconcerting to them was that these transactions were taking place very near the property of the complex, sometimes on it as well. A parapet wall, about six feet in height, which separated the condominium from the rest of the commerce in the area, perfectly shielded those who bought, sold, and consumed drugs – or, at least, so they thought. What they were unaware of – or simply uncaring about – was that from numerous other angles, including from up above, these transactions were plainly visible to the naked eye. This issue became a very serious point of contention – and acrimony – between the residents of the condominium and the management of the shelter. Respite only arrived when the wall was torn down by the condominium. This provided some relief to the condominium residents, but not necessarily to the area as a whole, since the drug trade simply moved to a parking lot across the street – to a lot, ironically, that bordered an entire wall of the shelter, so it appeared that the shelter itself was, in some way, complicit in such activities. This, unsurprisingly, posed even more concerns to management, including one particular supervisor, who was keenly invested in surveilling those engaging in such activities. In what can only be described as a hilarious incident, several employees once loudly mocked this supervisor who was so engaged – which they referred to as "recognizances" – when the supervisor was hiding in the chapel and looking out through a window to try to catch those buying and selling drugs. It was not so much that they were minimizing the problem itself that was laughable but that, as they saw it, the supervisor's actions, while laudable, were insufficient to even put a dent into the vastness of this problem.

The foregoing narrates the place of the shelter – its location and daily routine – in relation to the order of the city, one posing numerous concerns to myriad parties. From the outside, the shelter and its surroundings look disorderly at best, dangerous at worst, and raised serious concerns – even ire – for a variety of reasons ranging from aesthetics to the olfactory and the auditory. Primarily, these were concerns about the visibility of poverty and the bodies of such poverty as they traversed the spaces of the Square. This, while being a considerable concern to the order of the shelter, would pale in comparison to what was unfolding inside, as I explicate in the next chapter, and would have even graver implications to the conceptualization and deployment of care. Prior to so doing, however, it is propitious to explore and explicate the ethic of care that constitutes the shelter and the myriad ways it is conceptualized and made sense of by the personnel working there.

## The Shelter and the Ethic of Care

The shelter, as noted, is constituted by an ethic of care (Noddings, 1984; Held, 2006; Robinson, 2011; Slote, 2007; Thomas, 1993). Based on the meaning of the word ethics – as an injunction, grounded upon moral principles, to act – I use the term ethic of care to refer to the provision of myriad services, ranging from the essentials of life (e.g., food, shelter, and clothing) to miscellaneous services (e.g., treatment for drug and alcohol addictions), all of which is grounded upon and buttressed by a moral commitment, and thus, desire, to serve and help those in need. As Rob explained, the purpose of the shelter "has always been to ... be in service to the poor, to the less fortunate." In what follows, I unpack this term through the words of the personnel who work in the shelter.

As the foregoing suggests, one aspect of an ethic of care is helping those who are in need, in other words, to be in service to this group. This was clearly and explicitly mentioned by virtually all those working in the shelter, who saw it as their ethical duty to serve and help. "Well, *basically, we're here to help* people get back on their feet" (emphasis added), a senior manager stated. A supervisor echoed this sentiment in detail when it was explained that the purpose of the shelter is to aid "a person who's down on his luck or disadvantaged [get] back up on his feet with a foundation underneath him so that if they fall again they know where they can [go to] pick themselves up." Such views were unwaveringly shared by the employees also. "*Our first priority*," an employee stated, "*is to help people* and we know ... [that] we are here to help the homeless population" (emphasis added). Another employee similarly stated that the "shelter ... what it is supposed to do, is ... to help the homeless people." Elizabeth went even further by noting that the shelter "is a place where *anyone* can walk in for help" (emphasis added), an invitation that is, theoretically at least, open to anyone and everyone. Two commonalities underpin the beliefs of both management and the employees. First, the purpose of the shelter is defined clearly and explicitly as being about the provision of help, that is, helping those who are in need. Second, and related, the provision of help is defined not as an auxiliary function, but the primary one, occupying the "first priority" as the above quoted employee put it. This is best evinced in the reflection of an employee, who stated: "If we are here to really help the ... [clients] and we are not helping them, then that kind of defeats our purpose as ... [an] organization or as our role as an employee to help the ... people [who] are suffering." These statements, thus, locate the element of help (and helping) as the defining feature of the ethic of care (cf. Slote, 2007), one which serves as the primary objective both at the institutional and individual levels.

The provision of help necessitates that the shelter be "service oriented," as one employee put it, that is, and as a supervisor commented, "to provide resources," and, importantly, to do so continuously and consistently. As the same supervisor noted, "The building never closes," a comment which captures the ever present nature of help available to the clients, its veracity, however, as will be apparent later, is certainly debatable. That is, and put simply through the words of a caseworker, "essentially," the shelter "provide[s] a service." There is a wide range of services provided by the shelter. A caseworker, for example, explained that "there are many purposes to the shelter," and noted that "it is an emergency roof to one who does not have ... a roof. [As well], it serves as a place to feed the hungry and poor." What the caseworker alludes to concerns the basic necessities of life. As one employee put it: "We are supposed to be offering *the bare essentials* that help them stay alive and somewhat comfortable enough ... to put their lives back on track" (emphasis added). Another employee echoed this point as such: "The role of the shelter ... its purpose, is to ensure that we welcome everyone off the streets by providing them the basics that would make them generally comfortable." This notion of comfort, referred to by these employees, is profoundly important to both the conceptualization of an ethic of care and the daily ordering of the shelter, and it will form an important part of the discussion to follow. For present purposes, I simply underscore that the delivery of myriad services, especially the "bare essentials," is a crucial part of the provision of help.

It is important to stress that the employees, both front-line workers and caseworkers, are cognizant of what it means to provide help. They clearly understand that helping has important limitations and can only be stretched to a point – this view is also shared by management, but vocalized "loudly" and lucidly in these ways by the employees, perhaps because it is they, rather than their employers, who see these limitations firsthand. They, therefore, understand that it is important to set clear, rigid, and realistic expectations in regards to what can be

expected and achieved, and work within the constraints of the shelter system. "A lot of it," a caseworker commented in referring to the
provision of services and the problems associated with it, "has to do
with seeing the client[s] [for] where they are [currently], and not seeing
where they would be" – this also means the employees must distance
their own desires and visions for what they feel is best for the clients
when so providing services. There are several reasons for this stance,
but, in the main, the caseworker is hinting at the very limitations of the
shelter system itself. In other words, the provision of help, to be effective and, most importantly, pure and unadulterated – that is, help for
its own sake or help as an end in its own right – must take the client as
he exists in that very moment in which he has entered the shelter, complete with all his faults and limitations without any pretence of what
it could offer and afford him in the future. "I do think in some cases,"
the same caseworker continued, the shelter is "a Band-Aid. *We don't
fix things. We can help ... We can guide*. But we are not the ones fixing. It
is up to the individual" (emphasis added). In constructing the issue as
such, the caseworker explicitly locates the possibility of success, or lack
thereof, with the client, not the service provider, a practice visible with
many social service providers (e.g., Lindsey, 1998, 169; DeWard and
Moe, 2010, 122–4; Williams, 2003, 4). Hopper (2003), for example, writes
of the service providers he observed as being "in a peculiar bind, at
once agents and victims of a singularly desolate set of circumstances"
(96), a comment that captures these service providers' realization of the
limits of what they can and cannot accomplish.

Other employees relied on the distinction between "saving" and
"helping" to make the same point. As one employee put it:

> In this job, you cannot save nobody [*sic*]. You can *help*, but *you cannot save
> them* ... Let's say they needed a place to stay or something, "Okay, let me
> give you the resources to do it," but if that person doesn't want you to do
> it, you can't ... I find so many social field people ... [who] think they can
> save them. *You can't play God*. (emphases added)

Another employee similarly explained: "To a large extent ... the shelter is out there to help, but it will only help if, and only if, they [the
clients] make [read, take] that first step ... seeking that help ... We can't
shove it down their throats."

In these explanations, these employees are clearly and explicitly stating that the clients bear, if not all, then most of the responsibility to not

simply want the help that is offered, but also utilize it in a meaningful manner. What this means – perhaps based on their experiences, both first-hand and through the stories they have heard, imbibed, and made their own – is that they are somewhat, if not severely, jaded about the system. Help, as they see it, while an end in its own right – and, a pure form of an ethic of care (cf. Slote, 2007) – is rendered a mere means to an end, a means, rather unfortunately, that simply provides the basic necessities without much chance of meaningful change. In other words, the shelter system, its clients, and employees are caught in a system that repeatedly reproduces the same problems. The employees very clearly see and understand this – evinced in the comments of the case-worker who opined that it is necessary to see and, most importantly, accept, the client as he is, in that very moment, a type of wisdom that embraces and focuses on the present, not the future. In other words, help is provided on the grounds of ameliorating the present, without necessarily an anticipation of, or even an expectation about, what tran-spires next. This, as I explain later, is partly responsible for the ways the employees think about and make sense of the ethic of care and the ways they conduct their work lives. In what follows, I probe this further by exploring the myriad ways the employees think about and make sense of the clients.

## On the Limitations and Effects of the Shelter System

Although there is no doubt that many employees strongly believe that the problem lies with the clients, they also believe the shelter system is partly responsible because it coddles clients – ironically, as I explore throughout this work, this same sentiment is held by the management, who, however, believes it is the employees who are responsible for this coddling, especially the ways rules are bent to provide favours. While I use the word "coddle"' to mean to be overly protective, in the man-ner of a swathe, I underscore that this is mostly an unintended conse-quence of the shelter system. The employees claim that this coddling leads to dependency, which is difficult – even impossible – to shed. To make matters worse, employees also have to address the fallout of a culture of dependency. All this only compounds the difficulties related to ordering the shelter and deploying care.

Perhaps the best example of how coddled the employees believe the clients are is found in the numerous expectations the clients have, vir-tually all of which the employees – and the shelter itself – are simply unable to provide, a commonality in many shelters as well (e.g., Seider, 2010, 206). In other words, the expectations of the clients have ballooned to such proportions, often verging on the ridiculous, that they are often disappointed with what they receive – beyond disappointment, resentment is also a common feeling shared by both parties. A good example is the food provided to clients – discussed in greater detail in the next chapter. Simply put, and for many reasons, the clients are unhappy with what they are provided. On this matter, one employee noted, "I find that they are very spoiled," and added that in the country where she was born – a third world nation – "when you are hungry, you [are] hungry," a statement that suggests that even the, supposedly, insipid food provided to these clients will not – indeed, cannot – be an option to the poor in her country. Similarly, "Captain Delight," also speaking about his homeland – another third world country – and its ravaging poverty, commented, "they don't feed you for free."

What severely irritates some employees is that the food, while largely unhealthy, is nevertheless plentiful. For these employees, entry into a shelter is evidence of need, which means that one has little or no choice. Thus, to expect food of a particular type is unreasonable. This is precisely why, for example, an employee rather sardonically commented: "Some of these guys really think they are in a hotel," and explained that often she would have to tell the clients, "we don't really offer that kind of service here." Another employee raised the same point, stating: "Some people don't understand that they are in a shelter; what you get is what you get." In other words, like everything else in the shelter, there is little choice with respect to the food, something which the clients are either not privy to or refuse to accept, the latter the effect of being coddled.

It is not that these employees begrudge that the clients wish to have some choice, but rather that their wants are so extravagant and unreasonable – in fact, many employees believe that even they do not eat as well as the clients, who do so, they underline, for free. One elderly female employee, for example, ranted about this problem, the disgust in her voice clearly evident while she castigated not only the clients but the entire system. "Personally," she said, "I wouldn't leave [the shelter] if I can get ..." all the things the clients receive. "They're getting a good meal," she said, and added, *they are eating better than people living in homes*" (emphasis added). This is a powerful, yet sobering, statement not just about the lives of the clients (painted through a rosy lens) and the sombre life the employee is subjected to (painted through the lens of poverty and lack of choice), but of the entire system that rewards sloth and breeds dependency (see the next section). After explaining that the clients receive, for both lunch and dinner, a salad, soup, and a main course, in addition to a caffeinated beverage (tea, coffee, or a canned ice drink), milk, and a dessert, she, rather forlornly commented, *"I can't afford to buy all that"* (emphasis added). I underscore that for her – and the other employees – it is not jealousy or hatred that leads to resentment; there is, after all, an element of hyperbole that constitutes these descriptions. Rather, I suggest, the employees believe the clients are completely and utterly ungrateful and unappreciative of what they have, and this leads to bitterness (cf. Loseke, 1992, 121).

Partly as well, and to make matters worse, this type of coddling leads to a sense of entitlement, certainly an unintended consequence, so that these expectations, as grand, elaborate, and unreasonable as they are, are translated into a rights discourse. Thus, the clients believe that they, by right, are entitled to numerous services. "The thing I can't stand," one employee noted, "is that sense of entitlement that a lot of clients have." In explaining this further, another stated, "I think … [there is] a sense of entitlement because they feel that they *deserve* it [services] and they should have it." The comment of the latter employee highlights that the clients believe they deserve the aid that is due to them by right – not out of generosity or compassion, as in historical times (see Katz, 1986; Ranasinghe, 2010a). This point was nicely put by "Captain Delight": "A long time ago, I learned this from my co-worker … he used the phrase and I keep using [it], the phrase is, 'Are you requesting it or demanding [it]?' [This is] very important to me because we are not here to be abused … we are supposed to be helping." In constructing and narrating the issue as such, "Captain Delight," like his colleagues, clearly understands that his job is to provide help to the clients – this is a non-negotiable fact, one which all employees take great pride and joy in trying to deliver. However, he is also very clear that in this provision, he should not be abused – I suspect, as well, that he is hinting at the abuse of the system itself. This happens, he claims, when a request for service, one premised upon the compassion of the service provider, is turned into a demand, one premised upon the right to that service. This, he, and many others as well, abhor with great passion. This is why he noted: "For me, it is very important to ask them [the clients] to do something," a request – even, demand on his part – that is meant to offset the rights discourse within which the clients believe they can, rightfully – pun intended – exist, operate, and, even, demand!

## From Coddling and Rights Discourse to a Culture of Dependency

The effect of the coddling-entitlement nexus has significant implications for the conceptualization and delivery of care and the ordering of the shelter. One significant problem, alluded to above, is that it is believed that the shelter system breeds a culture of dependency (e.g., Desjarlais, 1997, 149; Liebow, 1993, 141; Williams, 2003, 70) or a culture of poverty (Lewis, 1966) – in a similar manner to the social reformers of the eighteenth and nineteenth centuries who wholeheartedly believed that unqualified aid did more harm than good (see Katz, 1989, 16–22; Greenhous, 1968; Ranasinghe, 2012b, 538–43). This point was repeatedly and forcefully made by many employees and all members of the management team, best evinced in the theorization of the concept of an emergency shelter itself. As they saw it, what is supposed to function as a temporary fix has become a permanent fixture in the lives of the clients. How each party made sense of this shift illustrates underlying disagreements that profoundly affect both the delivery of care and the ordering of the shelter.

A good explanation of the culture of dependency – its emergence, propagation, and continuance – is visible in the metaphor used by a supervisor, who explained that the shelter system as a whole has become a "crutch." "I am not going to be their crutch," the supervisor told me on the very first day I began my observations at the shelter, adding, for emphasis, that "we can't be holding their hands ... They have to be independent." This is a remarkable statement when considering that this was probably the first verbal interaction the supervisor and I had, and I was intrigued by it throughout the duration of my stay largely because the supervisor was making the claim that the shelter appears to be doing more harm than good, and the clients, well aware of this, are happy to be coddled. When I had the opportunity to converse in greater length with the supervisor – during an interview – I returned to this metaphor seeking further clarification. The supervisor's explanation was:

> The shelter has kind of been a crutch, it's kind of become a crutch where ... [the client will think] "No one is pushing me to really leave, I don't have to pay any rent, I don't have to [deal with] some of the stresses that I might have had in my day-to-day life ... I don't have to worry about shopping because I get three meals a day ... It's a free thing" ... I think

some people … get so used to staying that they almost start to believe this is … home. But it's not … home, it's just an emergency shelter.

A "crutch" refers to a tool that supports or reassures. On the face of it, there is nothing that is, or should be, problematic about a crutch – save for its very need – because it refers to something that is necessary and, therefore, good. The shelter, acting as a crutch, supports and reassures those who are in need (recall that this is how all the parties conceptualized an ethic of care, that is, as the provision of help). Thus, it is difficult to think that the supervisor finds fault with the system, one designed to provide help to those who are in need. For the supervisor, however, it is not the crutch *per se* that is problematic; it is its specific use – in fact, *abuse* – that is worrying. This is clear in the additional commentary the supervisor provided:

These shelters are … supposed to be temporary, transitional type things … Are all the individuals who are at the shelter using it for that purpose? No, and because everybody is kind of different and their situation is different, we've had to … *adapt* … The purpose of the shelter is … to get you back on your feet but not everyone is using it for those purposes. (emphasis added)

On the one hand, the supervisor is unequivocal about there being a significant problem: the shelter system, which is meant to attend to emergencies, is, in fact, dealing with long-lasting, even permanent, issues. On the other hand, the supervisor takes great pains to note that the problem is not systemic; rather, it is a problem found among some – perhaps many – clients, a fact that is underscored repeatedly in the commentary. At the same time, and in some ways in what looks like an apology for the system, the supervisor also speaks of the new "face" of the shelter, and, with it, seems to justify the culture of dependency that is part and parcel of it. In other words, the very survival and existence of the shelter depends on the task it performs, one which must be constructed as important. This is why the supervisor notes that the purpose and rationale of the shelter itself needed to be tweaked – "adapt," to use the supervisor's word – one which must also accommodate a culture of dependency. Thus, while the supervisor's commentary does speak of the grave problems of this culture, it is also couched within the reality of the life of the shelter, one which it must, unfortunately, oblige – in some ways, this represents the same concern that Rob raised when discussing the dramatic change in the clientele of the shelter over the course of a century or so. This is precisely why the supervisor called for "an ethic of tolerance" towards the clients and counselled the employees attending a staff meeting that "we are not going to paint people with the same brush; we are going to gather information and go on." The supervisor's counsel underlines that the problems in the shelter, in relation to clients, must be understood and addressed on an individual basis.

Some employees wholeheartedly agreed with the position of the supervisor. In locating the problem of dependency in human nature, one employee nevertheless made a concerted effort to underline that such generalizations are not only dangerous, but insufficient to understand what is taking place:

> It's human nature: some humans – I wouldn't say all humans – when some humans experience free food, free clothing, free shelter … it doesn't encourage them to want to work. So then the attitude will be, well, you know what I'm not capable of doing, I'm not capable of doing that or I don't want to do this. I'm not going to see no counsellor [sic] to get myself … reintegrated [in]to society.

There is no doubt that the problem of human nature – the natural condition of man as found in social contract theory, for example (e.g., Hobbes, [1651] 1985; Locke, [1689] 1982) – is invoked only as a somewhat sufficient explanation for the culture of dependence. In so doing, this employee, like his supervisor, does not locate the problem systemically: although the system might contribute to the problem, it is only found among particular persons whose natural condition is a proclivity towards indolence, and, thus, recalcitrance towards labour. Similarly, another employee spoke of how the shelter system can breed irresponsibility in clients, but, like his colleague, underlined that such an explanation cannot be generalized to everyone: "A lot of the people staying here, not all of them, are homeless; some of them, they just want to stay here because they don't want to be responsible for themselves … they do not want to be responsible."

Other employees, however, forcefully located the problem systemically, arguing that the shelter breeds a culture of dependency. One employee explained the problem in this way, the seething anger – and resentment – in her words palpably visible, even audible:

> Some of the people have probably been here five or six years. Why have they been here [for] five or six years if it is an emergency shelter? Don't

call it an emergency shelter because it's not, *it's a home*! That's where I get [into] conflict with the whole thing ... Because [in] an emergency shelter you only stay for a certain time and then you gotta go. (emphasis added)

Another employee echoed the views of his colleague in a more nuanced manner:

There is supposed to be a kind of point, they are supposed to only stay for a certain amount of time, and it's only supposed to be a kind of temporary, emergency, shelter, but what I'm finding here is guys are living here for years and *they are considering it home* ... You just see the level of comfort that shouldn't be seen here. And it sounds harsh, but *it shouldn't be comfortable to be here*. (emphases added)

In both positions, especially the latter, two significant issues are brought to light. First, the site is conceptualized as a shelter, that is, as a site that provides *temporary* relief to mitigate emergencies – for these employees, this is precisely why it is referred to as an emergency shelter. So constructed, the shelter is not – cannot be and, crucially, *should not be* – a home. For these employees, however, this is precisely what has happened: the shelter has been translated into the home of the clients.

The renouncing of the shelter as a home is constructed against the backdrop of what a home – what Gaston Bachelard ([1958] 1994) calls "domains" or "spaces of intimacy" (12) – supposedly, looks and feels like, invoking with it, particular, intimate, memories, which the shelter, it is said, cannot – and, most importantly, should not – mimic nor attempt to mimic. Here, light is also shone on the second aspect of this issue, that is, how something that should not be a home or home-like becomes one. Time is one crucial explanation. Ontologically, a home is fixated, constitutively so, on the permanent, which means that it does not and, cannot, represent the ephemeral. The home is, literally and figuratively, a permanent fixture: its structure – the house – is built for extended stay, often until death. The shelter, constitutively, is not the same: that is, although the site of the shelter is meant to be permanent, occupancy is meant to be ephemeral – in fact, it is premised upon relieving emergencies that are, themselves, fleeting in nature. Thus, the very ephemeral nature of the shelter's occupancy presupposes departure at some point, preferably for all parties concerned, sooner rather than later. This, however, has not happened, and is not happening. In other words, the transmutation of the mandate of the shelter – its new adaptation – has concomitantly transformed the way time is experienced in the shelter, that is, how it is spent and passed. In the conceptualization of the shelter as ephemeral, time was meant to progress and move – move towards departure, towards an end point. Now, however, it stands still, fused permanently into the client's psyche, and this means that there is absent an end point towards which the client can and must move. While time passes for most, for the client, it merely stands still, and so his reading of the space of the shelter moves from the ephemeral to the stable and permanent. Alas, the home in (and of) the shelter is born! (Recall that, like these employees, the supervisor was explicitly clear that the shelter is not a home and should not be treated as such; these words, however, belie the "adaptation" of the shelter towards a more permanent status, which, it appears, the supervisor and management more generally condone, even if only begrudgingly.)

A related, and crucial, aspect to this is the notion of comfort. I noted earlier that virtually all employees who spoke of the purpose of the shelter stated that it is meant to promote care, and part of that care had to do with the provision of help so the clients can feel comfortable. The commentary of the latter employee hints at the problem with comfort, if only implicitly. The problem – even paradox – is as follows. An ethic of care necessitates a semblance of comfort; care that is bereft of comfort would not only fail to do its job, but would be, in fact, the antithesis of care. In other words, to care for another, in some ways at least, presupposes comforting. It is, however, precisely this comfort, especially beyond particular levels, that creates an incentive to stay at the shelter. In other words, it makes little sense to depart from a place that is comfortable and comforting. Thus, the shelter, rather than being a temporary cocoon, becomes a comfortable oasis, and with it, what is conceptualized ephemerally is translated into a permanent fixture. As a permanent fixture, time becomes still, and with no end in sight, the shelter becomes home. This is a widely held view in the shelters, evinced, for example, in Amir Marvasti's (2002, 620–1) comments about a "board member [of the shelter he studied] who cautioned others during an annual meeting that 'if we make the shelter too comfortable, they would never want to leave'" – a belief, as noted above, extant in the past as well, where it was held that unqualified aid produced more harm than good (see Katz, 1989, 16–22; Greenhous, 1968; Ranasinghe, 2012b, 538–43).

Looked upon as such, it is possible to appreciate the ways the shelter system creates a culture of dependency. This is, unsurprisingly, a significant concern to many employees in the shelter, the example of the two discussed above aptly illuminating it. Perhaps the best example of how jaded these employees are can be gleaned from a comment-*cum*-question of one employee, whose words both shine light on the temerity of the clients and, ironically, on the fact that the clients believe the employees are credulous: "There are people who are there to abuse it [the system]. They'll come in and be like, 'Yeah, my house burned down.' [Yet] *how many times does someone's house burn down*" (emphasis added)? Without any doubt, the one thing that is captured by the employee's question is the frustration – even disgust – that pervades his thinking and the thinking of many others. All of this, I claim, hinders the deployment of care and jeopardizes the order in the shelter. As another employee put it, in regards to the entire system: "You give money you can't live on to people who can't function. *It's the most ridiculous system*" (emphasis added).

### From the Ridiculous to the Outrageous: The *Business* of Care

In the previous section, using the comments of a supervisor, I stated that the tenor of the shelter needed amending – an adaptation, as the supervisor put it – to reflect the climate of poverty that the shelter is called upon to address. This climate is visible in what appears to be the condoning or, at least, tolerance of, a culture of dependence, which, at least unwittingly, is a product of this adaptation. In fact, as management sees it, there is no choice but to adapt: survival, in other words, necessitates change. This is also brought to light in Rob's lamentations, discussed early in this chapter, where he revealed deep-seated concerns about the changing demographics of the clients: a dwindling in the numbers of those who can pay for their stay, from a 90/10 ratio to a 10/90 ratio (equally problematic is that these stays are, more often than not, long-term, if not permanent).

There is, then, "a business element," as an employee put it, to the daily ordering of the shelter and the deployment of care. This, as I explore next, is gravely important to the life of the shelter, in fact, its very survival. In the most direct and straightforward sense, part of the funding the shelter receives is directly dependent on the number of clients who occupy its beds: the more bodies spending a night in the shelter, the more funds it receives through the *per diem* allocations provided per client. This is well known among the employees, though not necessarily well received. In explaining the business element he had alluded to, the employee stated: "Yes, we are here to help, but at the same time though, they [the shelter] do gain an income. So there's *per diems*, so per bed you make ... income." He then further explained the paradox that constitutes the provision of care, one which must balance the fine line between compassion and profit or, at least, guarding against loss: "So ... you don't want people to be here [permanently], in the sense that ... you want to encourage people to find different housing and get out of the shelter; but at the same time, it's a business, where they [administration] want people to fill the beds: if you don't fill the beds, you lose money."

Another employee, also privy to this paradox, noted, "there's kind of two components: you have to balance that sort of societal function of housing homeless people ... [with the fact that] it's a business ... and it has to generate a profit. So, *a lot of the conflicts is [sic] between this*" (emphasis added). I underscore that the shelter is a not-for-profit organization and, thus, rather than looking to make money, seeks not to run a deficit. This is an important distinction which, it appears, these employees might not necessarily be privy to. However, what their comments do highlight is the fine line between the provision of care and the ability to so do, the paradox of care, in other words. This, as many employees see it, poses numerous conflicts regarding how care is conceptualized and deployed, conflicts which sharply separate the employees and management.

Many employees are circumspect, if not outright suspicious, of the "business plan," to use Rob's phrase, adopted by management – even *adapted to* given the changing demographics. As management sees it, however, this is a necessity. Yet, even management understands and is forthright that such a vision can – and will – gravely impact the type of care provided. Thus, Rob freely admitted that "it becomes more of a business thing ... [with regards to] what you're able to provide," and further explained:

> Well ... take the principles of business ... you gotta be able to pay your bills, pay heat and hydro ... pay your staff, and ... at the end of the day ... you have a bottom line. I mean we do balance budgets. We cannot, like the government, go into deficit and print our own money ... or go and get a loan. So, at the end of the year, whatever comes in and whatever we spend

have to equal. So from a practical and business point of view, nobody does that without using a business plan.

Similarly, a senior manager explained that "staying afloat" is crucial to the well-being of the shelter; that is, and simply put, the "bills need to be paid." The manager further explained that although the shelter is "a non-profit organization ... there's only so much that we can fall into the hole ... there's only so much time that you get before bills need to be paid." Thus, while management is cognizant that under a business model cut-backs will be necessary and this may compromise the care provided, it nevertheless justifies this as the only available option: not following a business model would mean the shelter would be unable to sustain itself, and without it, care, of any form, will become unavailable.

The employees do not disagree with this premise: as the foregoing suggests, they understand there is only so much that can be accomplished. What they are concerned about, however, is that when a business model takes precedence over care, the business model will severely impact and harm the type and quality of care provided, so that it is economic interests, rather than compassion, that will shape the tenor of the shelter. Equally, they also appear to be cognizant that the balance required tends to pose numerous problems to the ordering of the shelter. A good example, to return again to the foregoing discussion, is the emergency nature of the shelter and its relation to the occupancy of beds. As mentioned before, the shelter receives funding partly through the number of clients who occupy its beds: the more beds occupied, the more funding it receives. From an administrative standpoint, what has been troubling is the declining number of occupancies (a problem heightened in the months when warm weather prevails and clients prefer to sleep outside). Thus, as a senior manager put it, our "occupancy has been down [and] our occupancy basically pays all the bills; so due to our occupancy issues, we've been down the last seven, eight months, and it puts a cramp on the money situation."

This means the shelter has taken unprecedented steps to try to increase its occupancy, in ways, however, that not only run counter to the very ethic of care it seeks to provide but, as well, at the risk of utterly confounding, even annoying, the employees, thereby jeopardizing the order in the shelter. Elizabeth captures this well:

I don't think the help that they [management] want to offer is personal. I think it's – I don't even know what the word is – I think ... this company has changed a lot over the years. I have read up a little bit on it and how it started ... [and] I think now it's a business of money ... that's a whole other ball game. I think that they want us to be closed off from them [the clients], [and] they don't want us to get too close. I think they want us to do our job and go home. And I don't think the higher-ups realize that this is a people business, it's a community oriented business and ... I think us getting closer to them would help them.

Convoluted as these words are, they home-in on an important belief: a model of care delivered on the principles of a business plan cannot be meaningful. This is what she and others believe is happening to the ethic of care, and this, as will become apparent, poses significant problems to the ordering of the shelter.

## On the *Place* of an Ethic of Care: A Final Word

The shelter, I have suggested, is constituted by an ethic of care, one premised upon the moral commitment to help those who are in need through the provision of myriad services. Through a discussion of the history of the shelter, I suggested that the ethic of care has undergone profound changes that have numerous and significant implications to the ordering of the shelter. While the shelter was originally conceived and designed as a support to the city – in terms of its building and upkeep – currently, it serves to support those deemed in need of assistance. In so doing, it underpins a consumptive ethic that constitutes the heart of the city – in fact, contemporary urban public space itself (see Ranasinghe, 2011). It does so by essentially shielding those in need from a public eager to consume.

Inside the walls of the shelter, the ethic of care unfolds in profoundly significant ways. The words and deeds of the personnel who work in the shelter illustrate what an ethic of care is, looks, and feels like. There is no doubt that virtually every employee wholeheartedly believes that the purpose of the shelter is to help and serve those in need. What exactly this means, however, sharply divides them, creating a gulf that is visible not only between management and employees, but between the employees themselves. Thus, while the employees are cautious of what a business model will do to the implementation of an ethic of care, their problems are only confounded and exacerbated because what precisely an ethic of care means and, more importantly, how it should be administered, are grossly unsettled. This leads to an ethic of care that is polysemic. It is the polysemy of an ethic of care, I suggest and develop throughout the chapters to follow, that has serious ramifications for the delivery of care and the ordering of the shelter, one constituted by administrative chaos. In keeping with this line of inquiry, I turn attention, in the next chapter, to the visible representations of care, exploring and explicating what they look and feel like.

# 3 An Inside (and Closer) Look at the Shelter: Spatial Tactics and the Aesthetics of an Ethic of Care

In the preceding chapter, I examined how the shelter is viewed by various stakeholders. This involved paying attention to the relation between the history of the shelter and an ethic of care. As well, I examined the myriad ways the ethic of care is conceptualized by key personnel at the shelter, namely, the management team and employees. In so doing, I hinted at the problems that are a product of the polysemy of an ethic of care. This chapter explores and explicates the aestheticism of the shelter vis-à-vis an ethic of care.

This effort draws inspiration from the sociology of material objects, a valuable and significant endeavour in its own right that has now recast the ways subjects are constituted and produced through things – this certainly after the pioneering work of Bruno Latour (1988), especially his analysis of the door and its hinges which are said to replace the ineffective, inefficient, and, even, careless human (see also Greiffenhagen, 2014). For example, the output from the law and visual studies movement, such as that of Linda Mulcahy's (2011) recent work on how the architecture of buildings and the contents therein – for example, walls, tiles, bricks, as well as technological apparatuses such as wires and computers – profoundly shape the way courtrooms and, by extension, the law itself, are (re)constituted, thought about, and reimagined, is particularly fruitful to this effort. In exploring the aestheticism of the shelter, I focus on its *"physical and aesthetic fabric"* (Moran, 2012, 432, emphasis added). In so doing, I explicate how the physical layout of the shelter, concerning both the immobile – for example, walls and doors – and mobile – for example, tables and chairs – permit the administration of a particular type of care; additionally, the ways care is imagined in and through these objects will also inform this discussion. The fruits of such an effort can be appreciated in Robert Desjarlais's (1997) attempt to capture the spatiality of the shelter he studied and the effects its spatiality gives rise to, both real and imagined: "Spaces could have moods and physiologies as much as people d[o]. The features of buildings and apartments ha[ve] a contagious effect on the people who live ... in those spaces, especially when they spen[d] a lot of time in the same place and ... feel as if they ... [are] 'part' of a building" (58).

Accordingly, I provide a detailed and vivid *tour* of the shelter, an endeavour that draws inspiration from – among others – Fredric Jameson's (1984, 80–4) colourful description of the verticality that constitutes the Bonaventura Hotel in Los Angeles and the ways it reproduces the subjectivities of those who enter it, as well as the pioneering analysis of Gaston Bachelard's ([1958] 1994, 3–73) poetically charged and infused description of the intimate spaces of a house, again through the vantage of verticality. I mimic, albeit loosely, this same verticality as I simultaneously traverse the horizontality of the shelter.

### Entering the Shelter: Doors, Locks, and More Doors

Two separate glass doors, approximately fifteen feet apart, serve as the entrances to the shelter. These entrances can be accessed from the major arterial road discussed in the previous chapter. In practice, however, only one set of doors functions as the main entrance. This entrance is equipped with a ramp for those with physical disabilities. After entering the shelter through its principal entrance, there is another set of double doors that also serves an important purpose, namely, it is often and can easily be locked simply through the push of a button, either during pre-set times or when there might be a potentially problematic client or situation. This door serves much more than an instrumental purpose. It also serves an important symbolic function. Although the first door is never locked, thereby signalling that the shelter is always open to anyone in need – recall the words of a supervisor, quoted in the previous chapter, that "the building never closes" – this "openness," in fact, is neither absolute nor guaranteed. This is because this second door is locked, and not infrequently so; thus, the second door serves as a visible reminder that the shelter *can*, in fact, *will*, be closed given particular contexts. The openness of the shelter, in other words, should never be presupposed. This is vividly illuminated when clients, who confidently presuppose that the second door is open, try to enter, only to find out, after repeated attempts, that their efforts are futile; the shock and displeasure evident on their faces, along with questions posed to the employees in seeking clarification for their inability to enter, serve as powerful reminders of this. Thus, it is the second set of doors that serves as the official invitation to the shelter, thereby entitling the client to the receipt of care. The space between the two sets of doors almost serves as a "no man's land," where the client is uncertain whether he will be deemed worthy of entry.

There is an additional reason why this second set of doors is significant. To the right of the area between these two sets of doors – when facing the second set of doors – is a structure infamously known as "The Bubble." The Bubble will be discussed in detail in chapter 5, though for present purposes several points are worth noting. First, The Bubble has become symbolic of a fortress that literally and figuratively separates the employees and clients, creating an "us versus them" mentality. This separation is evident in how care is thought about and administered. In this sense, and second, it is in The Bubble that the switch to lock the second door is found. Thus, it is from the inside of this structure, one that already fortifies the employees and further creates a gulf between the caregiver and receiver, that a decision is (sometimes spontaneously) made about whether a client is permitted entrance. In other words, it is in that moment and space that the invitation to enter the shelter is extended or retracted. Where this invitation is denied, it is as though The Bubble itself – an inhumane, soulless structure – has denied a potential client care, sometimes even to get something as simple as a drink of water or use the washroom. This, as explicated above, is illuminated, though in a rather pitiful manner, when the client seeks to plead his case through a small opening in the window of The Bubble; this opening hardly permits sound to carry through, a powerful symbol that captures the limited leeway within which the plight of the client is considered, if it is considered at all. All this illuminates that the receipt of care comes with very stringent conditions that, theoretically at least, are carefully orchestrated.

The foregoing is important because The Bubble functions as the *de facto* reception area of the shelter and the *de jure* reception area for all clients, both before and after booking in. In other words, it is The Bubble that simultaneously provides and retracts care. An ethic of care "lives" and "dies" in The Bubble, in some ways, as will be apparent later, because of the decisions made in it.

Once inside the shelter, there are three directions in which movement is possible. For all practical purposes, however, clients are funnelled along one path, which takes them towards the lobby, which is found immediately to the right upon entrance and towards and past

The Bubble. Prior to describing the travels (and travails) of a would-be client, I discuss the two other directions open to clients, for these are also important for the discussion to follow. The first option is to move straight ahead past a set of unlocked doors towards the reception area *de jure*, a path that almost all non-client visitors to the shelter either take or are asked to take – though, as noted, The Bubble essentially functions as the *de facto* reception area. Several offices are located in this area, including the offices of the chaplain services and various other personnel who work for the city. This area also contains a locked door that leads to the administrative offices located on the second floor – the offices of human resources and most upper-level management, including the executive director. The second option is found immediately to the left upon entering the shelter where a set of double doors leads to the chapel where church services are held on some mornings during the week and every Sunday evening. The chapel serves other purposes as well, for example, to hold meetings or serve meals, as it was used for about a month when the kitchen was being renovated. The primary function of the chapel, that is, church services, deserves a final note. The chapel serves as a symbol that (dis)connects the past and the present, given that, as noted in the previous chapter, the present ethos of the shelter is quite different from what it was during its early days. The shelter, as noted, was founded upon a Christian ethic and, in many ways, it is this ethic, though largely diluted in present times – perhaps even unrecognizable – that links the two disparate times. Thus, when I asked Rob, a senior member of management, about the (dis)connection between the past and present, he spoke of the chapel and the Christian ethic it symbolizes to connect the founding ethos of the shelter to its contemporary existence – he noted, on three separate occasions: "We still have chapel services here." Despite this reminder – even insistence – on his part, this founding ethic, I learned from listening to others and observing their actions, has virtually disappeared, something, as I elucidate later, that is important to the conceptualization and administration of care. The final option, as noted above, is to turn right towards the lobby, an important – perhaps the most important – place in the shelter.

## The Lobby: The (Un)Making of Home

A short walk, about ten feet, along a narrow corridor – along which The Bubble is situated – leads to a large space that serves as the lobby of the shelter. This area, I would learn and observe, is as significant both instrumentally and symbolically to the clients as it is to the front-line workers and management. The lobby is designed as an open-concept area – which tends to magnify its space – but appears to exist, somewhat at least, in two sections because of a wall that partially separates one from the other. One section is long and rectangular in shape. It faces the major arterial road and contains large windows from top to bottom, adorned with white, transparent curtains, all conducive to the flow of ample natural light and visibility to the outside. This area contains several chairs placed along the sides of the walls along with a few tables. These tables often double as storage spaces, filled as they are with myriad personal goods of the clients. There is also a television that is mounted at the top of the far end of the section and it is turned on nightly between 7:00 and 11:00 p.m., permitting clients to view and enjoy television shows and sporting events. The other section of the lobby contains several chairs, two tables, and a vending machine. The communal washroom – the subject of detailed discussion to follow – is located in this area as well.

Many commentaries have homed-in on specific sites within shelters that are important not only to their constitution but also in how they shape the subjectivities of the personnel therein. For example, Irene Glasser (1988) states that the dining room of the soup kitchen she studied "functions as a symbolic living room" (3), because it was that area, more than others, where people gathered, mingled, and made sense of their lives. In what follows, I attempt to narrate the space of the lobby as a living or family room, one that is particularly tied to, and important for, the provision of care. Here, Desjarlais's (1997) commentary about the *place* of the lobby in the shelter he studied is informative. Drawing on the concept of "free places" discussed by Erving Goffman (1961, 230) in his classic *Asylums*, Desjarlais (1997) describes the lobby in this way:

> While the shelter was the staff's domain, the lobby belonged provisionally to the residents. Both groups understood that the lobby was not a part of the shelter and that the rules of the shelter could not necessarily be enforced in the lobby. Staff members would intervene when there was trouble and would often walk through or stand in the lobby, but they did not exercise the same authority that they did in the shelter. (79)

In this picturing, the lobby was a special place that belonged, first, to the clients: it was *their* place, their living room, so to speak.[1]

This is what I wish to narrate about the lobby, focusing on its aesthetics vis-à-vis the conceptualization and administration of an ethic of care. The lobby is the place where many – if not most – clients spend a considerable amount of time, and this is so especially during inclement weather. Even the most cursory observation of the lobby illuminates matters crucial to its constitution. First, the lobby has a set of familiar faces, both clients and employees (even supervisors and managers), and is composed of a set of routine, repetitive – perhaps mundane and monotonous – activities, again performed by both the clients and staff. It is as if – though not precisely that – time stands still here; or, at least, this is what the forlorn, if solemn, looks upon the faces of the clients and employees reveal. Each day, after breakfast, which is served between 7:30 and 8:30 a.m. like clockwork, the lobby fills up with clients who have managed to sit through what even they believe is unhealthy and insipid food. A few murmurings, a chatter here and there, a card game or two, the musings of many who are, even to the plain eye, mentally ill, and a host of others who pace around the area, fill and occupy the lobby and its space. All these activities have one commonality: they are designed to pass or "kill" time, a futile endeavour, given that for the clients, it is as if time stands still (as I developed in chapter 2). The vastness of the lobby and its apparent emptiness only reinforce this. Those who are fortunate enough to arrive early and find a chair will take a nap or fall into a deep sleep. This mundaneness proceeds until about noon when the clients make their way towards the basement for lunch. After lunch, the same (or a similar) routine unfolds until dinner, which is served at 5:00 p.m. After dinner, the routine tends to change slightly when the television is turned on, though for all practical purposes, it is the same monotony that unfolds until clients go to bed, either by their own volition or because they are subtly asked to do so at 11:00 p.m. What immediately resonates aesthetically, then, is a sense of calm, perhaps serenity, one mediated by the monotony of repetition. It is, however, the rather senseless repetition that tends to dull and numb the senses, thereby creating an aura that "all is well" – an aura, however, that belies what is unfolding on a daily basis.

Also plainly visible are the myriad personal belongings of the clients that "adorn" the tables, chairs, and floors of the lobby. This is a commonality in many shelters. As Elliot Liebow (1993) notes: "A principle difficulty was that most emergency shelters had only limited space for individual storage – often space for only two bags or two small cardboard boxes" (32). The aestheticism of these belongings – often crammed into large black or orange garbage bags, full to the brim, containing practically everything the clients possess, from clothes, shoes, and food to other personal documentation and papers – are stored wherever room can be found (see Figures 3.1 and 3.2). This, unsurprisingly, is a serious concern, certainly an annoyance, to management, one posing grave health risks to the entire shelter. Although this has been an ongoing problem, it was exacerbated because of a policy initiated by the shelter a few months into my observations. Ironically, this policy was instituted under the cover of attending to an impending health risk, namely, the rise in bed bugs. Prior to this policy, clients were allowed to leave their personal belongings in their lockers – every client receives a locker when he books into the shelter, which must be vacated either when he leaves on his own accord or is asked to do so. The new policy necessitated that clients empty the contents of their lockers every Tuesday and Thursday and leave them unlocked. This would allow the

Figure 3.1. Garbage and other bags stored in a corner of the lobby.
(Photo credit: Author)

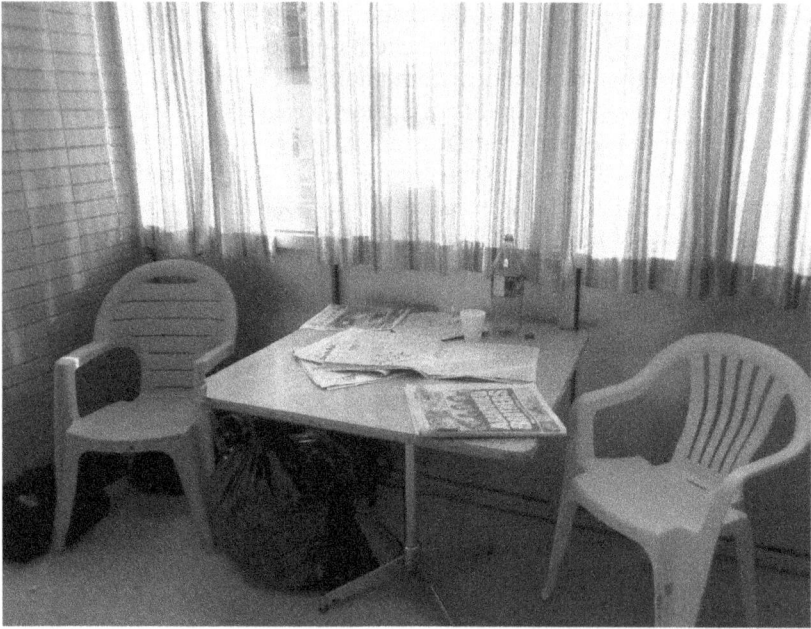

Figure 3.2. A table and chairs with garbage bags and other litter in the vicinity. (Photo credit: Author)

employees to search the lockers and, if need be, clean them. The belief and fear at the time was that the practice of hoarding was unhygienic and unhealthy and, if not caused, then certainly contributed to, the dramatic rise in bed bugs – clients would collect as much as they could of any and everything, including perishable items, and store them in their lockers for long periods of time, even months. This was a serious worry to all parties concerned (as I take up in a later chapter).

What resulted, however, was that while the clients begrudgingly followed protocol, the lobby – once a somewhat calm and serene place, the living room of the shelter, so to speak – essentially became one large "communal" locker. Thus, what was once in the background, shielded from plain sight, was now brought into the foreground, thereby illuminating the rather pitiful and unhealthy conditions in which clients live. The "living room" had become the dumping ground, so that even the modicum of civility, what Norbert Elias ([1939] 1978, 114–16) calls the threshold of delicacy and its relation to embarrassment, was not just ruptured, but this rupturing literally was a spillage of the backstage into the limelight (Goffman, [1956] 1959). This posed numerous problems, as I take up next, but how this policy was discontinued illuminates the significance of a particular sort of aestheticism, even in an emergency shelter.

The Alliance to End Homelessness – a major and powerful antipoverty organization in the city – held a press conference at the shelter, and, during a walkabout, one of its representatives noticed – not that it would have been difficult to do so – the rather large number of orange garbage bags in the lobby and questioned a member of management as to why they were there. In this case, it was an aesthetic norm – even the shelter has a particular code, so to speak – that was out of sorts and drew the representative's attention. The response that the representative was given – it was an effort to attend to the rising bed bug problem – however, was not well received, and the shelter was asked why this policy had been ongoing for six months without any significant improvement, especially when it unduly penalized clients and imposed unnecessarily taxing restrictions on their already difficult lives. Again, with optics in mind, the shelter reduced the stringencies of this policy, essentially allowing clients to leave their belongings in their lockers. In explaining the discarding of this policy to the employees during a staff meeting, a supervisor commented, "It's all about the optics; the optics don't look good." In many ways, this illuminates the aestheticism of the shelter and its relation to the administration of care, where concerns about, and over, aesthetic norms trumped a potentially serious health risk.[2]

The lobby, then, is a significant place in (and of) the shelter. If the foregoing only implicitly brings the aestheticism-ethic of care nexus into the foreground, a peculiar problem in (and to) the lobby further illuminates this. What immediately struck me as very strange – later confirmed by some employees and management as well – was that the lobby did not have enough chairs to meet the demands of the clients who wished to congregate in the area. This is something quite peculiar considering that the lobby serves as the *de facto* living room of the shelter. This problem is magnified daily between approximately 2:30 and 3:00 p.m. The shelter provides free meals to the community, that is, to anyone in need, both men and women, starting at 3:00 p.m. Beginning at about 2:30 p.m., people enter the shelter and wait for the doors leading to the basement to open so they can receive this meal. If there are chairs available, many sit. However, more often than not, chairs are not available, and what results is that about thirty people begin pacing around the lobby. The lobby, thus, has an air of disorganization and disorder, an almost chaotic atmosphere that is not part of its everyday climate – recall the semblance of serenity that constitutes the space. Such a feeling is often shared by the clients, who feel that "outsiders" have encroached upon their territory – this is especially so if an "outsider" has taken a chair, the result of which is that the "outsider" is subjected to a series of stern stares. This is a feeling also shared by the employees and supervisors who find it quite difficult to navigate the concourse of people who tend to, unintentionally, stymie the employees' movements.

Although this level of disorganization and chaos, during this time, is an aberration, it is not as if other times are bereft of such problems. The number of chairs, to put it simply, is insufficient to meet the demands of the clients who wish to sit. Other issues exacerbate the problem. First, more often than not, chairs are used to store personal belongings, and this means that one client will often use two, or even three, chairs – this was especially problematic during the six-month period when clients had to evacuate their lockers twice a week (discussed previously). There appears to be an unspoken code that a chair that is so occupied is spoken for, just as if someone is sitting in it, and moving belongings from the chair breaches this etiquette – one sanctioned by the threat of physical repercussions. The belongings of a client, thus, are of equal importance because often they are strategically deployed to occupy a chair or two while he steps outside, even if this absence lasts several hours. Often, when a client no longer wishes to occupy the chair, he will silently nod to the person he wishes to give "his" chair to – sometimes a friend, often times not – an act that garners a certain amount of respect and capital, perhaps to be drawn upon (i.e., "cashed in") at a later time. Interestingly, clients often gave their chairs to persons of similar racial or ethnic backgrounds, so that, for example, a person of colour would nod to another person of colour to take his chair. This is significant because this type of behaviour, which appears to be explicitly motivated along racial lines, is an important indication that the shelter is a racialized space, though not one easily visible at first glance. The chair, then, has a power, a social and cultural capital of its own (see Bourdieu, 1987; see also Wacquant, 1987; Dezalay and Madsen, 2012, for an explication of the different types of capital in Bourdieu's sociology); the capital associated with the chair, as I take up next, is intimately tied to aesthetic norms and the administration of care.

The lack of chairs posed numerous problems to the daily ordering of the shelter – the chaotic atmosphere beginning, every weekday, at 2:30 p.m. or so, is one example. There clearly appears to be a hierarchy among the clients: those who are stronger and (more) masculine occupy more social and cultural capital, and are easily able to monopolize the chairs for themselves, their belongings, and their friends. On one occasion, a client who appeared to have desperately wanted to sit, walked into the chapel and asked an employee whether he could take one of the chairs from the chapel into the lobby. His request was swiftly denied. In a few minutes or so – presumably after searching, even hoping, for a chair – he approached The Bubble and stated, almost on the verge of breaking down, "There is no chair for me to sit," and then added, "I know why there are no chairs – because *they are hogging them*" (emphasis added). The "they" he refers to are those on the higher end of the hierarchy, whom he, because he does not have the type of capital they do, is unable to compete with. The sympathy and empathy (or lack thereof) of the employees, his last hope for a chair – and, more broadly, fairness and equity – brought him no comfort, a fate that many others also endure. The situation is quite dire that even those who, for a variety of reasons – infirmity, old age, or a malady – require a chair, are often left without one.

It is possible to see that the aestheticism of the shelter is also grounded upon living bodies – often weak, dishevelled, and old – lying on the floors of the lobby of the shelter, its *de facto* living room. What was striking to me during the early days of observation – and one I would gradually get accustomed to – was the sheer volume of clients either sleeping or sitting on the lobby floor. These, mixed with the large number of garbage bags, created an environment that appeared quite disorderly. Even more appalling – even bizarre – was that many of these garbage bags were placed on chairs and tables while ailing human bodies were relegated to the floor. One event certainly drove this home. A cleaner was cleaning the floor one weekday afternoon, and, while personal belongings stayed in place on the furniture, the clients were moved from the floor. The aesthetics surrounding hygiene and cleanliness necessitated not the removal of garbage bags, but human bodies, only for them to be returned, just like things, to the same spots, but now clean and dry.

The employees, of course, were more than mindful of what was unfolding, best evinced in the comments of "Captain Delight": "[It is] [al]ways the same people sitting on the chair. You can see them leaving and when they come back the chair is still there for them." This knowledge was derived from close and personal observation – "I have been paying attention," he stated – though even a cursory glance at the lobby would have revealed that something was amiss. In addition, although some employees like "Captain Delight" spoke forcefully that such injustice needed to be addressed – "We as staff won't tolerate that" – more often than not, it was an apathetic attitude that seemed to constitute their outlook and behaviour, thereby condoning, if only tacitly, the hierarchical ordering in the lobby.

According to some employees, however, it was the vision of management that created this problem. "Captain Delight," for example, claimed that management did not want to add more chairs "because this is only an emergency shelter and they [management] don't want those guys to be more *comfortable*" (emphasis added). Here, chairs were equated with comfort; more importantly, the ordering of the shelter necessitated a particular type or level of comfort, anything beyond that would be counterproductive to the very ethos of an emergency shelter. Elizabeth echoed this sentiment as well, stating, though in a somewhat different context, "I think they [again, management] [a]re intending not to let people get *comfortable* in here ..." (emphasis added).

In some ways, and strangely, this is borne out in the comments of a supervisor who was both frustrated and flummoxed by this direction to withhold comfort. In what can be construed as a lengthy rant about the problematic state of particular rules and their relation to an ethic of care – explored in detail in chapters 7 and 8 – the supervisor noted:

> We used to have rules like "You cannot sit on the floor." It did not matter whether there were chairs left and it was the middle of winter, you [still] do not sit on the floor ...! There was another rule ... [that] you were not allowed to have chairs or hang out in that area [adjacent to the supervisors' office] at all. So can you imagine trying to enforce those things, and what's the point anyway? So if there is a point, if there is a door you would be blocking, and it's a safety thing, yeah, have the rule – don't be there. But why have all *these silly little rules* about, you can't put your chair there when there isn't really any reason for it and if it's in the dead of winter and there is no other place for these people to go and all the chairs are there, why are you going to make them stand for hours or until somebody goes to the bathroom and then they can nap [steal] their chair and then there can be a fight [*laughs*]. (emphasis added)

Even though this commentary ends in laughter, it belies an enormous amount of frustration, even acrimony. From the standpoint of the everyday organization of the shelter, the supervisor feels that it simply does not make sense to place rigid – in fact, "silly" – restrictions about when and where clients can sit. Equally, the lack of seating is a precursor for further problems of order, if and when, another client, perhaps unaware of the code, takes another's chair. The potential for violence, I suggest, is also a reason why some employees are wary of involving themselves in these situations, not only because of the threat of violence or danger to them, but also because this type of seating arrangement is best left to the clients to sort out; as the employees see it, the lack of leadership on the part of management, precisely what the supervisor bemoans, is the key problem. Beyond an issue of governance, however, also lies the issue of care that the supervisor's comments speak to, evinced in the invocation of inclement weather to paint a picture of the lobby filled with clients who cannot even be provided a chair to find comfort. For the supervisor, simply adding more chairs would address many of, if not all, these concerns. The chair – in terms of its symbolism and material effects – aptly and vividly illustrates the manner in which an ethic of care is conceptualized and administered, and how these are inherently tied to an aesthetic norm. The "heart" of the shelter, the "living room," is intentionally made uncomfortable – or, at least, not too comfortable – in an effort to promote what is seen as optimum care.

Again, when viewed from the lens of the "living room," there is another peculiarity of (and in) the lobby that illuminates the aestheticism-ethic of care nexus. Among other things (as described above), there is a washroom in the lobby that is located in the same section where the vending machine is situated. It is used predominantly by the clients as well other indigent persons visiting the shelter – never by the male employees, supervisors, or managers, or by visitors to the shelter on official business (I used this washroom on the first day of my observations only to be gently admonished by a supervisor, and later another employee, to use washrooms that are reserved for workers – I gladly complied).

To describe this washroom as filthy or disgusting would be to paint it in too rosy a light. There are several things that were striking upon entering the washroom, its stench was certainly one – a mixture of feces, urine, sweat, alcohol, occasionally tobacco or marijuana smoke, and a host of other smells that the limits of language simply do not allow a description of (similar to the way that pain, as Elaine Scarry [1985] describes, destroys language, that is, the ability to communicate the pain that is being endured).[3] Inside, pubic hair covered the surfaces of the urinal, toilet, and even other places, such as the sink and floor. The toilet was filled with toilet paper and, sometimes, drug paraphernalia. The floors, similarly, were often covered with toilet paper. Blood was also often found on the floors. Even the rather dim lighting could not mask these visuals and the visceral effects they gave rise to. Clients use this washroom not only to relieve themselves, but also to shave, cut their hair, wash their faces and sometimes their bodies, and dress their wounds, all of which make it even more untidy, unpleasantly odorous, not to mention leaving the floor wet, and strewn with blood and bandages. In addition, clients also consume drugs – either crack cocaine or marijuana – and, I have heard stories of, but never witnessed, homosexual sexual acts, both of the paid and unpaid type, inside the bathroom stall.

To further compound these problems, the toilet often overflows, spilling water not just onto the floor of the washroom, but into the lobby. Numerous times during my observation, I witnessed clients asking front-line workers to call maintenance workers to clean the washroom. Even though the employees never used the washroom, they believed that this was a serious problem to *their* health and well-being, not just the clients', and even went as far as conceptualizing it as a security issue (I develop this further in chapter 5). In describing this problem, an employee, clearly irate about the whole situation, rather dramatically noted, "There's stuff that are [sic] just run down, literally falling apart in this place. This washroom … out left here, it's flooded every single day. I mean we've had spills come out as far down as the caseworkers' desk" – approximately fifteen feet from the washroom. Though his description verged on the hyperbolic, such exaggeration was meant to capture his frustration, not just of the problem but of what he believed to be apathy on the part of management. "We're working on it," he said twice, the second time laughing rather sarcastically, in answering my query about the response that management has provided about this issue.

Despite these issues, ranging from aesthetics to health, what is peculiar about the washroom is that its entrance is bereft of a door. This means that from many places in the lobby – as well as from the supervisors' office – easy visibility into the washroom (and its activities) is possible. In fact, this visibility is considered essential to the ordering of the shelter. The washroom did, at one point, have a door, but it was removed because of numerous security issues, many relating to the sale and consumption of drugs and, to a lesser degree, the sale and performance of sexual activities. What is interesting is that the lobby, the *de facto* living room of the shelter, is also *the* site where the private, and in many ways unsightly and distasteful, behaviour are conflated, confounded, and brought to light, thereby eviscerating any pretence of civil(ized) behaviour (Elias [1939] 1978, 117–22, 129–39) – "the virtues of a certain kind of disguise," as Richard Sennett (1990, 79) describes it, are conspicuously absent. Thus, for example, from particular angles, it is easy to see someone urinating or defecating, though complete visibility is covered through a siding or the stall in the washroom. The bracketing or compartmentalization of space and its particular uses, as described by Jurgen Habermas ([1962] 1989, 43–50), now taken for granted as civilized, normal, behaviour, is a foreign concept in the shelter. Its spatial layout renders civility inexistent. In addition, even a modicum of privacy, in which a client can perform some of his most personal and basic daily needs away from the gawking eyes of his peers, is also absent, again, a commonality in many shelters (e.g., Desjarlais, 1997; Marcus, 2003). All this, I suggest, eviscerates comfort in the shelter. The lobby, the "living room" of the shelter, is designed precisely *to be uncomfortable* – or, at least, this is the appearance it gives. The ethic of care administered in the shelter is one that cannot be about comfort: it is, in fact, discomforting and must be so for the daily ordering of life within it.

I will further build upon this theme throughout this tour of the shelter. For present purposes, however, I briefly cast attention upon the offices located on the ground floor, which are important for the "backstage" (Goffman, [1956] 1959) activity of the shelter and the ordering of an ethic of care.

## The Offices and the Making of Order

The far end of the lobby contains another corridor that leads to the offices of the supervisors, a senior member of management, and the caseworkers. At the end of this corridor is a door that leads to four offices, three of which are allocated to the caseworkers (the other office is used for myriad purposes, two common usages being the provision of medical services to clients by a city nurse who visits the shelter once a week and the distribution of weekly stipends to eligible clients, who line up in the lobby and collect their money from a window that connects the lobby and the room in question).

Each client who is booked into the shelter is assigned a caseworker, to whom he must report within twenty-four hours of admittance, unless it is a weekend, when no caseworkers are available. For present purposes, I focus mainly on the offices of the caseworkers and their relation to an ethic of care (the work of caseworkers is discussed in greater detail in the next chapter). The large room that contains these four offices is very bright. There are several reasons for this. First, there is a large window at the very end of the room that provides ample natural light. Second, and related, the bright fluorescent lighting on the ceilings enhances the natural light. In addition, the walls are painted in a light yellow colour that further complements the lighting. The floors are quite clean and bright. What is immediately noticeable upon entering the room is its smell, which while not peculiar in any way, is very different from the rather repulsive odour that characterizes many other places in the shelter – there is an aura of cleanliness, and the room becomes a sanctuary of sorts for relief from what is otherwise the everyday noxiousness of the shelter. Partly, this is because the caseworkers – in an effort to create a pleasant work environment – make every effort to keep the place clean, including spraying it with air freshener. Partly, as well, because the space itself is quite small, the number of clients who can congregate in or near it is greatly reduced, and this has the effect of reducing the odour they bring into the area.

There are four caseworkers in the shelter, but only two are charged with the clients' files, and it is they who meet with clients and discuss their needs (the other two are in charge of clients on a different floor, clients who pay rent and, therefore, are housed two to a room and receive additional privileges that regular clients are not entitled to – essentially the exception to the norm that Rob, a senior manager, bemoaned in his narrative of the history of the shelter). Caseworkers are on duty to meet with clients every weekday between 8:00 a.m. and 4:00 p.m. These meetings can be initiated by the clients or the caseworker, but, for all practical purposes, an open-door policy is instituted during this time. At all other times, the main door to this room is closed, and clients are not permitted to meet with caseworkers. As noted above, there are no caseworkers on duty during the weekends.

Both instrumentally and symbolically, the offices of the caseworkers are important spaces for the administration of care – specifically, it is the doors of the offices that are significant. During meetings with caseworkers, clients discuss a range of matters. These range from logistical matters, such as filling out forms and obtaining the necessary paperwork they need, to requesting and receiving letters of reference, including asking caseworkers to make phone calls for them, to more personal matters, often entailing the discussion of past troubles, including abuse, and a host of other issues concerning addictions or personal relationships. Especially when sensitive matters are being discussed, many clients choose to close the door so that the outside world is not privy to what is unfolding (often, when standing outside the office, it is possible to hear what is being said even though the door is closed, but for the most part, it is difficult to follow the conversation closely – this, I learned when I was asked on several occasions to leave the office and the door was shut while clients conversed with the caseworkers). The door, then, is a kind of shield separating the outside and inside worlds of the shelter, a world – it should be remembered – that is virtually devoid of demarcations. The closed office provides the client a modicum of privacy. In fact, this privacy is a legal right the client is entitled to and often expects.

There is, as well, a significant symbolic aspect associated with the office door that cannot be minimized. The office of the caseworker illuminates that the administration of care is tailored to each client and his specific needs. At least on paper, this care is unique, specialized, and far removed from the generic manner in which it is deployed in practically every other place in the shelter. It is not, however, simply that the administration of this care is specifically calibrated, but that it is done so in consultation with the client, in private, with an expectation of, and right to, privacy. Even though caseworkers are terribly overworked and will (try to) rush through their meetings with clients – often even abruptly dismissing them – there is at least the facade that time is not an issue (in the office, however, time does not stand still as it appears to do in the lobby). This is because the door is closed and this means that the vagaries of the outside world – which trouble both the client and the worker alike – are held in abeyance. The door, then, is a powerful symbol of an ethic of care because of what it stands for, privacy; in this case, privacy is crucial to not just the administration of care, but also because it signals that someone actually cares. Thus, the one-on-one relationship that each client can have with his caseworker, where he can, at least for a brief moment, speak directly to and with someone, and only that person, knowing that his interlocutor will not be interrupted by the outside world, is made possible because of the door. How powerful a symbol this door is can be appreciated when recognizing that even when a client performs his most personal activities – for example, defecating or showering – his privacy, practically non-existent, is often interrupted by the procession of other clients in and out of the washroom. No such interruption takes place when the door is closed in the caseworker's office. Thus, while an open-door policy serves as a warm invitation that symbolizes care, it is, in fact, when a door is closed that this care can be administered, because the closed door and the space therein lead to and foster comfort, something that is difficult to come by elsewhere in the shelter.

For all it has to offer, however, the office is also the source of at least two serious concerns that affect the ordering of the shelter – these are introduced here and taken up in greater detail in later chapters. First, the office symbolizes the space where the "real" work is performed, that is, where caseworkers speak with clients, diagnose problems, and create a plan of action. The caseworkers, for their part, believe this as well, often claiming that they are directly in charge of the well-being of their clients. Such views, however, are poorly received by front-line employees, who feel that because they interact with the clients more frequently than the caseworkers, it is they, not the caseworkers, who truly know and understand the clients and what they need. This leads to a tense and acrimonious relationship between the two parties, which severely hinders the administration of care.

Second, the door has a specific relation to security, though in a somewhat counterintuitive manner. As a pliable device, capable of being opened and closed at will, the door symbolizes not just freedom, but security as well, so that a caseworker can close and lock the door when in jeopardy – the closed office functions akin to The Bubble, thereby protecting and shielding the worker from danger. However, the very act that creates comfort and enhances the administration of care for the client, that is, closing the door, could potentially pose a grave threat to the caseworker while he/she is behind that closed door, because he/she is then at the mercy of the client. The door, thus, is reminiscent of the dialecticism of the telephone that Elizabeth Stanko (1990) is mindful of: "By having a telephone women are forced to deal with sexual intrusions, potentially each time the telephone rings" (100). The door, then, perfectly captures the way an ethic of care is funnelled into a discourse of security, often at the expense of the former (also important, as I explicate in chapter 6, is the marked difference in the way the security of male and female employees, including caseworkers, is thought about and made sense of, which further affects the conceptualization and deployment of care).

There are two other offices along this same corridor that require brief commentary. The first is the office of a senior member of management, which is located directly opposite the entrance to the offices of the case-workers. Although the daily work life of the manager is composed of myriad activities, he is principally responsible for overseeing the work of the supervisors (and, indirectly, the caseworkers) and writing and amending the policies of the shelter. His powers, thus, are vast in a variety of ways. Given this, the location of his office is interesting for two reasons. First, it is removed from the visibility of, and everyday happenings in, the lobby. This means that he is often without direct knowledge of what is transpiring in the shelter, and the information he receives is provided to him by the supervisors and, occasionally, front-line staff or caseworkers. Second, and related, this distance actu-ally belies the keen interest – a fervent preoccupation of sorts – that the manager has of what is unfolding in the shelter. However, this interest is not necessarily with respect to the clients, but the employees and the manner in which they keep order and administer care. Thus, prior to moving into his current office, the manager's office was located closer to the reception area – the area, discussed before, where the offices of the chaplain services and other city employees are located. This loca-tion physically and symbolically removed the manager from the shel-ter. Thus, in deciding to move his office as he did, the manager sought to keep abreast of how the shelter is run, because, as he would later tell me, he believed that a certain sense of accountability was sorely lack-ing and he felt that his physical presence would help bolster this. This move aptly illuminates his vision of the shelter, one conceived by an ethic of care and requiring strict legality in the form of its policies – in many ways, the antithesis of what the front-line workers think. These different ways of making sense of the shelter and its mandate are seri-ously problematic to the provision of care.

It is in this context that the office of the supervisors needs elabora-tion. The shelter employs three supervisors who share one large office fitted with two desks (there are two supervisors who work the time period between the morning and evening hours and one who works during the overnight hours). This office is located in the same corridor that contains the offices of the senior manager and the caseworkers. The entrance to the office is through a large wooden door, one, how-ever, which is constructed so that the top portion may be left open while the bottom half is closed. The image, thus, is of an office that is simultaneously open and closed: clients can speak with supervisors but from an already determined distance, one with a physically demarcated boundary that separates the world of the client (the lobby) from that of the supervisor (the office). This door, then, serves the dual purpose of embracing and administering an ethic of care, and being open to it, while simultaneously enhancing security through its concomitant closure – in contrast, for example, to the doors to the offices of the caseworkers, which both because of their physical construction (a single door) and the nature of the work performed (matters requiring sensitivity and privacy) are different. The supervisors' door serves another useful purpose as well. Given that it can be left partially open, it allows the supervisors to hear what is unfolding in the lobby and its vicinity. This office also contains a rather large window that faces one section of the lobby, including the washroom, and provides an unobstructed view of several parts of the lobby. Thus, from inside the office, the supervisors are capable of both seeing and hearing what is unfolding in the shelter. Although the office certainly does not contain all the features of the perfect machine of surveillance, the Panopticon (see Bentham [1811] 1962, 498–503), it nevertheless works well to give the supervisors a portal into the life of the shelter.

The foregoing highlights the importance of visibility to the daily ordering of the shelter, including the administration of an ethic of care. By visibility, I do not simply mean the capacity to surveil, especially in the covert form that surveillance is often equated with – though, without doubt, this is an important component to the ordering of the shelter. Rather, I also mean visibility in the ordinary sense of the word, not just to be able to see, but also to be seen, the latter being crucial to an ethic of care. That is, the open-door policy of the shelter, both of the supervisors and caseworkers, presents an image that the clients are welcome and warmly invited to approach these offices. The ability to be visible and present, I suggest, is an important component in the provision of care, as important as the material things provided under its banner. That is, visibility seeks to create a comforting and comfortable environment.

There is also another aspect of this visibility that is important to the ordering of the shelter, and it pertains not to the clients, but the employees. Beyond providing a good view into the lobby, the supervisors' office provides the appearance of an unobstructed view of – though not into – The Bubble, the primary workspace of the front-line staff. In appearance, The Bubble is essentially hermetic, and, though it provides very good visibility into the lobby, its architecture leaves much to be desired for a variety of reasons. One reason that is particularly disconcerting to management and supervisors is that the employees can – and most do – retreat into The Bubble, thereby distancing themselves from the clients. This distancing, management believes, poses numerous problems to the administration of care, one being that it creates an image that the employees are not willing to help (for their part, many employees dislike The Bubble for a variety of reasons, one being that they are distanced from the clients – I take this up in detail in chapter 5). Although visibility into The Bubble from the supervisors' office is very poor, there is at least a facade that a supervisor might be watching what is transpiring, a fear that many employees have, especially when they are spending time talking and not working. I will delve into these issues in greater detail in the next chapter, though for now, it suffices to note the importance of visibility to the ordering of an ethic of care. This visibility, as can be appreciated, is important and readily available because of the prime location of the office, overlooking the lobby and The Bubble.

The ground floor, discussed in detail throughout the foregoing pages, is an important hub of the shelter in relation to an ethic of care. In what follows, I explore two other floors, beginning with the basement before moving upstairs to the second floor, with the purpose of further explicating the aestheticism of an ethic of care.

### The Warmth of the Cold, the Light of the Dark, and the "Comforts" and "Health" of the Basement

Abutting the entrance to the washroom on the ground floor is a door through which the basement and upper floors can be accessed (there is also an elevator close to this door, but it is used primarily by the employees and by clients with physical disabilities). This door is locked between 8:00 a.m. and 4:00 p.m., denying clients access to the basement and the upper floors. The exception to this rule is when lunch is served at noon, and when the community meal is served at 3:00 p.m. Even during these times, however, access is only granted to the dining hall located in the basement.

Just past this door, two sets of stairs, about fifteen stairs in total, lead to the basement. The walk down to the basement is quite pleasant. Despite the lack of natural light, the area is bright and well lit, especially after the fresh coat of paint the walls received about halfway into my observations. In addition, there is a pleasant smell about the area, far removed from the stench that envelops the lobby and other areas of the shelter. The kitchen, located in the basement, is partially responsible for this pleasant aroma.

The kitchen is located immediately to the left upon entrance to the basement. It is always locked to preserve and enhance the safety of the kitchen staff. It is believed that cooking utensils, especially sharp knives, can be used as weapons against employees, a belief that aptly illustrates the paranoia over violence and bodily harm that pervades the shelter, especially among management (discussed in detail in chapter 5). The kitchen is very small but tidily maintained, giving an image of cleanliness and salubriousness. During the day, that is, between about 6:00 a.m. and 8:00 p.m., the kitchen will be staffed by approximately three to five employees cooking, serving food, and cleaning the area. For the weary clients – their anguish palpably visible in their forlorn looks – the kitchen is a beacon of hope for what it purports to offer, a fresh, home-cooked meal. More often than not, as I explain below, the clients are thoroughly disappointed.

It is from the perspective of hope that the discussion of the kitchen and the dining hall is best made sense of. A large, bright, and well-lit, square-shaped area serves as a waiting area of sorts where clients congregate before being ushered into the dining hall. A few murmurings, along with a conversation or two occupy the room but, for the most part, the clients simply want to get on with what is otherwise their daily and monotonous routine, one important part pertaining to sustenance. In this sense, all eyes are fixated on the entrance to the dining hall, which is through a large set of double-doors. These doors serve as a powerful symbol that even nourishment will be administered according to the times and strictures of the shelter and its policies – and, often, the idiosyncrasies of the employees who are frequently oblivious towards the needs of the clients, evinced in the conversations they have with each other and the kitchen staff in the dining hall behind these doors, while the clients wait (im)patiently on the other side of the doors.

The dining hall is a large, rectangular room (see Figure 3.3). It is bright because of the fluorescent lighting and the beige paint that replaced the powder-blue paint that gave the room an institutional-type feel. No colour of paint or the brightness of the room, however, could ever conceal the institutionalized feeling, akin to a near-total institution that the shelter is (see Goffman, 1961; de Lint, 1998, 266, 281n1) – in fact, it has to be to function effectively (see Stark, 1994; DeWard and Moe,

Figure 3.3. The dining hall. (Photo credit: Author)

2010, for further examples). The top of one end of the wall contains small windows, each about a foot in height, that provide some natural light. However, these windows are covered with so much grime – the windows have the appearance of the forgotten, apparently never having been subjected to water, save for rain – that even the thin rays of sunlight that penetrate the windows remain inconspicuous. It also does not help that large trees and the apparently uncut grass on the ground above serve to further obscure the natural light.

Once the doors to the dining hall are opened, a sense of calm and order dominate the process of queuing, in many ways a surprise given the eagerness and anxiousness that pervade the waiting area – or, perhaps, this calm is a product of the rather jaded and defeated attitude that constitute many of the clients, especially given their past experiences with what awaits them. As the clients enter the hall, they are greeted by two employees seated at the front. The clients provide staff with their bed number – essentially their identification during their stay at the shelter – and proceed to pick up a plastic tray. They continue along the queue with their plates placed on a metal railing and wait to receive a plate of food from the kitchen staff. They then proceed to pick up a beverage – water, a caffeinated drink, or both; there is also tea, coffee, and milk – and a dessert, before finding a seat at a table. Everything unfolds quite smoothly: not once did I notice an instance of queue-jumping or other problems during this process.

There are thirteen tables in the dining hall, each lined up behind the other in neat rows with the appearance of an equal distance separating each table. Each table has six chairs. Thus, the dining hall can accommodate about seventy-eight people at a given time. Though these chairs are not necessarily uncomfortable, the arrangement of the chairs (and tables) so close to each other gives the impression that the meal cannot be consumed in comfort. Given what is essentially an uncomfortable experience, coupled with the large number of clients during the meals, the order of (and in) the dining hall can be precarious – especially considering the number of employees, including the kitchen staff. Yet, though I sometimes observed minor disputes – a verbal disagreement between a client and employee or among the clients themselves – serious physical disputes were exceptionally rare, with only one such incident occurring during my time observing the shelter.

Although this ordered state might be surprising, an in-depth examination of the space and its personnel reveals why it should not be. The order in the dining hall has little or nothing do with the policies of the shelter or their enforcement. Neither, surprisingly, has it much to do with comfort, which I have paid detailed attention to vis-à-vis an ethic of care. Rather, order is preserved and maintained by the clients themselves, according to what appears to be a code of conduct developed and policed by them, essentially a system of private ordering (see Mnookin and Kornhauser, 1979; Macaulay, 1963; Engel, 1984; Ellickson, 1991; Ranasinghe, 2014).

Thus, the most obvious factor that works in favour of the shelter and the employees is that the clients are hungry – some starving – and eager to eat as much as they can. Rarely do clients converse with each other during meals. What was striking about the dining hall during these times was how quiet it was – in fact, in some ways, even quieter than the sleeping quarters at night where the repeated and loud snoring, the more than occasional flatulence, and tossing and turning create a series of incessantly annoying sounds prohibiting many clients from falling or staying asleep. Any sound in the dining hall was essentially background noise emanating from the employees and kitchen staff – most of it random and idle chatter, the ramblings of weary and jaded employees looking to fill the monotony and boredom of their own lives with some, any, conversation. The clients would enter the dining hall by themselves, receive their food, eat, and leave, again by themselves – some never having uttered one word during the entire sequence, save for disclosing their bed number and the often perfunctory "Thank you" that is uttered before and after the meal. Solitude, rather than gregariousness, then, is the hallmark of a meal in this shelter, as it appears to be in others as well (e.g., Snow and Anderson, 1993, 74). Kim Hopper (2003), for example, writes that "drinking in the bars ... was curiously impersonal. Round after round would be set up and disposed of with barely a word of conversation being exchanged" (113), further illuminating the quietude and solitude that constitute the practices of the homeless.

The foregoing, however, does not imply that the clients are antisocial: they are simply not in the mood to talk because they are famished and want to concentrate on eating. Their sociality and affability were demonstrated in ways that illustrated not just cooperation among the clients, but that many truly cared for one another. In many ways, it was this cooperation and care that went far in ordering the dining hall. Thus, one of the common acts of courtesy is for a client who has found a seat to also save the chair beside him for a friend or acquaintance in the queue. Another act of cooperation is found in the act of sharing. Often, clients would give parts of their meals that they did not care for to others who wished to have more. Sometimes this act was in the form of a trade, but usually it was in the form of a gift. It also mattered little whether the recipient was a friend or merely an acquaintance, perhaps even having met for the very first time at that moment. Food is cherished among the clients, and, rather than being wasteful, it is freely shared. Another example of cooperation is when a client who would be getting up to get more of something – bread, water, or dessert – would ask the others at his table whether he could also get them anything. This gesture was frequently offered to those who were infirm and unable to freely move about. Thus, it was this code of mutual respect and cooperation, rather than the presence of the employees or the numerous policies of the shelter, that ensured the dining hall was orderly and that the provision of the meals unfolded smoothly.

What is remarkable, however, is that the aesthetics of this ordered space, one premised upon food, is neither pleasing nor easily palatable.

Thus, while the kitchen is a beacon of hope, one important aspect in the ethic of care, the food it furnishes, quickly and permanently eviscerates any pretence of that hope. The food simply serves to validate what each client already knows: the life he leads is tough and uncompromising, but perhaps not as tough as the food he chews – evinced beautifully in the rather witty and sarcastic comment of a client's description of a meal he had just consumed: "They are really BBQ *bones* but they call it ribs" (emphasis added). Despite what is most likely hyperbole, that the crux of his lunch was comprised of bones, the meal is viewed in negative rather than positive terms, such that it hastens the wear and tear on his teeth and, thus, unnecessarily strains an already difficult life. On another occasion, a client voiced his displeasure about the cuisine with the comment, "Another stunning example of culinary mediocrity." It should be noted that it is not only the clients who complain in this way. In comparing the food in this shelter to that of another, a caseworker noted, "They [the other shelter] actually have a cook, where[as] [here], *you have people cooking*" (emphasis added). This is an important distinction because it imagines the kitchen as one run by charlatans who somewhat (and somehow) extemporaneously manage to prepare a meal, one that leaves diners dismayed and flummoxed. To further illustrate this, the caseworker added that if, for example, pork chops were on the menu for lunch, the kitchen staff would have completed their preparation by about 9:30 a.m., "so when they serve it at lunch, *it is rock hard*" (emphasis added) – yet another reference to the texture of the meal that makes consumption difficult and places the health of the teeth in a precarious condition. To make matters worse, the food is believed to be extremely unhealthy, a complaint again raised by clients and employees alike. Although some employees believe the clients are well fed – at least with respect to the number of meals and variety of food provided, as discussed in the previous chapter – many, if not most, feel the food is unhealthy and use words such as "greasy," "fatty," or "oily" to describe it. That many will not eat food from the kitchen is indicative of their feelings towards it.

All this, then, illuminates the *place* of food in the shelter vis-à-vis an ethic of care, one which, both aesthetically and otherwise, leaves much to be desired. The volume of food cannot be disputed but, in many ways, the inimicalness of this volume of food is seen directly on the body; every step taken underscores the overweight, obese, anorexic, and overall extremely unhealthy frame of the client. Certainly, the food alone is not responsible for the clients' declining bodies, but the unhealthy nature of the food fails to alleviate the problem. In this way, the ethic of care is rendered harmful and dangerous by the food served in the dining hall, a place which, along with the kitchen, while symbolizing hope also symbolizes the eventual demise of the client. It is in this regard that the solitude that comprises the eating habits of the clients and the ambiance of the dining hall need to be understood: with respect to the unhealthy food that is served, this solitude vanishes and is replaced by sarcastic and acrimonious banter, all castigating the shelter. In many ways, however, this is precisely all the ethic of care can be. If the lobby is designed to be uncomfortable, and it can only be that, then the food must be designed to be unhealthy – it simply cannot be anything else.

The basement also contains one part of the sleeping quarters of the shelter. These quarters, referred to as an "overflow" section, were heavily used during the time of my observations, though, towards the twilight of my stay, they were being gradually phased out. The entrance towards the sleeping quarters is accessed through a very narrow and low tunnel-like structure that is located in the waiting area in the basement – the area clients congregate in while they wait for the doors of the dining hall to open. What is immediately striking about the entrance is that it bares very little light, a sign of what lies ahead. The tunnel is about ten feet in length and between six and eight feet in height, and leads to a large, again dimly lit, area that contains beds. There are thirty-nine beds in total – nine regular beds and thirty overflow beds. This distinction was never clearly explained to me, but, from what I gathered, it simply meant that these thirty beds, while part of the shelter's count, were not considered a permanent fixture – and, as noted above, they were being phased out towards the end of my observations.

The size of this area – about the size of a basketball court – is somewhat difficult to appreciate because it is compartmentalized by numerous parapet walls, about six feet in height and about three feet in length. Given the semi-closed nature of the smaller spaces created because of, and through, these walls, the sleeping quarters have the feeling of miniature rooms. Each area contains four beds, essentially separating the sleeping quarters from the others. Despite being more open than closed, these spaces provide at least some semblance of privacy, though, in practice, the murmurings, incessant and loud snoring and coughing, tossing and turning, and certainly the foul stench which permeates the area remind everyone that they are far from being alone – as discussed above, a sense of privacy proper, save for in the caseworkers' offices, is all but absent in the shelter.

The basement, as noted above, is largely dim, and artificial lighting is chiefly responsible for the visibility in the area. Yet, even with this light-ing, the area still has a dark and grungy look and feel to it, certainly darker than the rest of the shelter, in many ways symbolic of the ethic of care itself. Partly, this has to do with the lack of natural light. Although a row of windows – each about two feet in height and length – is situated on the top of one corner of the wall, just like in the dining hall, the win-dows are so grimy that sunlight is blocked from penetrating through. To make matters worse, the area is also quite cold, and, although this has some advantages, it is, for the most part, a problem for particular segments of the clients, namely, the elderly. They detest the cold and frequently complain, often requesting additional blankets – essentially thin pieces of cloth, symbolic of the ethic of care at work in the shelter, as I take up below. Frequently, these requests cannot be granted sim-ply because additional blankets are unavailable. Furthermore, the cold seems to make the air stale, especially during the winter. All these fac-tors do not bode well during the influenza season, and coughing and hacking are frequent noises emanating from the basement. If not for many, then at least for some, this sleeping area, with its dungeon-like look and feel, gives rise to an uncomfortable experience.

Despite these shortcomings, there are at least three things about the basement that some clients appreciate, especially in relation to the accommodations on the second floor (discussed in detail later in this chapter); these significantly enhance their comforts, many even specifi-cally requesting placements in the basement. One, rather surprisingly, given the foregoing discussion, is the cold. The second floor, especially during the summer, is unbearably hot, and clients find it impossible to fall asleep. To make matters worse, the thick and heavy air of the sum-mer tends to exacerbate the stench of the shelter. These problems, to some extent at least, are alleviated in the basement. Although clients do find the basement somewhat cold in the winter, they more than appreci-ate it during the summer and find it rather pleasant, especially because the stench is minimized, if not masked. Second, and especially because of its dungeon-like feel, the basement is perceived as very quiet. That is, very little sound penetrates the area, and the sounds in it are well masked given the basement's construction. For many clients, this is a welcome benefit, even a relief, as they seek respite from the travails of their lives. In addition, and again rather surprisingly, the basement is a welcome relief for those who are sick because it provides them with more "peaceful" rest. Finally, the washroom in the basement, equipped with shower facilities, is "clean," certainly in far superior condition to those on the second floor. It is not entirely clear exactly why this is so, though the smaller number of clients who use it on a daily basis, in comparison to the usage on the second floor, likely contributes to its cleanliness. Unsurprisingly, many clients prefer to use this washroom, again leading them to request a bed in the basement.

The basement, in particular its sleeping quarters, occupies a peculiar place in the shelter, not simply for its location, relegated to the invisible, but also because this location has a particular relation to the aestheticism of the ethic of care. Here, I refer specifically to light or, in this case, the lack thereof. What is significant is that the ethic of care and its administration, especially the objects mobilized for this very purpose – the beds, for example – and the very subjects to whom care is owed, are rendered somewhat inconspicuous. This inconspicuousness, I suggest, is symbolic of the ethic of care itself, which is often unnoticeable largely because it is lost in the commingling of other logics, namely, security and legality. The light shone in the shelter, as dim and murky as it is, illuminates the ethic of care that itself is incapable of reaching its aspirations. The basement aptly locates the place of an ethic of care, one essentially relegated to the bottom where it is almost unrecognizable.

Here, the bed, pillow, and blanket deserve attention. The beds that clients occupy are, for the most part, reasonably comfortable. The frame of the bed is made of thin metal with its ends drilled into the walls to give it stability, indicative of how unstable the beds are. The mattress, about three inches in thickness, is made of what appears to be synthetic material. It is, however, somewhat comfortable, even after being placed on metal coils which serve as the base of the bed. Thus, ostensibly, clients are provided with a reasonably comfortable bed to sleep in. This, however, is belied by the pillow and blanket provided to clients. Each client receives one pillow, which is about one-third the size of a "normal" pillow and appears to be made out of synthetic material. The blanket provided to clients is essentially a very thin piece of wool cloth, which while somewhat large enough to cover most of the body, does little to keep it warm. In other words, the potential comforts of the bed are rendered void or, at least, problematic, because of poor materials upon which the head rests and the body lies. What is significant, however, is that the shivering body is rendered inconspicuous in, and because of, the dim light, so that the only sign of discomfort that emanates is through sounds, especially of the constantly restless body (cf. Scarry, 1985, who discusses the place of sounds that replace language in the description of pain). It is almost as if while the employees know that a sense of discomfort pervades the shelter, they are unable to actually see it in full flight. It is true, as discussed above, that many clients repeatedly choose to stay in the basement despite the cold, dim, and grungy nature of it. This, however, aptly illuminates how problematic other areas in the shelter are: that is, despite all these problems, they still prefer the basement. The place of the basement, then, is significant to the ethic of care: the murky setting that renders suffering inconspicuous is reflective of the wider aspect of the dilution of the ethic of care throughout the shelter, where it is both invisible and unrecognizable. Sadly, however, as I explicate next through a detailed tour of the second floor, even the conspicuousness of suffering fails to ameliorate the deployment of care.

### The Second Floor: Sleeping Quarters, Bunk Beds, and the Perils of "Intimacy"

The entrance to the second floor is through the same door used to access the basement – the door abutting the washroom in the lobby. Two sets of stairs, each containing about eight steps, lead upwards towards another door, which, like the door in the lobby, is locked between 8:00 a.m. and 4:00 p.m. The pathway to the entrance of the second floor immediately, palpably, and unmistakably portends what lies ahead. This is because the pathway is poorly ventilated, and the stale and rather muggy air makes the odour in this area unpleasant. Yet, it is almost as if the surrounding area has a duplicitous character about it. Immediately upon entering the second floor, the large and bright corridor greets visitors and clients alike with an image of cleanliness and hygiene. To confound matters further, the laundry room, situated immediately on the right-hand corner upon entrance, enhances this feeling through the sweet and pleasant fragrance of detergent and soap. For a moment, and rather unfortunately an all too brief one, it is as if the site is *not* a shelter, but some place of distant memory. It is a feeling, however, that vanishes as quickly as it emerges.

Next to the laundry room, on the same side, is a door that leads to a washroom. At the very moment this door is opened, even if only slightly, the reality of this place, one far from clean and hygienic, is palpably and vividly illuminated, a reality that powerfully and forcefully

serves as a reminder, just in case amnesia or wistful thinking had overcome the senses, that this is, in fact, a shelter. The smell inside is palpable: a mix of feces and urine, sweat (especially from clothing), and
alcohol and drug use, seamlessly combine to create air that is both foul
and nauseating – no amount of air freshener, which is sprayed liber-
ally, can mask the putrid odour of this room. The place smells as if it
is rotting, a powerful symbol because it captures not just the idea of
the physically rotting body, but that the very lives of these clients are
slowly but surely rotting away as well. In this way, the shelter serves
as a museum of sorts, putting on vivid display the very process of this
putrefaction which it may, either indirectly or directly, contribute to –
recall, for example, the unhealthy food or cold temperature discussed
previously.

The images inside the washroom serve as a vivid reminder of the
quality of this place. Immediately upon entering the washroom, on the
left hand side, are three toilet stalls. They are filthy and probably only
subjected to mandatory, and most likely cursory, cleanings. The interior
walls of the stalls are covered in all types of profanities and comments.
The toilets themselves, often unflushed and overflowing, are both a visible and odorous reminder of the place in question – numerous times
employees who did spot checks would need to "tip-toe" around the
water that had overflowed, presumably, from the toilet. In front of
these stalls are three urinals, which are equally, if not more, repulsive.
A profusion of pubic hair covers the urinals and the floor immediately
underneath them, another vivid reminder that the washroom is either
not cleaned frequently or properly or, more likely, both.

Before describing the rest of the washroom, an interesting aspect
about the toilet stalls is worth highlighting. This concerns the doors of
the stalls, which, as noted above, are covered with myriad comments
and images, often vile and containing sexual content. I am mindful that
many public toilet stalls contain similar comments and images. In this
sense, the doors of these stalls are not unique. It is important, however,
to remember that most of these public toilets are public in nature, that
is, regardless of whether they are located in public spaces proper – a
park, for example – or semi-public places – a mall, for example – they
are frequented by a plethora of people from different walks of life who
are invited to these spaces. At least in some ways, the shelter is different
from these spaces. That is, in many ways, it is not a public place proper:
while any adult male is theoretically welcome via an "invite," it is only
a particular segment of the population who accepts this invitation. This

means that, in many ways, the shelter functions as a quasi-home for the indigent because it is by nature more private than public, this despite the lack of privacy that is a constitutive feature of the shelter – the preceding discussion of the lobby illustrates this homelike nature. Yet the very fact that clients write or draw on these doors suggests that they may not view the shelter as home or, at least, not *their* home. If it is reasonable to claim that private possessions are cherished, often to the point of giving rise to a sense of paranoia about their well-being (see Ranasinghe, 2011, 1933–5), and that homeowners are protective of their homes, then the vandalized stall doors signify that the clients view the shelter ephemerally (i.e., they do not believe they will be there for long) and as a thing devoid of the need for responsible ownership (i.e., it belongs to someone else, and clients can, therefore, do as they see fit). In this sense, the "new Golden Rule" of communal life, that rights presuppose responsibility, as Amitai Etzioni (1993, 1–11; 1996) explains, has little meaning to them. This is unfortunate because it feeds into the stereotype that clients of the shelter live for the present, including their inability to respect the property of others (see Ranasinghe, 2011, 1933–5; see also the distinction made by Edward Banfield [1970] 1974, 57–63, between the upper and lower classes and their views on life). For present purposes, I merely wish to underscore that although particular places such as the lobby are thought of as, and turned into, a home, thereby leading to a homelike feeling, the behaviour of the clients in other places illuminates a different belief: they are without homes, and their temporary – what is in reality a permanent – situation is not constitutive of them nor their lives and, most importantly, they do not wish it for themselves. In many ways, it is the clients themselves, then, who appear to renounce the very ethic of care that, supposedly, constitutes the order of the shelter.

In the middle of the washroom there are several sinks and above them there are several mirrors. This is a heavy traffic area because it is used for the purposes of washing and shaving. It is an area that is, like the entire washroom, filthy. The washroom also contains two shower stalls that are similarly unclean. There are several windows located on one side of the washroom but they are so stained with grime that unobscured sunlight is a virtual impossibility – a common feature throughout the shelter, as the preceding sections have documented.

Beyond the aesthetics of cleanliness and hygiene, the daily routines in the washroom give further impressions of its chaotic nature. To fully appreciate this, it should be remembered that this washroom is shared and used by close to ninety clients. Given this number alone, the aes-theticism of filth, dirt, and grime is not surprising. What adds to these, however, is the sheer volume of activities, some conventional for a washroom, some not. Thus, the daily gauntlet of clients going in and out of the washroom, brushing their teeth, washing their faces, show-ering, urinating, and defecating, is part and parcel of its daily charac-ter. Beyond this, however, other activities also consume and frame the character of the washroom, including its smell. First, there is rampant drug use, crack cocaine and marijuana being the two most popular and most frequently consumed. Cigarettes are also frequently smoked. Employees are exhorted to perform routine inspections of the wash-room and to do so during different times of the day so as not to tip off the clients about the times of the inspections. The problematic nature of this issue is evinced in the explanation of a client, who, in not only admitting to the frequency of the problem, but seeking to shed light on it, commented to an employee, "They [the clients] know the timing" and, therefore, could coordinate their activities as such. In response to the employee's comment, "I am pretty oblivious," the client expanded, "My eyes can see more than what yours can see," and then, for good measure, noted, "sometimes, you don't want to see what I see." This lat-ter statement only skims the surface of the disorder – from the perspec-tive of management and employees – rampant in the washroom. It also hints at the difficulty of governing and ordering the shelter because it highlights that more often than not, the employees are unable to attend to all the rule violations in the shelter, if they are even aware of them. In addition, and related, it highlights that the clients know this very well and behave accordingly.

On other occasions, the washroom is used for rather peculiar pur-poses in the sense that these activities take up much time and space, issues that are important given its rather small size. One example is particularly illuminating. I watched as a young female employee gave a client a haircut that she had promised him earlier in the day, something that is not part of her job requirements. After cutting his rather long hair with scissors, she proceeded to use the rather blunt razors provided by the shelter to shave his head – about six razors in total were required to complete the task. What was striking is how matter-of-factly and nonchalantly all this proceeded: the client sat in an area between the two showers and the sinks while his hair was cut and his head shaved, all the while, a procession of clients went in and out of the washroom, some bare bodied with only a towel around their waists, attending to their needs. Given that all of this was performed after dinner meant that the washroom was very busy, and the manoeuvring required to navigate the space aptly illuminates the rather chaotic nature of the washroom.

It is important not to lose sight of the *place* of the washroom in relation to the shelter. At its core, it represents the space reserved for some of the basic necessities of life – intrinsically and inherently tied to an ethic of care. In particular, however, it is a space reserved for the most private of acts, though the presupposition of privacy that is inexorably linked to this space is practically non-existent – yet another reminder that this space is not like others. It is true that the washroom on the second floor affords more privacy than the washroom on the ground floor, where even a door that is supposed to shield the inside from the outside is absent. Yet, even on the second floor, privacy is absent because in a place such as a shelter this is something that is impossible to facilitate. As elucidated before, an ethic of care in the shelter is one that is unable and incapable of respecting, preserving, and delivering privacy. In addition, the aesthetics surrounding this care point to its core features, namely, that a space that caters to numerous individuals on a daily basis, and one in which the permanent and the transient seamlessly blend, cannot provide care of a superior quality, in many ways, not even of a mediocre sort. Partly, this has to do with the clients themselves, who, because they do not appear to view the shelter as home – *their* home – tend to use it in a manner that leaves much to be desired, both by them and management. The resulting dirt, filth, and untidiness is as much a product of the architecture of the space, its policies, and its everyday ordering, as it is a product of the people who pass through it daily. The washroom vividly brings this to light, as do the sleeping quarters, to which I now cast my attention.

At the end of the corridor – the one immediately visible upon entering the second floor – there is another corridor, also very clean and bright, along which the sleeping rooms are situated (see Figure 3.4).

There are ten rooms in all, containing ninety beds in total. On one side of the corridor, there are six rooms. These rooms and their accommodations are of better quality than the other rooms and are preferred by the clients, some even expressly asking whether they can be accommodated in them. Each of these rooms contains two beds and two lockers (see Figure 5.3, in chapter 5). This means that, at any given time, a client will only have to share the space with one other client. This has significant implications in relation to privacy – already practically

Figure 3.4. The hallway of the sleeping quarters on the second floor. (Photo credit: Author)

non-existent in the shelter – and collegiality. Second, and related, unlike the other rooms that have bunk beds, these are single beds, which, in some ways at least, facilitate some level of privacy and additional comfort. Third, and unsurprisingly given the number of persons occupying the rooms, they tend to be cleaner. Fourth, the odours in these rooms are not as repulsive and the noise not as loud. There are additional advantages as well. These rooms have windows that overlook the major arterial road. The clients, therefore, are not completely cut off from the outside world and life (the other rooms have smaller windows overlooking a parking lot). These rooms are reserved for those clients who have steady employment. The occupants of these rooms do not pay a fee for them, in contrast, for example, to the clients who are housed on the fourth floor and who sleep four to a room and pay a monthly rent. Instead, the purpose of these accommodations, as management sees it, is to reward those who are seeking to sustain their lives independently.

(Again, here, the concerns of Rob are aptly visible: that is, that 90 per cent of the clientele do not pay for their stay, and that he would prefer them to be [somewhat] self-sustaining; in this case, those assigned to these rooms are, at a minimum, believed to be capable of functioning on their own, if not now, then at least at some point in the future.) The other rooms, located on the other side of the corridor, house the remaining clients. There are four such rooms. These rooms are large, and each houses between sixteen and twenty clients. The typical room contains four rows of beds on each side, each a bunk bed, for a total of sixteen beds – some rooms have an additional bunk bed or two (see Figure 3.5).

Certain features, vivid and palpable, define the sleeping quarters. First, and only during the night, its space is overcome by myriad sounds, all loud, incessant, and annoying to employees and clients alike. Loud snoring is a common sound – the sounds brought on because of sleep apnea create tension and acrimony among clients, some resorting to, some receiving, threats, others launching complaints to employees

Figure 3.5.  A sleeping quarter on the second floor. (Photo credit: Author)

asking to be moved. Other sounds range from flatulence to loud and "violent" coughing, along with the often, but sometimes drowned-out, restlessness evinced in the constant tossing and turning. Easily falling and staying asleep, then, is a luxury that many clients simply do not have. Second, just like many other places in the shelter, this space is overcome by a rancid, almost putrid, smell, a mix of sweat, body odour, and unwashed clothes (especially socks). These combine to give the sleeping quarters a repulsive stench, equally unpleasant as the adjacent washroom, though palpably different – certainly ninety men occupying a relatively small area can only lead to unpleasantness, both of the olfactory and aesthetic kind.

The problems associated with odour are made worse by the presence of the lockers in the rooms. As noted before, each client is assigned a personal locker upon registering at the shelter. The practice of "hoarding," discussed briefly in a previous section, where clients collect and store a variety of items – ranging from old and unwashed clothes, sometimes shoes, perishable and non-perishable food, alcohol and drugs, magazines to a host of other items – is a significant issue. To make matters worse, clients do not clean their lockers, and this means these products remain in their lockers throughout their stay. Thus, unsanitary conditions created by this practice gravely threaten the salubriousness of the shelter and its personnel, both employees and clients alike, evinced, for example, in the rampant paranoia about bed bugs (the subject of chapter 5). For present purposes, however, I merely wish to underscore the manner in which the air in the sleeping quarters is putrefied through, and because of, this practice. Here, the sock is particularly relevant and revealing. Perhaps more than any other item or piece of clothing, unwashed socks, both on the feet of clients and in their lockers, contribute to the pungent stench of the sleeping quarters. Many clients sleep with their socks on, and this practice provides a visual reminder of the putrid and rancid atmosphere that defines and envelops the second floor (a sad, but at the same time funny, recollection of my time at the shelter involves a particular employee who, when doing rounds – canvassing the area to ensure that all was in order – would use her jacket or some other piece of clothing to cover most of her face and speed walk through the sleeping quarters, the speed at which she performed this task belying her heavily overweight and unhealthy frame). Thus, the symbol of the sock in relation to the indigent body, the shelter, and its ethic of care cannot be overlooked. The very item of clothing that protects and cushions the foot, an important part of the body that is crucial to mobility, is also aesthetically repulsive: a white cotton sock now turned into a mixture of black, brown, and other colours, covered with filth, unwashed perhaps since it was first worn, juts out from what is otherwise a thin blanket that is too small to cover the entire body – a commonality of the homeless body characterized by "inattention to personal hygiene, appearance, and dress" (Elias and Inui, 1993, 399). The sock, however, is not just a visual symbol: the stench that goes with it is a powerful reminder that, in this space, an ethic of care can only be deployed to a certain extent.

In this light, it is important to examine the locker vis-à-vis the comfort it provides clients and how this comfort leads to particular problems in ordering the shelter. Regardless of how small it is, at its core, the locker is *the* space that belongs to the client. That it is locked and can only be opened by a key owned by, or a code known to, the client, establishes this space as *his* space and reinforces his presupposition of it – the lock can be cut, and often is, but legitimate grounds approved by a supervisor or manager, is a requirement. In fact, the relationship of the locker is not just one between the client and the employees of the shelter but one between the client and other clients as well, separating their spaces from each other. In that sense, both instrumentally and symbolically, the locker is meant to enhance the comfort of the client and, therefore, is crucial to the deployment of care. Yet, in this very attempt to create comfort, an additional, and from the perspective of management, a dangerous health problem is created. Thus, to combat this problem, the employees were directed to frequently clean and, where appropriate, empty some contents from the lockers – the policy described earlier, requiring clients to empty the contents of their lockers on certain weekdays, was an effort to attend to this problem. The employees, however, and understandably so, abhor this practice and find it repulsive, many often trying to trade this task for other chores with their colleagues. Beyond the olfactory and aesthetic concerns – the latter is particularly a concern for female employees who have to deal with pornographic images or the underwear of the clients – health concerns are also a major worry, specifically in relation to bed bugs or being pricked or cut by needles or other drug paraphernalia. Cutting oneself is another major safety concern for employees: in fact, an employee once brought into The Bubble a knife with a rusted, nine-inch blade that had been found in a locker.

From the perspective of management, these fears need to be balanced against an ethic of care, one which seeks to create a space that is comfortable and comforting. This very space, however, is open to a variety of threats and puts at risk the very personnel who are tasked with deploying care. This, then, is a good example of how the logic of security comes directly into contact and conflicts with an ethic of care, the subject of discussion in chapters 5 and 6. For present purposes, I underscore that this contact and conflict can be visually mapped in the aesthetics of care, one which also has an olfactory dimension to it.

In a similar vein, it is worth exploring two other material dimensions of the sleeping quarters in the shelter and their relation to an ethic of care: first, the door, and second, already discussed in some detail, the bed. The word "room" is, in some ways, a misnomer, because these rooms do not have doors, a crucial element to what constitutes a room. This, however, has not always been the case. These rooms, at some point in their history, did have doors, evinced in the still easily visible marks of door hinges. I immediately noticed the absence of doors during a guided tour I received from a supervisor on the first day of my observations. In response to my query as to why these doors were removed, the supervisor explained that transparency is important to the daily ordering of the shelter, and the doors physically curtailed transparency and permitted clients to freely engage in a variety of illicit activities (these were breaches of the shelter's policies despite being, in some cases, legal in the broader sense, such as consuming alcohol or drugs or engaging in homosexual sexual acts, some involving the purchase and sale of sexual services). Therefore, in order to eliminate such behaviour and to clearly outline that such behaviour was not tolerated within the walls of the shelter, the doors were removed.

Again, what this act reveals is that privacy does not exist in the shelter. It also illustrates that the shelter cannot meaningfully seek to preserve or enhance privacy. That is, its daily operations must be undertaken and performed in such a manner that the principles of visibility and transparency must trump those of privacy. Thus, while on the surface it could be said that an ethic of care cannot facilitate privacy, on a deeper level, it is the daily ordering of the shelter, in relation, for example, to safety and security, that renders privacy unfeasible and a threat to its order.

This is also brought to light by way of the shelter's beds, which I have already paid detailed attention to during the discussion of the sleeping arrangements in the basement. For present purposes, I wish to underscore the *place* of the bed in relation to other furniture and material products in the shelter. Unlike most other objects, save for the locker assigned to each client, the bed is a quintessential symbol of privacy – each bed belongs to a client and is, therefore, his. Thus, whether the bed is comfortable or not is almost unimportant to the ethic of care – though, for the most part, it is somewhat comfortable. Rather, it is that the bed is *comforting* – a symbol not just of rest and relaxation, but privacy – that is significant. In that sense, the bed is a representation of an ethic of care in action. What it signifies, however, is that this very ethic is continuously eviscerated and destroyed because, in the very comfort it symbolizes and purports to deliver, the communal trumps the private. That is, comfort can only be extended as far as the space allows it: in this case, that some fifteen to twenty men must share a small space on a daily basis. Examined in this light, an ethic of care can only be deployed to a certain extent: the objects relied upon to enhance care – the locker, the chair, and the bed as examples – also bring this ethic into direct conflict and, thereby, destroy it. The aestheticism of an ethic of care is a powerful and visible reminder of this.

### The Materiality of Space and the Aestheticism of an Ethic of Care: A Final Word

In this chapter, I have examined and explicated the space and place of the shelter. This involved focusing on spatial tactics and material objects and the way these are mobilized for an ethic of care. As well, attention was paid to how these objects are tied to, fuel, and even circumscribe this ethic. I have provided a sensory tour of the shelter and homed-in on the aestheticism of an ethic of care, comprising the aesthetics, the auditory, and the olfactory. I have suggested that these dimensions provide a means by which it is possible to think about and make sense of an ethic of care. Beyond the discursive practices that make up an ethic of care – the subject of the next chapter – these dimensions not only (re) produce this ethic, but are also visible in the very concept and practice of care. Thus, the materiality of the shelter, from the immobile (such as walls and rooms) to the mobile (such as chairs and mattresses), shine light upon an ethic of care and its daily mobilization. These materials, in other words, contain numerous insights about the care that resides in – in fact, is said to be the hallmark of – this space. The discursive and the material, then, must be viewed simultaneously and as complements to each other.

# 4 From the Mundane to the Chaotic: The (Un)Making of an Ethic of Care

In chapter 3, I examined the space of the shelter to shed light on how the materiality of this site, as well as the spatial tactics and their deployment therein, aptly illuminate the aestheticism of an ethic of care and what it reveals about the daily ordering of the shelter. This chapter casts its gaze on the key personnel in the shelter, introducing them and their work. This forms the foundation upon which an exploration and explication of the discursive production of an ethic of care vis-à-vis the logics of security and legality will be undertaken in later chapters. In the preceding pages, I suggested that the ordering of the shelter is constituted by a type of administrative chaos that renders the deployment of care difficult, even impossible. There is a different type of chaos – related to the formalized one but, perhaps less visible, perhaps less inimical and potent – that is also a significant part of the daily life of the shelter. In this chapter, I describe the ways the mundane and humdrum of the daily work lives of the key personnel of the shelter and their relations with each other and the clients contribute to this chaos. It is this chaos – deemed problematic and, therefore, addressed through more formalized means, such as rules – that further contributes to the administrative chaos I have referred to.

There are three principal parties involved in this discussion: the clients, the employees – comprised of a variety of groups, two of whom, namely, front-line employees and caseworkers, will receive detailed attention – and the management team, comprised of managers and supervisors. Other parties also play an important, though secondary, role and they and their work receive attention through the contact they make, and the relations they have, with the primary actors noted above.

## The Clientele: The Making and Unmaking of Homelessness

The ethic of care that constitutes the shelter necessitates that, at least facially, the shelter have an open-door policy – recall the comment of a supervisor, quoted in chapter 2, that "the building never closes." This also means the shelter will attract a panoply of people from myriad walks of life, representing a variety of age groups and racial backgrounds, each constituted by a particular and, often, troublesome (and troubling) history. Examples of the broad range of people found on any given day include the homeless or otherwise visibly poor; persons recently released or discharged from jails, prisons, mental health facilities, or hospitals; persons travelling from one city to another who are temporarily looking for a place to stay; persons who are new to the city; persons who have been either evicted by their landlord or asked to leave by their spouse or partner; and, in a handful of cases, young adults who have run away from home. Despite the apparent visible poverty uniting this disparate group, the eclecticism that constitutes it is ripe with problems, especially given the rather small and restricted space in which clients cohabitate. It is, then, the very ethos upon which the shelter is founded and operates, that is, an ethic of care, which poses significant problems to the organization of the shelter. The employees, as a result, are tasked with dealing with a plethora of concerns, ranging from the mundane and minor (e.g., loud noises or the stench within the shelter) to more serious and dangerous matters (e.g., physical assault, threats and verbal abuse, both in regards to their well-being and the well-being of the clients). Despite this open-door policy, it is worth recalling, as discussed in chapter 3, that there is a somewhat careful vetting system in place through the spatial tactics of doors and locks (along with other practices that will be discussed in later chapters), which serves to, at least momentarily, provide employees the opportunity to assess the potential client and determine whether he should or should not be granted entrance. This system anticipates and portends the trouble to follow and take hold of the shelter, something which suggests that even within a space that is designed for care, serious problems, some dangerous, are part and parcel of its daily life.

While homelessness is difficult to precisely define and make sense of (see Hopper, 2003, 15–24; Rossi, 1989, 10–13, 45–81; Takahashi, 1996, 292–3), especially given its changing dynamics over the past sixty years or so (see Rossi, 1994, 344–5), what is crucial for present purposes is that there are numerous disagreements between employees (both front-line workers and caseworkers) about whether those persons who walk through the doors of the shelter are homeless and, therefore, deserving of assistance. Here, even the visibility of poverty which, apparently, "adorns" the bodies of these persons, does not alleviate the uncertainties and disagreements at hand. While some employees see the visibility of poverty as an indication of the sad plight of these persons, for others, it is merely a ruse on the part of the clients who are adept at exploiting the system and profiting from the sympathies of others. The comments of "Captain Delight," perhaps the most outspoken critic of the clients and the shelter system itself, aptly capture the suspicion that shapes his thinking (and that of many others as well). After noting that "they [the clients] are *manipulating* us ... They know to work the system ... [and] they know how to read us" (emphasis added), he underlined that the clients are not poor. *"They have money,"* he said, and then commented, *"I don't know what it means to have money,* but ... people [are] using laptops ... [and] you don't see them getting desperate or anxious to be here. For them, this is [a] life they have made ... a way of living. *They are not homeless ..."* (emphases added)!

Notice how "Captain Delight" arrives at his conclusion, one presented as factual and derived from careful and detailed observations of the clients conducted over the course of the ten or so years he has worked at this shelter (along with many years in others) – his own ethnography, so to speak. These experiences have clearly revealed to him that those who enter the shelter system are not poor. This is evidenced in the material goods that are part and parcel of their lives. Here, this belief is derived from a particular type of "othering," that is, one that *a priori* paints what it means to be, and look, homeless – the "performance of homelessness," as Robert Desjarlais (1999, 477; Desjarlais 1997, 214; see also Desjarlais, 1996) puts it. As "Captain Delight" sees it, the condition of homelessness is a difficult one. What he witnesses – the property the clients possess (e.g., laptops) and their behaviour and attitude (they are not anxious or desperate) – reveals exactly the opposite of what he expects. For these reasons, he questions the veracity of poverty that is worn as a visible mark, one, as he sees it, meant simply to elicit sympathy. In many ways, such a way of thinking is far from aberrant, not simply in relation to workers in the shelter, but in other spaces as well. For example, one participant observer, who, in commenting about "the shiny new low-rider convertible truck ..." driven by the boyfriend of a client she knew, wrote: "Such possessions are uncommon for a homeless family on welfare" (Connolly, 2000, 3). This suggests that particular material goods, perhaps those connoting wealth, are not part of the fabric of the homeless. Thus, when "Captain Delight" sees the clients of the shelter with an abundance of material goods, his suspicions about the veracity of their plight are strengthened because he is merely subscribing to a widely held belief about what it means to be homeless.

Even if only subtle, there is also an element of anger, perhaps disgust, in his comments, one which has grave implications for the ethic of care (Held, 2006, 10). In the "othering" he partakes in, that is, in the construction of what homelessness is and, therefore, looks and feels like, it is possible to see that the subject of the other is, surprisingly, him. That is, he wishes to clearly reinforce that it is *he* who is poor and, it is he who is *the* victim – this process relies upon a duality or binarism in the ways that Homi Bhabha ([1989] 1994, 19–39) both speaks of and castigates. In commenting that "I don't know what it means to have money," "Captain Delight" is stating that if the condition of poverty describes anybody in the shelter, it describes him, not most of the clients. This frustration and disgust is clearly visible in his comment: "Those guys, just sitting there, get more money. *Come on*" (emphasis in original)! Such a belief is shared by other employees as well, evinced, for example, in the comments of a female employee who, as noted in chapter 3, rather disgustingly admitted, "These guys make more money than me sometimes" and "they are eating better than people living in homes." Thus, for "Captain Delight" and others like him, the visibility of poverty that adorns the clients is a sobering reminder, one driven home on a daily basis, that it is he who has been left behind.

For present purposes, I underscore that how the clients are viewed – as homeless or not and, with it, deserving or undeserving of service and assistance – is fundamental to the ways the everyday ordering of the shelter unfolds. What results is a chaotic environment. The tenor of this environment profoundly impacts the deployment of care and speaks volumes about the ethic of care, the cornerstone upon which the shelter and its mission are founded and operate.

Thus far, while mentioning the clients, I have cast little attention on them. In what follows, I construct a biography of the clients, one mindful of the disparities (rather than commonalities) that constitute them. In this vein, it is important to recall one key demographic about the clients, perhaps the one thing that unites them: the clientele in the shelter are men – the shelter provides services solely to men. The shelter, therefore, is quite different from many others where men and women commingle (see Glasser, 1988; Desjarlais, 1997). This, as I discuss later, has important implications for the ordering of the shelter, as the dynamics relating to gender (a male clientele served by both male and female employees) pose numerous difficulties, one particular concern relating to perceptions of safety and security.

Most, if not all, of the clients in the shelter, as I have discussed in some detail in the previous chapter, are unhealthy and saddled with a variety of medical illnesses ranging from hepatitis and asthma to more serious conditions such as cardiovascular or pulmonary diseases. Some are also physically immobile either because of amputations to their legs or, because of broken bones or, even old age and, therefore, are largely restricted to wheelchairs or crutches. In addition, many clients suffer from mental illnesses such as bipolar disorder, schizophrenia, depression, and paranoia. Most clients, as well, are severely addicted to alcohol and drugs (in particular, alcohol), which bodes poorly for their salubrity, not to mention the daily ordering of the shelter.

A majority of the clients are middle-aged Caucasians. The rest of the clientele are composed largely of African descent (a majority being from Somalia) and Aboriginal descent. The latter are, as it is widely believed in the shelter, heavily addicted to alcohol. This poses serious problems to the non-Aboriginal employees who must attend to them and their needs while always mindful and sensitive of the racialized aspects of these relations – this, even among those employees who are minorities. As I explicate below, race relations in the shelter are a particularly concerning matter, though not as palpable or visible on the surface.

## A Racialized Ethic of Care

One particularly sensitive aspect about race relations in the shelter concerns the francophone clientele, who make up a not-so-negligible portion of the clients. Given the city is close to the Province of Quebec (a francophone province), there is a heavy francophone community who lives in or visits the city. Thus, the influence of the French (or Québécois) culture in the city is palpable. This is also reflected in the indigent population. The problem, however, is that many employees, especially those working on the front-lines, either have no working knowledge of French or very little of it. It is now taken for granted that language, as a key marker of culture, is, if not explicitly, then, at least implicitly, violent both in the instrumental and symbolic sense. In its usage, in the very utterance of words, competence and belonging are clearly and explicitly conveyed to the interlocutor, regardless of whether or not the grammaticality of the language is sound; thus, other aspects associated with speaking, such as pronunciation or the enunciation of words (through, for example, particular accents), work, *a priori*, to "other" the speaker in relation to his/her interlocutor (see Bhabha, [1989] 1994, 66–92; Bourdieu and Wacquant, 1992, 140–74). This "othering" – even if occurring unwittingly – unfolds theatrically in the shelter when a client of francophone descent who is not well versed in English communicates (or *tries* to communicate) with employees either of Caucasian or minority descent who cannot speak French or speak it very poorly. Thus, because the francophone client is well aware that his every word will be microscopically scrutinized to decipher its meaning – because, presumably, his accent stymies "correct" pronunciation and enunciation – the conversations he has with employees are fraught with tensions, whether implicitly or explicitly so, and are, therefore, heavily racialized. What results is that the francophone clients treat every interaction with a non-francophone employee transactionally; that is, each client seeks to convey as quickly and briefly as possible what it is that is required, and, by extension, wishes that he is responded to and receives his request in the same manner. Any pretence of cordiality, even professionalism, is, *a priori*, bracketed by the client. This is the only means by which he can find some dignity in the act of communication, a process in which he his constructed as virtually incompetent.

To some extent, the Caucasian employees are quite sympathetic to the plight of the francophone clientele, though in many situations they are not in a position to help. At a minimum, however, they recognize and acknowledge that there is a problem and that the francophone clients are marginalized. What is most troubling concerns the employees who are of minority descent, especially those who, themselves, have very poor or mediocre knowledge of English and certainly none of French. Given they struggle with English – and, as well, have only begrudgingly accepted that they have to learn, and communicate in, a foreign language – they tend to be less sensitive to the francophone clients because they feel that they, rather than the francophone clients, are oppressed and marginalized (in fact, they see the francophone clients as one aspect of a larger pool of Caucasians who have discriminated and oppressed them).

The foregoing underlines the space of the shelter as heavily racialized (at times, explicitly so), and this strongly influences not just the ordering of the shelter, but how care is thought about and deployed – the discussion in the previous chapter about how clients of minority descent would "reserve" their chairs for others of minority descent is illustrative of this. Just how disconcerting this is can be gleaned from a comment of a caseworker who linked racism to safety: "Let's say a Native gentleman doesn't like the way that [a] white person is looking at them, so … you don't want to see people … getting hurt, you don't want a risk to … the staff." Here, the precarious nature of order in the shelter, in relation to safety and security, is linked directly to the racialized nature of the space: and, it is underlined, this can be precipitated through the most simple and humdrum activities of everyday life, such as a look or a particular gesture. All this poses problems to the clients and employees alike, thereby jeopardizing order.[1] To give further colour to the racialized space of the shelter, I provide as an example an episode that transpired when a man of minority descent tried to reserve a bed.

It was just before midnight when a middle-aged black man entered the shelter, walked up to The Bubble where two front-line workers were seated, and said (or mumbled) the words, "Hassan, Hassan" – which probably sounded more like "Hssn, Hssn." It was immediately clear – at least to me, a man of colour – that he hardly spoke English and the little he spoke contained a thick and heavy accent that appeared to be of Somalian origin. A young employee, who seemed perplexed as to what was happening, asked the man, "Do you speak English?" The employee repeatedly asked him this question and the man provided the same response, "Hassan, Hassan," though, to make matters worse, would also add the word "king," so his response sounded as "Hssn, Hssn – king." While there appeared to be some confusion about whether the man was drunk, for reasons that are not clear, the employee was unable to figure out that the man could not speak English well. Partly, the problem was exacerbated because, as a young white Christian male, he appeared to be oblivious that the man was, in fact, telling him his name, one that was not, however, anglophone, and which was, therefore, strange to his ears, just as the man standing in front of him was a stranger (and strange to him). Thus, because of his apparent inexperience with such persons, and his unwillingness to listen carefully to the man, he tended to dismiss him as intoxicated until his colleague pointed out that perhaps he was stating his name. At this point, the employee asked the man to provide him with some identification so that he could verify his name – a standard policy at the shelter for anyone who wishes to reserve a bed. The man, however, was unable to fully understand what was requested of him. After repeated failed attempts to elicit identification, the employee provided the man with a small piece of paper and asked him to write his name on it. The man, who now seemingly understood what was required of him, proceeded to do so, but what he wrote was, because of the illegibility of his penmanship, so unintelligible that it was impossible to decipher his name. The employee continued to tell the man that he could not read what was written and persisted with his request for identification. At this point, the other employee took out a piece of his own identification, showed it to the man and asked him to do the same. After sifting through a stack of papers, the reasons for which are not readily clear, the man then took out his health identification card from his wallet and, after initially toying with the employees about whether to hand it over or not, finally did. At this time – a period of some ten minutes after the man's entrance into the shelter – the employees were able to determine that the man's name was, in fact, "Hassan, Hassan," just as he had stated or, tried to, from the outset.[2]

Much more transpired after, the details of which I refrain from narrating for they are not pertinent. For present purposes, I simply underscore the difficulties surrounding the ordering of the shelter which are, in some ways at least, a product of the racialized space in (and of) the shelter. I do not claim that the two employees are racist or harbour prejudices towards those of minority descent. However, there is a certain simplicity that constitutes the young white Caucasian male who was unable to recognize that the client was stating his name – a simplicity that has little or nothing to do with intellect or acumen but, rather, with social standing, where his surrounding environment and its history is largely Anglo-Saxon. Explored in this light, his actions were a reflection of his history, one that would make it virtually impossible for anyone of his background to know that "Hassan, Hassan" is a name. His ears, in other words, trained only to detect particular accents and particular ways of pronouncing words and enunciating them, could not register the attempts of a middle-aged black man who did not speak English well, who repeatedly struggled to not only state his name, but highlight that it was, in fact, a name that he was stating.

This employee saw nothing problematic – that is, racist or prejudicial – with his actions, save for, perhaps, the logistical issues of spending about fifteen minutes with the client. Yet, the client – primitive and backward as Frantz Fanon describes the colonizer's description of the colonized, castigated as the wretched of the earth ([1961] 1968; see also [1952] 1967) – appears to have recognized the "othering" that took place, be it implicitly or explicitly, and the racialized aspects of

the entire conversation, where his very name was foreign to a Caucasian man. Thus, towards the end of this episode, the client accused the
employees of racism and, then, rather ironically, hurled racial insults
at the employees, especially towards a white female employee (whom
he believed to be of Scottish descent) who was not even present during
what transpired and had only entered The Bubble at the end. Interestingly, and again in the Fanon-ian infused hostility of Jean-Paul Sartre's ([1961] 1968) vitriol for violence as the only means upon which
the emancipation of the colonized can be achieved, the client similarly
hurled his own violence, in the form of racial epithets, as an antidote
to the violence of racism he believed he was subjected to, even if only
unwittingly.

What this episode clearly illuminates is that not only is the space
racialized, but that – and given this – the very ethic of care and its
deployment is, itself, racialized and, therefore, made complicated and
cumbersome. In other words, even the simple request to enter the
shelter, a routine and humdrum practice, can not only be difficult, but
acrimonious as well, laden with vitriol and spite, precisely because
of a culture that privileges particular norms over others. In this case,
because the client's name could not be understood – mapped onto the
lexicon of names, *as a name* – he was rendered nameless and, therefore,
ineligible to receive a bed for the night, a basic aspect of care.

*Gender and the Production of Chaos*

As noted before, although most of the clientele are middle-aged, there
are clients who are young-adults, that is, between the ages of eighteen
and thirty. Most of these are Caucasian (both anglophone and francophone) with a handful of minorities. More so than not, they have left
home at quite an early age (due to a variety of reasons, though, more
often than not, difficult family relations appear to be a driving factor)
and have immersed themselves into a nomadic lifestyle moving from
shelter to shelter in various parts of the country (it was not uncommon
to find young adults who had come to the shelter from as far west as
British Columbia or as far east as Nova Scotia). Some of these young
adults enrolled in either a trade school or college in an effort to better
their lives.

From an organizational perspective, and with respect to the daily
ordering and governance, these young men pose specific difficulties. It
is not that they are young *per se* that is the issue, but that they are *young*

*men* that is significant, and this is particularly problematic given the number of young female employees. Before explicating this problem in greater detail, it is important to note that age as a whole – just like race, noted above – is a particularly important demographic trait that poses significant problems to the ordering of the shelter. For example, as noted, many of the clients are either middle-aged or old and, more often than not, find it extremely difficult to take directions from those who are much younger. This is viewed not just as insulting and disrespectful, but also as silly, because the clients wholeheartedly believe the young employees simply do not have enough life experience to understand and discuss the problems they face.[3] It is not only the clients who so believe. In fact, and rather surprisingly, many employees subscribe to the view that many of their colleagues are not suitable for the job. A woman in her mid-thirties, for example, stated, "A lot of staff are young [and] inexperienced." Similarly a woman in her forties noted "that most clients will come to me because, I guess ..., of the age factor and most kids, some in this field, they don't know how to have a conversation without either shouting or putting a person down or letting them feel bad for being there." It is interesting that she equates the younger employees to children – when she speaks of "kids" – who, because they are inexperienced about life, are not knowledgeable of how to engage and interact with this population. In fact, equating them to children means that, by extension, she is also implying that the younger employees require strict supervision and close guidance – as children do – and this responsibility falls upon the shoulders of the mature employees, further adding to their responsibilities. This point was made forcefully and directly by a male employee:

> You see the staff are young and for the most part they are very immature in the way they carry themselves around, let alone dealing with some of these clients ... So it's kind of tough working in such an environment because you feel for the client. We are supposed to be a compassionate organization ... we are supposed to be caring in treating them. In treating them in a different manner, we are not emulating the basics of the organization.

The employee's lament captures two related concerns that are significant to the life of the shelter. Here, immaturity is not simply a problem with respect to the everyday ordering of the shelter – in terms of, as he puts, creating a tough work environment – but to the ethic of care and its deployment as well. As he sees it, the incompetence of the young workers, brought upon by their immaturity, makes it difficult, if not impossible, to put into practice the basic values that the shelter stands for. In other words, the space of the shelter is not simply chaotic for the workers, but one bereft of care for the clients as well. Just how dire a problem this is can be gleaned from the comments of Elizabeth, who is, in some ways, mature enough to understand the very immaturity that constitutes her and the problems that emanate as such: "I don't like the fact that there are so many young people like myself working here. I don't understand it. I love these girls, don't get me wrong, but I think that there is a certain lack of maturity sometimes."

I will return to this issue in a later chapter, though for present purposes, I simply use the foregoing to underscore the problems that are inherent in (and to) the shelter, problems that are precisely a product of the types of personnel and their biographies that cannot be extricated from their work lives. The other problem with respect to age, already introduced above, concerns the relations between the young male clients and young female employees, which I now turn to.

What was clear from the outset of my observations was that the relationship between the clients and female employees was very cordial and friendly, certainly far more than the relationship between clients and male employees, which was, at best, tepid and characterized by circumspection. Specifically with respect to the young clients and the young female employees, this relationship was more close and warm. The male clientele often flirted with the young female employees who, for their part, were quite smitten by, and very much appreciated, the attention and affection they received, so much so that they would encourage this behaviour. In explaining the appeal of the young male clients, an elderly female employee, who simply could not understand it, juxtaposed the "dirty old homeless men …" whom the women encounter frequently, to the young clients who "are gangsta, gangsta [and] … trying to change their lives." Perhaps the infrequency of young men entering the shelter explains the appeal; or, perhaps, it is that they are seeking to build a future that explains it. Regardless of the reason(s), this "relation" and "appeal" are of a serious concern to management. It is also a serious problem for the male employees who find it difficult to interact with the clients, so much so that they fear for their safety.

I draw on an example between a young male client and a young female employee to give colour to the foregoing discussion. A young man, in his early-twenties (perhaps, late-teenage years), took a keen liking to a young female employee in her mid-twenties. During his short stay at the shelter, about two weeks, he would come and speak to her every day after dinner (at least when I was present). He would then proceed to finish his homework (he was enrolled in some type of school program) and would again come back to see her. Each time they would converse in a very friendly and flirtatious manner for about ten minutes. The employee, for her part, was quite charmed by the attention she received and reciprocated with her equally coquettish behaviour.

This brief "relationship," however, posed significant problems to the ordering of the shelter. First, the female employee was quite distracted from her duties while conversing with the client. More pertinently, perhaps, several of her colleagues were quite uncomfortable with her actions because they were forced to be overly friendly to the young man as well. Partly, many understood that her actions blurred the boundaries between employee and client, in terms of what is and is not acceptable. Thus, in excoriating actions such as hers, "Captain Delight" once commented to me: "I won't cross that *friendly line*," because "that will destroy what we do" (emphasis added).

While the employee's actions may seem innocuous, they were, in fact, quite inappropriate, as the following example illustrates. One day during an afternoon shift, an intoxicated client found a female sex toy – commonly referred to as a dildo – in a garbage bin in the lobby. He showed it to a female employee and asked her whether it was her cat (with all the sexual puns intended). This brought a raucous laughter and exchange between the employee and several of the clients who passed by the vicinity. Later, the young female employee in question – who had now found the toy which had by then been placed in The Bubble – told her admirer, just as he had walked into the shelter after his program, "I found your instrument." He was unsure as to what she was referring to, so she continued with the joke by saying, "I found it under your pillow," indicating that she had visited the dorm room where he was sleeping. When she displayed the toy, the young man was both shocked and embarrassed, though the humour was not lost on him. This example, highlighting a narration of a sexual joke, clearly breaches protocol, because, as noted above, many clients, who are starved for female attention, flirt heavily with the female employees. In this particular case, this young woman's actions could have been read as an encouragement of such behaviour. It is precisely such behaviour that management believes is both inappropriate and dangerous. In fact, just how problematic this situation is, I would learn on another occasion during a conversation with a representative of the human resources team who stated that these relationships were a major worry for management.

It is not, however, as though management is exaggerating or embellishing this problem. According to what was disclosed to me by both the employees and management, though not necessarily a frequently occurring practice, it was, nevertheless, not uncommon for some young female employees to commence intimate relationships with younger clients. This practice poses a variety of concerns to management as the following rather lengthy lament, which is almost a diatribe, by a supervisor illustrates:

> Oh, boundaries, boundaries [are] an incredibly big thing in working behind the desk. I'm sure that you've seen all kinds of boundary breaking [*giggles*], and as soon as you let your guard down and let someone in psychologically then that's a problem. We ... got somebody engaged now to somebody she met here as a client and someone else was having an affair with a client. *This is nuts.* She should know better, you would think. [She] had all the training, all that sort of thing, was working here, somehow or another hooked up with one of the clients who was here, invited him home, he went home, stayed with her, stole her cell phone, did something else, came back here ... after they had some sort of an argument, something like that and, yelled at the top of his lungs to [her] coworkers all about the relationship and made quite a ruckus, [and] got kicked out. So the person [the employee] thought "fine, I've been outed, I guess I'm going to have to tell management that I've hooked up with this guy," and she ended up getting fired. (emphasis added)

What this relationship signifies to the broader governance of the shelter is deeply disconcerting to management. Such a relationship connotes the blurring of an important boundary between worker and client, that is, between caregiver and receiver. Such a boundary, paramount to order and governance, creates an important distinction between "us" and "them." While many employees (and clients as well), abhor such a distinction and feel it severely hinders the deployment of care, for management, this "line" is crucial to the ordering of the shelter. Thus, a relationship between an employee and client signifies not just the evisceration of this boundary, but with it, the very glue that binds the everyday life of the shelter.

This is why management has unequivocally stated that *any* relationship between an employee and a client, even of the platonic sort, is strictly forbidden. This, however, appears to be borne out of a certain paranoia which can, in some instances, run counter to an ethic of care. The following example highlights this. One evening, a female employee commented to her co-worker that she had "received a lecture" from a supervisor for "crossing the boundaries." She was admonished for barbequing twelve hamburgers and eighteen pieces of chicken – she had used her time and money to buy and prepare the food – and then eating a meal with the clients in a picnic-style lunch near the vicinity of the shelter. To her surprise, what she thought was an act of kindness was met with severe reprobation, all of which was shocking to her as evinced in her comment, "I guess I was the only one who thought that there is nothing strange with what I did." In explaining her actions to her co-worker, she explained that the clients "work really hard and deserve" a break.

There is no doubt, even to this worker, that protocol was breached. What shocks her is that the very kindness which she showed could not even be mapped onto the extant protocol: that is, in this case, the provision of a basic necessity such as food, a key part of an ethic of care, was met with severe criticism. It could, of course, be said that, in some ways at least, this employee's gesture, though kind, thoughtful and generous, was unnecessary given the plenitude of available food (though, it could also be said, that her gesture provided a home-cooked meal, which the clients very much appreciated, especially given, as discussed in the previous chapter, the rather unhealthy and insipid food served at the shelter; similarly, the thought behind the actions, a personal gesture rather than the run-of-the-mill type meal, perhaps made more of an impact than the food itself). Yet the issue has to do with more than the provision of food. That is, I suspect that if this act was performed by a male employee, it would not have received the type of admonition it did or, perhaps, not received any admonition at all. In this case, what was troubling is that it was a young female employee who ate a meal with twelve young men, all the while alone and in their presence, that is, without supervision. In other words, what is at stake here are the optics, and the optics point to a space which is, at least in the eyes of management, not only disorderly but also unsafe. Thus, according to the employee, the supervisor's words (and tone) made it seem that this was an intimate episode, one akin to an "orgy" – the phrase "candle-light meal" was used by the supervisor. Here, the optics pointed not just to (the potential of) an intimate sexual encounter, but one that is taboo, verging on the pornographic. Thus, the supervisor was invoking the rules in an attempt to protect this young woman; that is, what appears to ground the supervisor's concerns was the safety of the employee. Thus, it is possible to appreciate how the provision of food – a basic tenet of care – when delivered outside established protocols can clash with concerns about order and safety.

To a large extent, paranoia about the (potential) relationships between clients and young women shapes some of the policies of the shelter. In other words, many of these policies are grounded by a patriarchal and paternalistic ethos of order and safety, one premised upon particular performances of masculinity and femininity (see, Butler, 1990, 2004), which presuppose the male figure as strong and virile and the female as weak and passive – one that originally framed my own reflections about safety and fear in the shelter (see Ranasinghe, 2013b). Interestingly, however, as I explicate in chapter 6, this very paternalism is not only valued immensely by some of the (young) female employees, but is one that works in their favour to make the shelter safe(er) for them, certainly far more safe than it is for the male employees, at least as they perceive it. In addition, some of these policies and ways of thinking are not only reasonable, but prudent as well, as the following example demonstrates.

At about 4.30 p.m., when her shift was close to finishing, a caseworker entered The Bubble and began earnestly looking outside through its window. While so doing, she commented to me – the significance of which I would learn a little later – "You know, stalking is an occupational hazard that we get at working at a shelter." After looking out in such a manner for a while, she, along with a younger caseworker who was standing near The Bubble, left the area. By happenstance, and still oblivious to what was happening, I decided to go outside because I desperately needed some fresh air – the air in The Bubble (as described in the next chapter) and throughout the shelter as well (as already discussed) can be suffocating and nauseating at times. While I was walking towards the front entrance, the two caseworkers entered through a door, quickly glanced outside and then hurriedly left again, not forgetting to say "excuse me" as they pushed me aside to make their way. While I was standing outside, still unsure as to what had just transpired, I noticed the two caseworkers who had by now approached the front of the building from its rear entrance. In the interim, a tall, slender, black man, about forty years in age, whom I had noticed numerous times in the shelter, began to approach the two women. The women had already spotted the man and walked speedily towards the entrance of the shelter.

It is at this point that I began to make sense of the caseworker's comment about stalking. For at this moment the older caseworker told the man that she was going to call the police, to which the man, rather cockily, told her to so do. She went inside and the man followed, but the doors to the reception area – as described in chapter 3 – were (apparently) locked by an employee who was privy to the situation. The man continued to hover around the front entrance. I am unsure exactly what transpired inside, but in about five minutes, I spotted the two caseworkers who had again made their way outside from the rear of the shelter. When the man noticed them, he came outside and began to lean against the railing at the front of the entrance. He watched them while they, in turn, carefully monitored his behaviour. They quickly crossed the street and hurriedly walked towards a parking lot directly in front of the shelter – the one belonging to the condominium described in chapter 2 – where they got into the older caseworker's vehicle. At this point, the man walked towards the car, shouting out to them that he simply wanted to talk. Two clients who were standing against the railing, presumably observing what was transpiring, told the client, "You leave [her] alone," stating the caseworkers wanted nothing to do with the man. The client and the other two men then got into a verbal altercation with the client challenging the two men to a fight. The caseworkers drove away and the man went back into the shelter.

About a week later, I had the opportunity to speak with the older caseworker about the incident. She told me that the man in question had been stalking the younger caseworker for a while and she had intervened on that day to protect her because the man's actions were threatening. She also revealed that the very next day after the incident, she called the police to file a report, but the two officers who arrived were apathetic and rude. The officers, she claimed, wrote very little in their report, even failing to take down a description of the man, simply telling them that the man, like all other middle-aged black men, was crazy.

I am unsure how this situation resolved itself, though I did not see the client again after the day in question. For present purposes, I rely on this incident to describe particular difficulties and concerns regarding the safety of the (young) female employees. While I did not observe further incidents such as this, I was told by numerous employees that such happenings are far from aberrations and that female employees are threatened, harassed, and stalked in this fashion. In fact, the very caseworker who was stalked was also dating another employee during this time, and sometime after the incident, he commented to me that the two had decided not to openly disclose their relationship because of fear that a client who may have taken a liking to her might harm him. The decision taken by the two illustrates how precarious safety and order can be for the employees.

Given the foregoing, the preoccupation over safety and security, evinced in particular protocols, cannot be considered imprudent. This is because the order in the shelter is quite tenuous and fragile. If, as described in the earlier section, the racialized aspects of the space pose particular difficulties to order, then, as discussed in this section, the young men in the shelter pose additional problems to this order when they come into contact with young female employees. As I have shown, these relations can be of the mundane type, such as a platonic friendship, but can also blossom into more serious and intimate relationships and, as well, into more threatening and dangerous behaviour. All these cases are serious concerns to management who have taken every step to secure the space and its personnel from the chaos that can, and often does, ensue. The preoccupation with security, however, tends to shift the focus away from the ethic of care.

Thus far, I have discussed the employees somewhat indirectly, as they have presented themselves through the clients. In what follows, I focus specifically and directly on the employees and illustrate how the mundaneness of their work lives tends to impede and occlude an ethic of care and its deployment.

## The Employees and the Deployment of Care: The Routine, the Boring, and the Ridiculous

The daily operations of the shelter are undertaken by a host of personnel working closely with each other in various settings. Among others, they include the kitchen staff, cleaning personnel, security guards (discontinued towards the twilight of my observations), the chaplain services, the administrative staff, and various volunteers, many of whom I have already introduced briefly in the previous chapter. In this section, I focus on two immensely important groups, namely, front-line employees and caseworkers, and explore their daily work lives and their interactions with clients and each other. It is in this work and the relations that emerge therein that the significant problems that shape and constitute the order of the shelter are revealed, thereby illuminating a space that is chaotic.

*On the Front Lines: (Un)Making Homelessness
and the Deployment of Care*

The front-line employees bear the bulk of the responsibilities of the
shelter (they certainly underscore the importance of their job, that they
are treated poorly by other employees and management, including not
being appreciated for the work they perform, and that they are remunerated unfairly). These employees are the first faces a client sees when
he walks through the doors of the shelter. As discussed in chapter 3, the
employees and their workspace – The Bubble – act as the reception *de
jure* for the clients and, as well, the *de facto* reception of the entire shelter,
including matters that have little or nothing to do with clients. Front-
line employees are tasked with myriad functions, which range from
specifically prescribed tasks to virtually all other types of work which
concern the clients that are not preassigned to other employees. In other
words – to put it somewhat crudely – any work that can be labelled
"miscellaneous" automatically becomes the responsibility of the front-
line staff. They, as Herbert Gans (1972, 278) puts it, perform the "dirty
work" in the shelter.

I do not intend to diminish nor dismiss the work performed by front-
line employees. Their work is crucial to the ordering of, and the order
in, the shelter. In this regard, several of their daily tasks deserve mention. First, front-line employees are responsible for booking the clients into the shelter, a process that is rather straightforward, though
mind-numbingly dull and boring. When a person enters the shelter and
approaches The Bubble, an employee will ask him for his name, date
of birth, a piece of identification along with a host of other information
such as his social insurance number, phone number (if he has a cell-
phone), or place where he can be contacted (e.g., the residence of a rela-
tive or friend), whether he has any type of income, where he slept the
previous night, whether he is on any medications, the health concerns
and medical illnesses that he has (or might have), whether he has a family doctor in the city, whether he has any alcohol, drugs or weapons on
him and, finally, whether he has been previously booked in at the shelter. The client is then provided the registration sheet which has been
filled out by the employee (based on the information the employee
received) and asked to sign it. At this point, the client is asked to turnover his medications (if he is taking any) to the employee who puts
them in a clear plastic bag, labels it with the client's name, and stores it
in a locked cabinet (this procedure is designed to ensure that overdoses

do not take place; the client can request his medications from the front desk when he needs to take them). After this, the employee logs into the Homeless Individuals and Family Information System (HIFIS) – a national system coordinating shelters, where a click of a button allows employees to find out pertinent information about a client, such as, for example, whether he has been recently banned by another shelter and why so. After this process is completed, the employee assigns the client a bed. The client is then provided with bedding (sheets, a blanket, and a pillow) as well as a towel and, if needed, other toiletries such as shaving cream, a razor, shampoo and soap, items which, as discussed in chapter 3, are quite paltry in form and substance. Finally, the client is notified of some of the rules of the shelter, including meal times and, if any questions need to be answered, these are answered before the client is directed to his bed. In total, the entire process takes about ten minutes, though more seasoned employees can complete it in about half the time.

The process described pertains to those persons who do not have a bed reserved in their name, and it takes place daily after 7 p.m. and lasts until about midnight, depending on the availability of beds. However, if there are beds available, a client is provided one no matter the time of night or early-morning hour that he enters the shelter. Each client who has a bed reserved in his name (in other words, he slept in the shelter the previous night) must reserve that bed the following day if he wishes to keep it. Failure to do so would result in him foregoing his bed and he would then be required to rebook one anew, should he wish to have a bed for the night. The process of reserving beds in this manner takes place daily between 4 and 6 p.m., and this is another important function front-line workers are tasked with. While a client can speak to a front-line worker in person to reserve his bed (those clients who are in the shelter or near its vicinity reserve their beds in this fashion), this is not mandatory. Instead, a client can also call the shelter and speak to a front-line employee and reserve his bed in this way. Thus, between 4 and 6 p.m. the two telephones in The Bubble ring incessantly and a large part of the employees' energy is geared towards answering the phones. As I explain in chapter 7, this rather simple, straightforward, and boring practice poses an inordinate amount of confusion and disorder in the shelter leading to an immense amount of frustration and anger among the clients, employees, and supervisors.

Beyond these functions, front-line workers also perform a plethora of other duties, including supervising the four meals that are served: three to the residents of the shelter (breakfast, lunch, and dinner) and one, in the afternoon, to the community, which is open to anyone – male or female – in need. In addition, the employees patrol the shelter to ensure that everything is unfolding smoothly. The bulk of the time, however, is spent attending to the numerous and incessant requests from clients. These range from requests for toiletries, bedding, clothing, and food to fielding questions about the shelter and the meals, to name a few. Significant time is also spent listening to and conversing with clients. As mentioned before, any work characterized as "miscellaneous" falls under the jurisdiction of the front-line employees and they begrudgingly perform these.

The front-line workers can be grouped into three types, these groupings having serious implications for how the work is performed and, by extension, how order is procured. The first comprises workers who work on a full-time basis, work which largely involves shift work. The second is composed of those who work on a part-time basis. Many of these employees either have other jobs and/or are enrolled either in a college or university program. Usually, part-time employees work about two to three times a week. Finally, another group is comprised of those who are referred to as "on call," that is, employees who do not have a minimum set amount of time they must work (nor are guaranteed a particular amount of hours). Instead, they take shifts at their choosing when there is availability. Thus, it is common to find an employee working only once or twice a month or, in some cases, even less frequently (during the year that I spent at the shelter, there were two such employees whom I met only once).

The structure of this form of employment poses immense problems to the daily operations of the shelter. Not surprisingly, clients have better relationships with full-time employees (and, to a lesser extent, part-time employees) because of the familiarity between the parties. This is not the case with on-call employees who can be (essentially are) strangers to the clients and vice versa. In addition, the working relationships between the employees run smoother when the employees know and understand each other and this happens when there is more interaction between them. In particular, the enforcement of rules becomes a very difficult matter that poses myriad problems to the workers, the clients, and the supervisors; as a result, the order in the shelter is made precarious. Partly, if not mostly, this is because many employees are unaware of what the rules are, a product of the vast and frequent changes to the rules, both officially and unofficially. Working infrequently only serves to exacerbate this problem. While I discuss this in greater detail in chapters 7 and 8, for present purposes, I provide one example to illustrate how problematic this situation can be (and, in fact, is).

By happenstance, I interviewed a front-line worker on the same day he had undergone what was, according to him, a very frightening and disconcerting experience during a shift – it had taken place just a few hours before. This incident, as he narrates it, was brought on by management's concerted effort to reduce operating costs, and one aspect of this involved the reduction of the workforce and hours. What had resulted was that on this particular morning, this employee had been scheduled to work with two new and inexperienced employees. I draw on, in great detail, his words to vividly capture the agony as it unfolded for him and the anger and dismay still palpable at the time we spoke:

> A client comes in, a person I've never seen before … So he comes in and he looks under the influence, so I say … "Have you been drinking?" He said he never drank. So we asked him, "What have you taken?" "Oh, I've taken OxyContin," [he stated]. So I tell him, "Because … you are under the influence, [and] we have a 'zero-tolerance' policy [relating to drugs and/or alcohol], you have to leave. So basically if you've drank anything, taken anything, anything that makes you inebriated in any way, you have to leave" … I said this to him and my co-workers didn't recognize [that] we had this policy, so I explained to him as well as my co-workers at the same time but because they … are not fully aware, one of them was continuing to talk to him in a casual manner. And, I'm like, "No, no, no." First of all, this conversation you're having … shouldn't be happening. If I had an experienced co-worker they would have been [backing me up, and maybe saying,] "You know what, I'm going to back my [co-worker] and [ask you to leave." Instead, I said] "Sir, please move it along." But this person [the new employee] kept on going and I'm like what are you doing, in my mind, like, what's going on? So basically this guy did not in fact leave and because he didn't leave, I'm like, "Sir, you're going to have to go" again in a more forceful way, and when I told him this he's [says], "You know what, I've taken OxyContin, but I'm also going to shoot you," and … bells went off … and I'm like, "You know what, for that I'm going to ask you to leave and, if you don't, I will be calling the police." And I pick up the phone … and fake dial, which is basically [I] pretend[ed] to call 911 and a lot of times that convinces them to leave. But in his case he slowly takes off his bag, puts his hand in the backpack, and when he puts his hand in the backpack right after the statement where he said "I'm on OxyContin

and I'm going to shoot you," for me alarms are going off, I'm freaked out, I'm thinking this guy is going to pull a gun. My two co-workers, they're not even aware, so I'm like, "All right, you know what, cause we're in a bubble and The Bubble is designed in a way … it's a desk and it has [a] glass enclosing but it's not bullet proof and really if someone were to have a weapon, what do you call it, a fish in a barrel where you have no real avenues to escape because the two exits are covered … So when this guy was like this, I went to the door. So when he went to put his hand in the bag I actually got closer … I know it doesn't make sense, usually you run away but I got closer, because I knew there was no other escape. So I went to [the door], maybe, if he pulled something, [I could] fight him right … but I've got these two co-workers who don't even recognize that this guy might, you know, really have something or that we're actually in danger or don't even know the security risks here.

The angst and trepidation the client felt was palpable and he spent close to half the time during the interview speaking about the incident. I am mindful that this is an extreme example, which the employee would admit as well. However, as he narrated it, while the client was the start of the problem, it escalated because his co-workers simply had little or no knowledge of the protocols of the shelter. This inexperience and lack of knowledge, I am suggesting, is, if not directly, then at least partially, a product not only of the high turnover rates of the employees, but also the high number of part time and on-call workers. Many of these employees are simply unaware of the rules of the shelter (and, to make matters worse, more than apathetic as well). This example illustrates how the structuring of work – a simple and mundane aspect about the everyday life of the shelter – gravely disrupts the flow of work relations and, by extension, makes the space of the shelter not only chaotic, but also potentially dangerous.[4]

What also uniquely shapes the order in, and of, the shelter are the different temporalities that serve to structure the space, though, ironically, this very structuring vividly illuminates how disorganized the space is. I focus on the distinctive shift work of the employees to explore and explicate this.

The afternoon shift, which begins at about 2 or 3 p.m. and lasts until about 10 or 11 p.m., is a time period unlike any other. The afternoon and early-evening simply look chaotic (hereinafter, I will refer to this period as the afternoon). Whether this is a product of the quietude of the morning and night or that the afternoon is constituted by a hustle-and-bustle is not clear. Regardless, it is not just that the time is busier or more congested, but that it feels disorganized, even clumsy. There are, of course, good reasons for this. First, there are more clients who are visible, either congregating in the lobby or outside. As noted in chapter 2, the spatial organization of the lobby, both with respect to the paucity of chairs and the use of the space as a living room-*cum*-storage space, replete with garbage bags, gives an anything-goes type attitude and feel – the type that, perhaps, the authors of the now infamous "broken windows" (Wilson and Kelling, 1982, 1989) would shine light upon as a perfect example of what happens when order, in particular, civility, is either absent or breaks down (see also Ranasinghe, 2011, 2012a). Second, and related, it is not just the sheer volume of people that is important but what they are doing or, more importantly, not doing. The afternoon is characterized by a constant flow of people, both clients and employees, who are, more so than not, on the move. Visually, the constant and incessant movement is, or can be, disturbing, because even a modicum of respite appears unattainable. To make matters worse, this movement also has a particular auditory aspect because even without words other sounds fill and consume the space – sounds of footsteps, chairs being moved around, or the sounds of the ever-present illness that permeates and envelopes the shelter, such as a cough or a sneeze. There is, in other words, a constant reminder that the private (and privacy) is not to be found in the shelter, and this absence vividly highlights its chaotic nature.

Ostensibly, while this hustle and bustle paints an image of chaos and disorder, it is, rather interestingly and bizarrely, "silences" or "absences" that truly illuminate the chaos at hand. I will refer to these silences or absences as a sense of "nothingness." In other words, it appears as if movements are without purpose, without, that is, direction; a client moves in and out of the shelter simply because he has nothing else to do and, thus, this "doing" keeps him occupied, even though what he is doing amounts to nothing. For the homeless, Amir Marvasti (2002, 619–20) writes, "idleness was more of a nuisance than a luxury." Similarly, Irene Glasser (1988, 20) writes of the homeless life as one "filled with boredom and despair," and Elliot Liebow (1993, 29) speaks of "boredom … as one of the great trials of homelessness." The focus here is not to explicate the boredom that constitutes homelessness – the subject of a future project – but to underscore what it implies to the ordering of the shelter. The "nothingness" underlines the disorder and chaos of the shelter because the stationary body (or the stationed body) – one sleeping, passed out, or simply sitting in or occupying a chair – is not only a vivid reminder of the problem but also serves to make the space look and feel (even smell) disorderly. In other words, even in the very quietude that is so cherished by the employees, what is revealed is a profound sense of disorder that tears at the very core of an ethic of care, which has literally grounded life, including the desire to purposefully move. It is in that sedentary moment that some modicum of order is restored for (and to) the employees, though it is hard to dismiss that the sedentary is out of order because it represents not just the absence of an ethic of care but, in some ways, even an *unwillingness* to care. This, as I have suggested, has to do not only with the sheer number of people in the shelter during this time, but also with what they are (not) doing. I have focused on the temporality associated with order and care because, in the brightness of the day – when visibility is at its best, certainly unadulterated – what this ethic of care is truly about is plainly shone: the sad state of a stationary being who (only) moves because he has nothing else to do, and employees, who are either apathetic towards the entire problem or understand that there is little they can do to profoundly change the situation.

To put this into perspective, I focus on a different temporal period, the nighttime. It is a time when the shelter is overcome by a different climate, a different mood, so to speak. This time frame vividly highlights how the mundane and the humdrum cohabit in the boredom of the space, thereby eviscerating any pretence of care.

For the most part, the nighttime and the overnight shift, between about 11 p.m. and about 7 a.m., is very quiet and, unsurprisingly, this is because most clients are asleep. Often, clients who have trouble falling asleep can be found sitting in the lobby or quietly mingling with others. Occasionally, clients will go outside to get some fresh air or smoke a cigarette. The weekends are busier or, at least, give the sense of being more chaotic, largely because of the location of the shelter in the entertainment district. The hustle and bustle and drunken revelries of bar and club patrons are a vivid reminder that despite the monotony of the shelter, life in the city is in full flow, and the clients, especially the younger ones, relish the opportunity to stand outside and gawk at the scantily clad young women who stagger along the sidewalk. These sounds and activities aside, the shelter is enveloped by a palpable quietness, almost akin to a feeling of loneliness, that envelops the clients and, as I would slowly come to understand, the employees as well. In fact, it is not simply the quietude that is significant, but that several places in the shelter, such as the lobby, are virtually empty; this emptiness removes the visibility of the clients and their problems from the gaze of the employees. This, the employees appreciate very much. However, this benefit comes with an acute disadvantage, one of utter boredom. It is in this boredom that an important aspect of, and about, the shelter and its employees is shone.

To put this into perspective, I describe in some detail the proceedings from one night. The night was so quiet, dull, and boring that the two employees on duty were finding it difficult to stay awake and were trying to so do through a series of irrelevant and ridiculous conversations – it was, conversing for the sake of conversing. A member of the management team (hereinafter, the manager), perhaps because of this very problem, entered The Bubble around 3 a.m. and began conversing with the two employees. This time period, between about 4 and 6 a.m., an employee once described as a "dead zone" – when nothing happens – and, in expanding upon this, the manager added, "That's when you're fighting to stay awake."

While these personnel were "fighting" to stay awake, a severely inebriated man entered through the main entrance of the shelter and stood between the two main doors – the entrance into the shelter itself was locked. It was not clear whether the three personnel in question noticed the man or not, but after standing for about ten minutes, the man fell asleep – likely passed out – while standing! Suddenly – as if to provide comic relief to the monotony of life at the shelter during the night – the man fell to the ground bringing with his fall a loud noise. He was startled and sought to sit up. At this moment, the female employee began laughing in a loud and uncontrollable manner. While the male employee went outside to check on him, the manager remained in The Bubble and continued reading a newspaper; the manager did, however, tell the female employee that she needed to either stop laughing or go somewhere else where she could not be seen by the client. Here, the manager was making it very clear that the employee's behaviour was far from professional. What is interesting is that while admitting to the manager that her actions were unprofessional, she sought to excuse them by stating that the night had been long and boring up to that point, and this episode provided the necessary relief for her to get through the rest of the night. Equally important, she also told the manager that the man – who by now had been brought to his feet by the male employee and was seated on a bucket that was in the area – would fall once again and that she could not guarantee that she would not laugh.

When everything had been restored to its "normal" state, the male employee, who by now had returned to The Bubble, told his colleague, the manager, and myself, that he had recently watched a very funny video on YouTube and thought that it would be fun if we all watched it – another desperate attempt on his part to pass time. While he was searching for the video on the Internet, the manager, who clearly was not happy with the idea that the employee was using the computer for personal reasons, left The Bubble, stating that the manager did not find such videos interesting. The video in question is titled "Unforgivable 1," an amateurish-type production of a young black man recalling particular exploits about how he poorly treated a woman he met, a video laden with a panoply of expletives, including the word nigger (or nigga). The employee, to whom the video was shown, was a woman of colour and she did not find it particularly funny, though she watched it in its entirety. Interestingly, however, while this video was playing, the employee who suggested that we watch it, a young white male, left The Bubble, the reasons for which are not clear. Sometime after this, the telephone rang and the female employee picked up the phone and spoke to the caller, completely oblivious that the video, with its expletives, was playing in the background – the call did not appear to be a personal one. When the male employee entered The Bubble, he quickly realized what was happening and immediately paused the video. When the female employee had finished the phone call, he told her, rather matter of factly, "Pause, if you are on the phone." It is only at this point that the woman understood the gravity of what had transpired and, in apparently what appears to be her trademark, burst into another uncontrollable fit of laughter.

This incident is interesting because it illustrates how the humdrum – a video clip or a telephone call, for example – can symbolize the chaotic nature of the shelter. Here, the employees were not only spending their time on personal matters but did not have the wherewithal to understand that a video clip that could be overheard over the phone, not to mention the racial epithets it contained, sends a very specific image about the space in question. As discussed previously, the shelter is one that is heavily racialized. How much this is, is evidenced in this example, because, here, the irresponsible manner in which the employees behaved can be read as a sign that this is not even mapped onto their consciousness. This male employee, the same one I described in the "Hassan, Hassan" incident, appears to be unmindful that he was showing this video to a woman of minority descent, illustrating how oblivious (or insensitive or both) he is to the ways that race constitutes being.

Things that night, however, were only beginning to get worse. At about 5.30 a.m., a loud sound emanated from outside of The Bubble in the area between the two main entrances to the shelter. The same man who had fallen in this same area about an hour before, had – just as the female employee "predicted" – fallen once again; this time, however, the fall resulted in a cut on his forehead, leading to significant bleeding. The female employee muttered something to the effect that she cannot laugh about this incident because it looks very serious and went to where the man had fallen. The other employee called 911 for assistance. She and I lifted the man and sat him on the same bucket that he was placed on before. The man told us that he was fine and did not need medical assistance. At this time, the female employee went into The Bubble and came back with the First Aid Kit. While she was in the process of getting ready to clean the man's forehead, he realized (how, I am unsure) that an ambulance had been called and immediately got up and left. While I accompanied the male employee who described what happened to the police officers who arrived on the scene, the female employee resumed watching video clips.

This incident aptly captures both the hilarity and sadness that encapsulated the night. It is interesting that both the employees and the man ager appeared either to be oblivious or apathetic that a man who was clearly drunk was standing some ten feet away from them. Partly, a product of this obliviousness is that they were too preoccupied with their conversations, itself a product of the utter boredom and dullness that permeate their work lives. In other words, in the effort to do something, anything, to keep them occupied and awake during the night, the very man who needed desperate attention remained unnoticed and neglected.

It took, then, a fall for them to realize what was transpiring. Although one employee sought to help the man – while the other was too engrossed in the laughter that consumed her, presumably brought on by what was, to her, a hilarious moment – his actions leave much to be desired. In seating the man on a bucket, the employee showed both a lack of compassion and foresight for what could possibly – and eventually did – happen. Equally, the other employee and manager were remiss in their duties as well – at least the male employee got up from his seat to help, while they made no such attempt. It is interesting that all three knew – or certainly should have known – that the man needed to sleep. Yet, while they provided him a seat, it was not on one of the chairs in the shelter; nor was a chair brought out for him. Rather, a lowly bucket, already outside, was used as a seat, suggesting that this very man who needed care, in a place meant to provide it, could not, for a variety of reasons – apathy, neglect, irresponsibility – find it. In other words, here, at this precise moment when chairs were abundantly available – a rarity, as I have discussed in chapter 3 – none was provided, and more astonishingly, it probably did not dawn on these workers to do so. Thus, what transpired later was not only comical, but expected. In underscoring the comical aspect of this incident, I do not mean that a man falling on the floor is funny. Rather, I mean that the actions of the employees are comical. Clearly, at least one of the three knew that the man would fall – the female employee said this much – but none thought that it was irresponsible to place a drunk man on a bucket. This, however, is exactly what happened, a sign of the ethic of care that constitutes the shelter. Even the very visible signs of distress are not treated responsibly and seriously when they appear, until blood, the signal that things are not well, arrives on the scene. Thus, it took yet another fall, one accompanied by the spillage of blood, for the employees to show concern.

What I seek to underscore through the example of the overnight shift is that the very work itself, boring and dull, contributes to the chaotic environment of the shelter, one where care is far from the primary concern and what is deployed is mostly superficial and determined by the conveniences of the employees. Apparently, video clips and superficial conversations take precedence over caring for the clients.

None of the following, however, is to imply that the employees do not care about the clients. This is far from the case, and as I have already discussed, there are concerted efforts on their parts to care deeply for the clients. In other words, removing these employees and replacing them with others, I suggest, will probably do little to improve matters. It is, then, the very systemic manner in which the space is organized and an ethic of care conceptualized and thought about that is harmful to the deployment of care. In other words, for present purposes, I underline the institutional barriers to compassion and care; one important, though often neglected, aspect about social services work concerns the sheer boredom and dullness of it, which itself is significantly responsible for how care is practised.

## Dirty Work and Movie Stars: Front-Line Employees, Caseworkers, and the Disappearing Ethic of Care

Thus far, I have focused on the front-line employees discussing how the very constitution of their work makes the deployment of care difficult. This problem is made worse because of the rather tenuous relationship between front-line workers and caseworkers. This has significant implications for the administration of an ethic of care.

It is an understatement to claim that the relationship between front-line employees and caseworkers is problematic, one filled with, and consumed by, resentment, acrimony and distrust. Practically every front-line employee spoke negatively not only about the caseworkers but about the working relationship between the two. Elizabeth, for example, described the relationship as "a little bit tattered," while an elderly female employee said that "it is ... strained." To a large extent, the poor working relationship is a product of the way each group feels about how the other views its members. For example, a front-line employee commented that the "front-line staff tend to *resent*" the caseworkers because "the majority of caseworkers don't really consider front-line employees on the same level" (emphasis added). This, it appears, is a product of a particular hierarchy, both formal and informal, which leads to "power tripping," as one front-line employee put it. Another echoed the same sentiment more bluntly and acerbically: "The caseworkers think they're amazing ... I mean, they seem to think ... they're God's gift to the shelter. They seem to be competing for ... this elitism and I don't fully understand it ... I don't think they are as amazing as they think they are!"

"Captain Delight," like many of his colleagues, was equally forthright. "They [the caseworkers] think they are better than all of us," he said. He underscored the gulf between the two by adding: "It is like we are *a different race here*" (emphasis added). He used this analogy another time as well, when he commented that one particular caseworker "believes [that] caseworkers are a *special race*" (emphasis added). The invocation of race is interesting, because, as noted before, the shelter is heavily racialized and this alone leads to particular difficulties in ordering it. In this context, however, "Captain Delight" is not speaking of a problem of race, nor the racialized dynamics of (and in) the shelter. Rather, in invoking race – itself a loaded term – he is consciously underscoring a particular problem at the very heart of the chaos in (and of) the shelter. As he constructs it, the problem has nothing to do with the clients; it is almost as if they are absolved from any responsibility, largely because they are rendered intentionally irrelevant and, therefore, inconspicuous (a remarkable statement because, as elucidated earlier in the chapter, "Captain Delight" strongly believes that most clients are undeserving of service, and they are a significant problem to the very "being" of the shelter). In this context he is highlighting that the front-line employees are treated as a different and inferior group – like racial minorities – and this makes the ordering of the shelter arduous and fraught with complications. If this is only implicitly brought to light in these comments, his additional comments, that the caseworkers *"interfere* with everything we do here," leaves little doubt in this regard. To further shed light on the problem he also noted: *"Their behaviour is a little risky* in the sense that *they put everybody in danger"* because "they don't recognize the *boundaries,* and then we have to jump in" (emphases added). There is little doubt that what "Captain Delight" is hinting at has to do with more than inconveniences. He is drawing attention to a problem of safety. When he invokes the notion of "risky behaviour," he is stating that the problem is the behaviour of the caseworkers who fail to follow established protocol. This is an important point because, as I take up in chapter 7, to some extent at least, this is a (or, at least as management sees it, *the*) significant problem facing the shelter. Here, it is possible to see that one reason for the disparate manner in which the rules are thought about and enforced is because the caseworkers, at least as "Captain Delight" sees it, believe that they are superior than the other employees – recall his comment that "they think they are better than all of us."

"Captain Delight," certainly more than other employees, was extremely vocal about the hierarchy between the front-line workers and caseworkers. On one occasion, when a caseworker walked passed The Bubble in which "Captain Delight" and I were seated, "Captain Delight" ridiculed the caseworker, stating, "That's a … [person] who behave[s] like a movie star." At another time, he made this same comment in a more generalized manner directing it towards all the caseworkers: "To be a caseworker, you have to behave like a movie star." The implication here is damning: it is not just that the caseworkers wholeheartedly believe they are different from the rest of the employees (recall the analogy of race), but that their actions tend to mimic this very thinking. Thus, as "Captain Delight" sees it, the caseworkers are pretentious, arrogant, and insolent, characteristics which make them difficult to work with, and certainly unsuitable for the line of work they are tasked with. This much was very clear to me on the day when I was scheduled, for the first time, to spend time with caseworkers in their offices, at which point "Captain Delight" said to me, both as a cautionary note and a sympathetic gesture, "don't let them try to impress you!"

For their part, the caseworkers were more than mindful of what the front-line employees thought about them and their work. Here, the reflections of one caseworker are illuminating. The caseworker was upfront that "some of them [front-line employees] feel that because we are caseworkers, we have a hierarchy [sic]." The caseworker, however, underscored that the caseworker did not subscribe to such a view by speaking not just of a "mutually dependent relationship" between the two parties, but one where the front-line employees perform absolutely crucial work, without which the caseworkers would be unable to perform theirs. "They are my eyes and ears in the night when I am not here," the caseworker said, and added, "So, *I depend on them*" (emphasis added).

The latter acknowledgment of the importance or necessity of the front-line employees, however, should not be read as an approval of the work performed by them. In fact, the caseworker was exceptionally harsh in assessing their work, noting that some, if not many, are not performing their job well:

> If they don't know the answer ... or if they're tired or lazy or whatever that's going through their mind, they send ... everyone to us for whatever it may be. Yes, anything that happens in the shelter, essentially ... [the] front-line workers are like, "Go talk to your caseworker, go talk to your caseworker" ... It's frustrating; it's tough.

The caseworker's frustration is further evinced in the following comments:

> I want the front-line workers, if they know the answer, [then] do it. And if they don't know, go on the Internet and search it so then they get the answer right away instead of waiting till I come in, because my case load is very large so I may not ... have that time for everybody. [Also] if it is a simple thing like, "Can you print me out something, [for example], directions," don't wait till I get in so I can get directions ... [So] whatever they are able to do on their own, please do it. Alleviate [me from] it.

The foregoing illustrates not simply the caseworker's annoyance, frustration, or even anger, but almost a cry for help, evinced in the exhortation at the very end. One aspect of this frustration is that the front-line employees are either not knowledgeable of what to do in particular situations – they have poor problem-solving skills – or they are habitually indolent and, therefore, seek to delegate their responsibilities to others, a criticism that is not necessarily unfair. Perhaps, however, what really irritates the caseworker is not just a combination of incompetence and laziness, but that the caseworker is not just saddled with more work, but *front-line work*, that is, work that is not part of the job description of a caseworker.

This is evinced in the comment, "They just delegate it [work] to us [caseworkers] *when it is their job*" (emphasis added). This statement nicely illuminates the inherent hierarchy and power struggle (the "power tripping," as one employee put it) between the two groups. While not directly subscribing to the hierarchy between the two groups, the caseworker's comment about the belongingness of work – "it is their job" – tends to reproduce this very hierarchy. As noted above, any and every task that is not specifically assigned, that is, what can be called "miscellaneous" duties (or "dirty work," as Gans, 1972, 278, puts it), automatically falls within the domain of the front-line employees. This, the front-line employees abhor, and they seek, as much as possible, to distribute these tasks to other employees, such as the cleaning personnel or housekeeping staff, or, and rather ironically, back to the caseworkers themselves. The front-line workers view the distribution of sundry work to them by the caseworkers as a sign of disrespect, and this occurs, they believe, because the caseworkers feel they are superior to them. Thus, when this particular caseworker demonstrates indignity towards the employees because the caseworker feels they are not performing "their job" – what is, in terms of the job description, a truism – the caseworker is, in fact, subscribing to, and reproducing, the very hierarchy that the caseworkers are accused of fostering and maintaining (as can be appreciated from the foregoing, in many ways, management itself bears some, if not all, of the blame in this regard, considering that this is governed through protocol, as I take up later in the chapter).

What is even more interesting, and significant, is that while this caseworker is – or, at least appears to be – cognizant of the rather fragile and tenuous relationship that underpins the interactions between the two groups, the caseworker is nevertheless oblivious to how grave the situation is. Thus, on occasions the caseworker would speak of the supposed hierarchy between the two groups by saying that some front-line employees "are cool with it" and "they are pretty receptive ... they are pretty good" – even the most sympathetic employees were not, and this comment is another example of the ways the caseworker, perhaps unwittingly, tended to subscribe to the very hierarchy the caseworker wished to be distant (and distanced) from. This is best captured in the caseworker's assessment of the relationship: "If it's not friendly, *then it is at least professional*" (emphasis added).

The problem, however, is that this relationship was far from professional, and this worked to render the effectiveness of an ethic of care insignificant. The problem had reached such grave heights that the cordiality that ought to govern the relations between the two had all but eviscerated, with each group – certainly the front-line employees – even resorting to *ad hominem* attacks, something certainly not lost on management. On one occasion, for example, a caseworker was standing in front of The Bubble in conversation with, it appeared, a worker from the city. Two front-line employees who were on shift in The Bubble began heckling the caseworker who appeared to be totally oblivious to what was transpiring. They mimicked the caseworker's actions, took turns impersonating the way the caseworker was speaking, and one employee even commented that the caseworker would enter The Bubble after the conversation and complain to them about how tired the caseworker was because of the heavy workload. Sometime later, after the caseworker had left, "Captain Delight" stated, "Everyone is pretending here." When I asked him exactly what he meant by this, he simply stated, "working," and then immediately added, "Lying and pretending." While not necessarily straightforward, he seemed to be suggesting that the caseworkers are so unprofessional that they do not perform the work they are tasked with (this comment, however, is unmindful of the unprofessionalism of the two front-line employees). It is precisely this unprofessionalism – bordering on hostility, acrimony, scepticism, and cynicism – that characterizes the relations between front-line employees and caseworkers, the end result, as explicated in detail below, is a chaotic and disorderly space that is far from conducive to the administration of an ethic of care.

Here, it is worth exploring some reasons behind the unprofessionalism. One reason, though by no means the main point of contention, is that caseworkers are paid at a higher rate than front-line staff (all employees are paid on an hourly basis). It is important to remember, as already discussed in chapter 3, that the front-line employees believe they are paid very poorly and, to make matters worse, the constant reminder of what they see as the comforts – in some instances, opulence – in the lives of the clients, only irritate them (recall, the comment of "Captain Delight" that he does not know what it means to have money). I remember vividly, for example, the rather sobering response of a young female employee, who, in commenting on the way an elderly female employee mocked the Christmas bonus provided to the employees that year – $45 and a calendar – stated that she would use the money for petroleum for her car. While the young employee believed that the bonus could (in fact, should) have been more, the way she put into perspective the importance of this sum is indicative of how poorly the employees believe they are remunerated; as paltry a figure as $45 might be, it nevertheless was a significant difference to her disposable income.[5]

Poor pay is, of course, a commonality in the field of social services. Lisa Ferrill (1991), for example, who, in discussing her managerial work as a social worker, writes, "It frustrated me that a master's degree, very hard work, and doing something that I felt was valuable to society in general was given relatively little monetary reward, but I knew what I was getting into when I went into social work so I could not complain" (85–6; see also Loseke, 1992, 71). With regards to Ferrill, she, as her biography shows, was well educated and still poorly paid. Most, if not all, of the employees at the shelter are, if not poorly educated, then even uneducated (none had a university degree; one was registered in a university program, and another in a college program). Thus, their prospects for high remuneration are capped at slightly above minimum wage.

Interestingly, it is not only the front-line employees who feel they are poorly paid. The caseworkers feel this way as well. During the considerable time I spent in the office of one caseworker – the movie star, as "Captain Delight" mockingly called the caseworker – this aspect of work was, almost painfully, revealed to me. "I really do enjoy my job," the caseworker said, but also underscored that it is "*very thankless and frustrating*" (emphasis added). This was directly a product of poor remuneration. The caseworker explained that caseworkers at the shelter (Residential Case Workers, as they are called) are exactly like social workers (Registered Social Workers, as they are referred to) in terms of the work they perform; indeed, as the caseworker saw it, caseworkers perform more work than social workers. However, because their title is one of a caseworker and not a social worker, they are paid at a lower rate. "It's a name game," the caseworker stated rather jadedly. What is interesting, of course, is that in this assessment of different pay scales, the caseworker refuses to account for the fact the caseworkers are not accredited through education – though some caseworkers had undergraduate degrees in a variety of fields, none possessed the equivalence of a social work degree, and none had a graduate degree. Despite this, however, the caseworker, just like the others, not only saw fit to criticize the pay scale, but, in fact, elevate the caseworker's own status to that of a social worker.

While the (perceived) poor remuneration could, in fact, unite the caseworkers and front-line employees, this has the opposite effect. This is because of how the issue is conceptualized and thought about. For example, as noted above, one way the caseworker underscored the poor pay of the caseworkers was by equating casework to social work. However, to further underscore this – in fact, illustrate how insulting the pay is – the caseworker went as far as claiming that the caseworker is paid only marginally more (about $1) than the front-line employees. In this very juxtaposition, the indignation the front-line workers feel is aptly brought to light. As this caseworker sees it, pay scales are structured in a particular manner, with those performing important work being paid more than others. Thus, the caseworker's indignation was of two sorts: the first, as noted above, in relation to other social workers and, second and most importantly, in relation to the caseworker's colleagues. The comparison to the caseworker's colleagues, however, was in the form of distancing, where the caseworker first distanced and then separated the self – and the work performed – from the front-line employees. It is precisely this way of thinking that further fuels the acrimony over hierarchy, which, despite the comment of the caseworker about a "mutually dependent relationship," clearly exists and is subscribed to and propounded by the caseworkers. The end result is that both groups feel slighted and discriminated leading to a relationship that is acrimonious and fraught with tensions.

While financial remuneration is a significant issue, it is, however, merely a reflection of a larger problem with deeper roots. In part, this problem concerns the ways each group is perceived by its superiors, that is, managers and supervisors and, related, how these perceptions are internalized and made sense of by each party. The hierarchy between caseworkers and front-line workers is one that is, at its core, (re)produced and maintained both consciously and unconsciously by management, and this, to a large extent, is the basis upon which this problem is founded and sustained. Management is certainly cognizant of the extremely fragile relations between front-line employees and caseworkers. A supervisor, for example, readily admitted that "there is *animosity* towards each other" (emphasis added), and further explained some bases upon which this is founded and situated:

> Because they [the caseworkers] are given more freedom in terms of making decisions, that kind of becomes a power item ... [and] a caseworker will go up to a front-line [employee] and say, "Why did you do this? I noticed that you did this, can you explain what your thought was behind that?" But, it's more of a "why did you do that?" so the person being approached gets immediately defensive and there becomes kind of a hierarchy where one thinks one is better than the other.

The supervisor's explanation leaves little doubt of a hierarchy (or, at least a perception of one) that constitutes the working relations between front-line workers and caseworkers. What is, however, only inconspicuously revealed is one fundamental reason for this, one systemically (re)produced and maintained: it is the protocols of the shelter that give caseworkers more authority and leeway in their decision-making powers.

One aspect of this power is the right to use discretion in enforcing rules. This right, it appears, has been accorded through the "blessing" of management, so that what was originally sanctioned via the practice of custom has now been translated into a *de facto* right. It is here, through this *custom-cum-rule*, that the seeds of animosity and resentment have been sown. In explaining the logistics of discretion, the same supervisor noted, "If there is any room for grey ... the supervisor is going to hold that kind of authority or power and *the caseworkers still have an element of grey*" (emphasis added). This comment illustrates that the power to contravene the letter of the law, a necessity as the supervisor understands it, lies with the supervisors. Yet there is also an implicit acknowledgment of the messy realities of everyday life (see Lipsky, [1980] 2010), which lead concomitantly to bestowing the right of discretion to caseworkers, albeit to a lesser degree. This means that the supervisors and caseworkers are put on very much the same level; additionally, and more gravely, this right places the caseworkers above the front-line employees. This is very clear in the additional comments of the supervisor: "We're going to go back to black and white at the front desk because ... in ... offering them [front-line employees] grey, *there has been just too much ... chaos*" (emphasis added).

Interestingly, this last statement shines light on a particular aspect of the problem. It appears that both caseworkers and front-line employees were provided the right to use discretion. It does, however, also appear that the front-line workers were perceived as unable to use this power in a reasonable and appropriate manner. The end result, as the supervisor put it, was not just chaos (which is, perhaps, tolerable) but "too much chaos" (which poses grave threats to the ordering of the shelter and, therefore, cannot be tolerated). Thus, based on this history, the caseworkers have been deemed responsible and, therefore, trustworthy enough to use discretion. In fact, the supervisor also explained how the abuse of discretionary power by the front-line workers led to significant conflict among the two groups: "That actually leads back to interpersonal relationships because if so and so is interpreting these policies this way and so and so is interpreting it another way, then they are going to have a conflict when ... a guy [a client] addresses them both at the same time and they have different ideas on how the policy goes." The end result, which elevates one group over another and bestows to it the power of discretionary practices, also ends up creating a hierarchy, even if only unwittingly. This hierarchy, as explained, is underwritten directly into the rules that govern the life of the shelter.

As management sees it, caseworkers require discretionary power to effectively and efficiently carry out their work. This is because they are most "intimately" in contact with, and connected to, the clients and, thus, more so than any other group, best suited to "know" them and opine about their needs. This is plainly clear in the comments of the same supervisor:

> Ultimately, the caseworkers are the ones who are meeting with the clients. The caseworkers have more information about the clients than ... any supervisor or even a front-line worker. Front-line workers are there to handle the immediate things, the caseworker is interviewing, assessing... discharg[ing] a client, [that is], just getting right into the meat of what this person's problem is. So, ultimately ... we really have to defer to what the caseworker[s], what their opinion is, because they have spent the most time with them.

The work performed by caseworkers – interviewing, assessing, and discharging, for example – is conceptualized as not only quantitatively more but, as well, more important and essential to the delivery of care. Conversely, the work performed by front-ine employees is almost relegated to the marginal – they "handle the immediate things" – essentially what I described earlier as "miscellaneous work." Such a characterization paints the work of front-line staff as "dirty work" (Gans, 1972, 278). This, they seem to have internalized, evinced, for example, in the comment of one who claimed, "We're *doing the dirt*" (emphasis added). Thus, many front-line workers view their work as meaningless. This defeated attitude is evident in the words of "Captain Delight." "In general, *I feel I lost my skills in here*" (emphasis added), he said, and then added: "Waste of talent. I feel that way." This type of feeling has led him to ponder leaving the job and look for new work: "I believe the solution can be looking for another job. So that can be the solution." This, he believes, "can help me recover my peace!" He is, sadly, not the only one who feels this way. Elizabeth, for example, explained how the restricted power she has drastically curtails how she can help clients:

> They [the caseworkers] have a lot more power where our jobs are concerned: they can give out leave passes [and] overnight passes. *They can help them in a lot more ways than we can.* And I don't think … they are higher than us, but they have a lot more to offer in … in terms of what they [the clients] need in life, you know [a] health card is very important, SIN [Social Insurance Number] card is important and your mental health is important, and those things are better helped by them. (emphasis added)

This is particularly distressing to the front-line employees because they firmly believe that they, not the caseworkers nor the supervisors, "know" the clients. The end result, they believe, is not only are the clients provided poor(er) services, but their work lives are impoverished. "I like to think," an employee said, that "*we are dealing with a little bit more* because we are front-line [and] we are seeing everybody first" (emphasis added). The little bit more he refers to, I suggest, implies that front-line workers do more work than the caseworkers. What is also claimed, however, and explicitly so, is that the front-line workers are in a better position to gauge the needs of the clients because they are the first to come into contact with them. A female employee explained this in greater detail:

> We're the one[s] *who see*; we're the front-line workers. They call it front line for a reason, [be]cause we're the front people. *We see what others do not see* [be]cause *they're not there to see it on a daily basis.* We are! So if someone … needs to be informed because they're not taking showers, they're not

taking their med[ication]s, they're getting very agitated and stuff like that, *we should be able to communicate that.* Sometimes the lack of communication is, we tell them [the caseworkers], but they don't follow up with ... what we say. Because sometimes they, caseworkers, I find, because we are front-line workers, [they think] that we don't know nothing. *We're the eyes, we're the eyes of the shelter,* that little bubble is the eyes of the shelter. *If it wasn't for us, the shelter would not be running like it's running ... We're eyes and ears of the shelter.* (emphases added)

The employee's position is simple: the daily life of the shelter functions effectively and efficiently because of the work performed by front-line staff. As her colleague put it, *"We're doing the dirt, we're in the trenches, we're doing the work"* (emphasis added). This comment equates their work with the trenches where one has no choice but to get dirty; anything else, such as the work performed by the caseworkers, is not real work, because it is not in the trenches. The reason front-line employees are paramount to the order of the shelter, the above quoted employee explained, and then repeatedly underscored, is because they serve as the eyes and the ears of the shelter – something, it should be recalled, a caseworker admitted to as well. This metaphor is important for several reasons. First, front-line workers welcome clients to the shelter. Their faces are a reminder of the care that awaits clients. Much more, however, is intimated by the employee. She is also speaking of the presence of the front-line employees, especially in relation to surveillance. This is important, she notes, because the caseworkers are "not there to see it on a daily basis," hinting that the absence of their presence makes their ability to do the job difficult, even impossible. Thus, as she sees it, without front-line employees, the shelter would fall apart. In other words, the daily presence of the front-line workers is a constant reminder that someone cares. Without them, care ceases not only to exist, but to even facilitate an image or impression of its existence. In this way, she is seeking to salvage some worth, some respect, for front-line work, which has been all but eviscerated by management through the policies of the shelter which privilege one class of employee over another.

Also problematic is poor communication between the parties, something raised not only by this employee, but many front-line employees as well. What this employee underscores is that what the front-line workers have to say is not taken seriously – despite pretences to show otherwise – and this is because they and their recommendations are seen as less worthy. This, she and others find particularly problematic, because, as she repeatedly noted, front-line workers are the ones who not only see, but see in ways others do not (in fact, cannot, given their absences). This would mean, then, that when front-line workers are not taken at face value, not only is this seen as a sign of disrespect, but it also directly affects the administration of care. All this only serves to exacerbate the poor relationship between the two.

An example aptly illustrates this. A client, ABC, required special attention due to a plethora of maladies, some serious, others less significant, and still others fabricated (in many ways, he was like numerous other clients). According to front-line workers, what ABC was particularly adroit at, again like many clients, was being able to "abuse" and "manipulate the situation" and the system as a whole. One particular concession that ABC had succeeded in obtaining was to have water, in some instances even food, personally brought to him by the front-line employees. The front-line employees were frustrated and irritated not only about having to do these additional chores for ABC, but, perhaps more frustratingly, that ABC had successfully managed to fool both the supervisors and caseworkers – as they saw it, yet another example that it is they, rather than other employees, who truly know and understand the clients and what is happening in the shelter. "He expects us to fetch for him," one employee once said disgustingly while exiting The Bubble to take some water to ABC.

In fact, it was not just that ABC had managed to have water delivered to him, but to have bottled water delivered to him – an allowance not granted to any other client. This was granted to him by a caseworker who, after initially speaking with ABC, decided that it would be prudent for him to drink plenty of water given the high level of his blood sugar. Thus, for the one night in question, the caseworker suggested that he be provided with a bottle of bottled water. ABC, however, seeing an opportune time to "abuse" and "manipulate" the situation, as the front-line workers put it, continued to request bottled water and steadfastly refused to fill his bottle with water from the water cooler. Thus, in seeking to resolve this issue, the caseworker who originally recommended bottled water, reasoned that ABC's immobility precluded him from freely accessing the water cooler; additionally, because the cone-like cups used to drink the water are small, the caseworker reasoned that bottled water would last ABC a longer time, which would reduce the frequency the front-line employees would have to provide him with water. Not once in this reasoning, it appears, did the caseworker think it prudent to simply ask the front-line employees to fill the bottle with

water from the water cooler, which would have provided ABC a sufficient quantity of filtered water.

Thus, for an entire week, bottled water was provided to ABC. This
practice was then extended for another week. While this was unfolding, the front-line workers were becoming increasingly agitated with
the caseworker who made this recommendation. They were more
frustrated, however, with the supervisors who permitted this practice,
especially because it represented the discretionary power of the caseworkers in action. An employee once scoffed at a supervisor who went
to the nearby grocery store to buy a case of water for ABC; as the supervisor left, she sarcastically commented, "Good job, Jackass. Way to go."
At the end of the second week, the supervisors and the caseworker
realized that they simply could not allow this practice to continue and,
thus, ABC was no longer provided bottled water.

This example illustrates how discretionary power bestowed to caseworkers can, at times, pose problems to the ordering of the shelter.
Here, what exacerbates the situation is that communication, at least
as the front-line workers see it, appears to proceed in one direction:
the supervisors and caseworkers provide directives which the front-
line workers must follow; however, what they have to say is not given
proper due or respect, even though, as the female front-line employee
put it, not only are front-line workers "the eyes and the ears," but the
other personnel are not constantly present and, therefore, do not – in
fact, cannot – "see." This, as they view it, poses problems to the ordering of the shelter and they are frustrated by it. It is this type of frustration that manifests itself in discontent, resentment, and acrimony and
poses grave threats both to the ordering of the shelter and the deployment of care. Both symbolically and in practice, the working relationship between front-line workers and caseworkers eviscerates the ethic
of care that constitutes the shelter.

## On the Chaotic and Mundane: A Final Word

In focusing on key personnel in the shelter, from the clients to the
employees, I have shown how the relations among these groups, ranging from the mundane to the significant, play a vital role in the everyday order in the shelter, including the implications for the ethic of care
and its deployment. In so doing, I have argued that the mundane events
that unfold in the shelter, from how a shift is organized, how employees combat boredom, to how different employees interact with others,

coalesce to shape the tenor and climate of the shelter. The result is that even in the humdrum and mundane of the every day, chaos is the norm. This makes the conceptualization of an ethic of care and its deployment that much more difficult and, as well, ineffectual and inefficient.

One notable absentee thus far, at least explicitly and in detail, is management (i.e., senior managers and supervisors). Management is crucial to the order and ethic of care in the shelter, and will receive detailed attention in the following chapters. It is management, recognizing and seeking to attend to and alleviate the mundanity of chaos, which tends to exacerbate matters leading to administrative chaos. This, as I show in what follows, is because of the logics of security and legality that management seeks to implement in order to combat this chaos. The resultant order, thus, is more chaotic, and administratively so, and this has grave implications for the ethic of care and its deployment.

# 5 The Securitization of an Ethic of Care and the Administration of Chaos

In the two previous chapters, I examined the ways the aestheticism of an ethic of care is visible in the architecture of the shelter, especially in the spatial tactics deployed. As well, I discussed the daily practices of various personnel, ranging from the mundane and humdrum to the more serious and significant. In both instances, whether pertaining to material objects, such as doors or chairs, or the actions of registering clients or dealing with boredom, I paid attention to the ways these significantly shape the everyday order of the shelter. I suggested that this order is constituted and characterized by chaos. Here, I hinted that management is mindful of this chaotic environment. Given this knowledge, management has sought to be overly proactive in attending to and rectifying this problem. Ironically, however, as I show in this chapter and the chapters to follow, these endeavours exacerbate the problems in the shelter and create an environment that is constituted and governed by what I have called administrative chaos, one gravely inimical to an ethic of care.

This and the next chapter explore how administrative chaos comes to constitute the ordering of the shelter. To this end, this chapter examines an important logic that underpins this order, namely, security. Paying heed to the vast and eclectic literature calling for a more robust analysis of precisely what security looks and feels like from the ground up (e.g., Loader and Walker, 2007, 3; Shearing and Johnston, 2010, 496; Valverde, 2001, 2011; Waldron, 2006; Zedner, 2003a), I examine the production of security in the shelter. I explicate how the attempt to create a secure – or securitized – environment leads to conflict and acrimony between two major parties, namely, management and employees (both front-line staff and caseworkers). Even a cursory observation of the

shelter quickly reveals that what exactly security is and, most importantly, ought to be, is profoundly unsettled and subjected to a series of
struggles. These struggles unequivocally highlight that security is characterized by its polysemy (see Ranasinghe, 2013a; see also Zedner, 2009,
9–25). By this I mean that different people can, and do, think of security
in different ways despite being subjected to the same place. In exploring and explicating the discursive production of security, I conceptualize security not necessarily as a thing (cf. Valverde, 2011) or a public
good (cf. Loader and Walker, 2007) – though they can be both, among
many others – but, rather, as a site of struggle (Ranasinghe, 2013a,
2013c). I show how in this spatial struggle, the concept of an ethic of
care is diluted and rendered secondary to the logic of security (and, as
will become apparent later, legality). I begin with a discussion of the
history of The Bubble – introduced in chapter 3 – and provide a tour
of its structure in an effort to locate the *place* of security in the shelter.

**The Bubble as a Safe Haven**

It would be hyperbolic to claim that the shelter is extremely anarchic
and dangerous as some emergency shelters are said to be, such as the
infamous Armory in New York City (see Dordick, 1996). Nevertheless,
it is quite typical of many others where "crime is a pervasive aspect
of shelter life and includes the use of drugs … and theft," and where
"everything is up for grabs – the resident's personal belongings, his bed
or locker, his bodily safety, and his privacy" (Grunberg and Eagle, 1990,
523). Thus, the threat of physical violence and bodily harm is a serious
concern to many employees and is taken very seriously by management, to the point of paranoia.[1] Thus, it is not surprising that a supervisor described the place as "volatile" and used the metaphor of war to
describe the space and its environment: "We are front-line workers. *We
are in the trenches*" (emphasis added). Similarly, when I asked another
supervisor, "Is this a … safe place?" the answer was an immediate and
emphatic "No," and elaborated upon as such:

> People come in and they're intoxicated and they're high and a lot of them
> have weapons and a lot of them don't have the skills to get along with
> each other without resorting to … yelling [and] fighting … and so we
> don't know who's walking through the door, [because] anybody can walk
> through the door, and anybody can have anything in their pockets or their
> backpacks, and we have no idea what they've got … So, it's not safe.

If such a feeling generally permeates the climate of the shelter and its personnel, especially the management team, this feeling was exacerbated because of a particular incident which gave birth to The Bubble and drastically reshaped the tenor of the shelter.

The Bubble was a direct result of a very rare, unfortunate, and extremely violent incident that occurred in approximately 2007 or 2008 – the narration of the story contained numerous ambiguities, including when it happened. It is a commonality for front-line workers who work overnight shifts to be tasked with, among other matters, waking clients who request to be awoken during the early morning hours, whether for work (which is often the case) or for a variety of other reasons (one being, as "Captain Delight" so comically sought to put it, because the clients simply want to control the employees; another is that at least one client likes to walk the streets in the early hours of the morning looking for spare change and other valuables that drunken revellers may have misplaced). On one particular night, a client had requested a wake-up call and a male employee went up to the second floor to wake the client. When he approached and woke the client, the client, who was supposedly suffering from a severe mental illness, was startled and attacked him. The employee was repeatedly stabbed in the stomach – "gutted" as an employee put it, "eviscerated" as a supervisor claimed. The worker survived the attack but, unsurprisingly, was never the same again and, supposedly, still finds it difficult to maintain even a modicum of stability in his life. It was this incident and its aftermath that vividly highlighted the need for significant changes in the shelter's safety procedures that eventually led to the erection of The Bubble.

Prior to The Bubble, front-line employees worked in a semi-enclosed space. The large reception area that operated as the intake centre for clients was, like many reception areas, enclosed only by a counter at the front, about three-and-one-half feet in height. Behind this counter stood a fibreglass-type shield that served as an additional barrier of protection, which employees could utilize if and when they felt that an interaction with a client was getting out of control or becoming dangerous. However, clients could easily gain direct physical access to the workers by simply jumping over the counter, which, as recalled by some employees and management, did happen, even if only infrequently. As one female employee said of the set up: "No protection whatsoever! None, none, zero!"

It was precisely this lack of protection that deeply worried the management team who thought it imperative to safeguard employees from the potential for further catastrophic incidents – and, with it, minimize any legal issues that might emerge (as I take up later, the essence of The Bubble as a mechanism for, and of, security is inextricably linked to legality). Management began by inviting security consultants to survey the space and provide recommendations as to how it could be better secured. Numerous recommendations were put in place, but the most significant was the erection of The Bubble.

The Bubble, as it is referred to fondly by some workers and pejoratively by most, is a fully enclosed space that, being a "protective cocoon" of sorts (Giddens, 1991, 126–33), fortifies the space front-line employees work in. It is approximately ten feet in height and length, but only some six feet in width and, therefore, ends up being a very small space given it must accommodate at least two to three employees at a time, often more given the heavy traffic in and out of it (see Figure 5.1). It is virtually rectangular in shape with the front being oval-like. The front of The Bubble has a counter that is about three feet in height from the bottom up and another two feet or so from the top down; the remaining

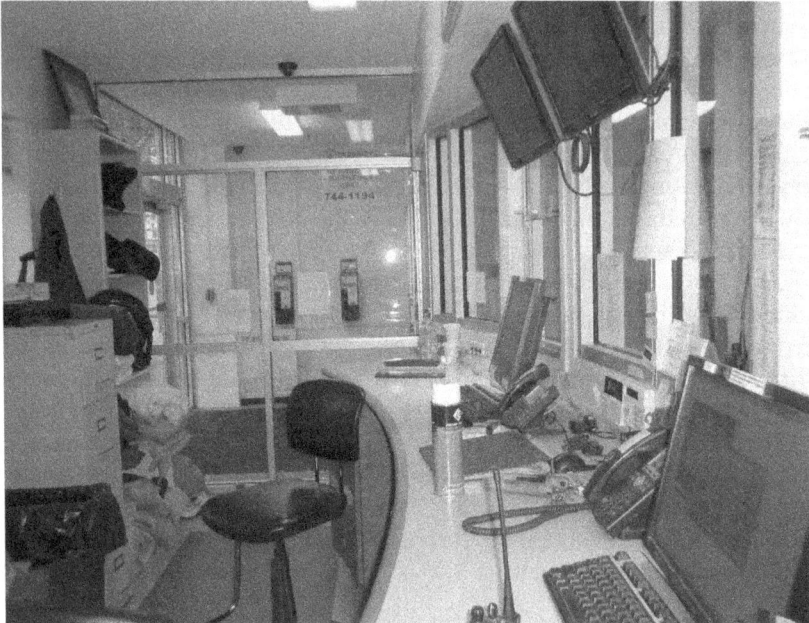

Figure 5.1. A view of The Bubble from the inside facing the entrance of the shelter. (Photo credit: Author)

middle portion is made up of glass panes. This glass portion also has two windows that allow employees and clients to interact. At the ends of The Bubble are two doors that have glass in the middle to enhance visibility. Both sides of The Bubble overlook the two entrances to the shelter, one, the main entrance, the other, a side door, and both sides are fully composed of glass from top to bottom and thus provide good visibility.[2] However, the visibility from within The Bubble overlooking the lobby area is quite poor and employees must rely on the surveillance cameras or the large oval mirror situated on the upper-right hand corner outside The Bubble to circumvent this blind spot.

Ostensibly, then, The Bubble is meant to be, and is symbolic of, a fortress, one designed explicitly with the physical safety of the employees in mind. This is often referred to as "primary safety" (Valverde, 2001, 84; cf. Spitzer, 1987), that is, "the basic physical safety of oneself and one's loved ones" (Valverde, 2001, 84). This is also referred to as "the pure safety conception" (Waldron, 2006, 461), or that which closely parallels what Anthony Giddens (1984, 50) calls "ontological security." The crucial point to underscore is that security, as envisaged, conceptualized, and acted upon by management, is solely and directly equated with violence and bodily harm – this will be referred to as primary safety.

It would be remiss to suggest that management is either unmindful of other issues beyond violence or neglects or overlooks them. Rather, my contention is that in these cases, there is a tendency to treat these as less important than concerns about primary safety, and in some cases, such as concerns over poor pay, as unimportant. In addition, when these concerns are taken up, they are often funnelled into the logic and discourse of violence and bodily harm so that if they are not part and parcel of such a characterization, they are not constructed as an issue of security. One example illustrates this. A major concern that management has had is the use of personal laptops or communal computers by employees to "surf" the Internet for private purposes. At a staff meeting this was raised by the supervisor who conducted the meeting. In gently admonishing the employees to refrain from this practice, the supervisor, rather adroitly, turned the problem into an issue about primary safety. The supervisor suggested that if employees are preoccupied with surfing the Internet, they will be unaware of their immediate surroundings and what is taking place. This, the supervisor noted, would put them in danger: "We have to be aware of our surroundings. The minute we are not is when someone gets hurt ... Always be aware of your surroundings, personal space *and be safe*" (emphasis added).

Rather than criticize the employees for their dereliction of duty to serve the clients, the supervisor turned this failure into one about *their* safety, and thus, was able to use the discourse of security to promote an ethic of care, This, however, was more than a tactical shift. Rather, it is also representative of a preoccupation with primary safety, where a variety of issues are funnelled into its logic and rationale. The Bubble is perhaps the clearest example of this.

Symbolically, as noted above, it is impossible to deny what The Bubble stands for: a fortress of protection, akin to the metaphor of the cocoon that Giddens (1991) utilizes to locate the place of security in late-modernity (126–33). This is precisely what management had in mind when it conceptualized, designed, and erected The Bubble. It also cannot be denied that at least some employees think quite fondly of The Bubble and its protective capacity. One example illustrates this. While interacting with a severely inebriated client in the lobby, a female caseworker was physically threatened by him. He called her a "bitch" and threatened to stab her and, later, while being escorted out of the building by the security guard, warned her that "This ain't far from over." The caseworker entered The Bubble and called the police. While on the phone, and presumably in response to a question about her well-being, she replied, "I am in this bubble, so *there is nothing he can do to me*" (emphasis added). This statement nicely captures how, at least for her, The Bubble is a safe haven that shields and provides solace from the chaos of the shelter: the mere entrance into it provides a sense of safety that is unmatched, because, in this case, "there is nothing" that clients "can do" to employees when they are in The Bubble. The Bubble is a symbol of security and hope. In this instance, The Bubble provided this woman, who believed the shelter to be safe, protection and respite during an occasion when her safety was jeopardized.

Related, The Bubble signifies a particular way that management *imagines* its employees, particularly, front-line workers; this imagining, as will become apparent later, has serious repercussions not only for the conceptualization of an ethic of care, but for its deployment as well. In discussing the problematics of safety, the same supervisor who emphatically stated that the shelter is unsafe, further explained one reason for this:

> One of the problems … I think, with some of the front-desk people, [is that while] I'm always vigilant … – I think … that you have to be … aware of your surroundings and you always take precautions and all of that sort of

thing, [that is], just make it second nature ... – an awful lot of people here, it's not in their second nature and ... they'll go and talk to someone ... [and] they've got a coffee in one hand and a clipboard in the other ... and they're telling somebody that "Yeah, sorry, you can't be here," and their body is exposed ... If you are going to do something like that, make sure you don't have your coffee in your hand, make sure that ... you are ready to move here and there [or] whatever. I've seen people just let their guard down and it shouldn't be [like that].

In this somewhat lengthy explanation, the supervisor bemoans the absence of the prudential employee, one who understands the volatility of the space he/she is working in and the clients with whom he/she is interacting. The Bubble, in other words, is the solution (or a response) to the irresponsible worker who fails to take such precautions – for example, in regards to the employee who was stabbed, that he failed to undertake this task with another employee, as laid out in the protocols. In a similar fashion that the hinges on a door ensure that it will close automatically – and, thus, serve as the antidote to the forgetfulness, discourteousness, or incompetence of the human (Latour, 1988) – The Bubble functions to shield the irresponsible and incompetent employee from bodily harm and violence, thereby enhancing security in the shelter, not just for the employee, but for all concerned. In other words, material objects – which I previously explored in relation to an aestheticism of an ethic of care – are mobilized for security, which, by extension, are meant to, if not enhance, then, at least preserve, an ethic of care. In reinforcing this narrative, another supervisor explained how these material objects seek to impress and, thereby, enhance, a culture of security where the employee is forced to recognize the problem and take responsibility for it: "So they've [management] done stuff ... by putting a security door, we've got magnetic locks that can lock the ... [entrance to the shelter], we've got panic [buttons] ... Safety, I think, goes to the culture of security, to the *instruments* that are brought into ... keep everybody secure" (emphasis added). The Bubble, then, is a representation not simply of a horrible and unfortunate incident. It is, as well, a representation of, and solution to, the incompetence of humans, in many ways, the ways management imagines its employees. Ironically, it was because of this very incompetence – one which led to serious bodily harm – that the shelter, at least theoretically, was made more secure.

While The Bubble was envisaged as such, more often than not, it failed to live up to its ideal, not only because of inherent flaws in its structure (see below), but also because of the complacency and non-chalant attitudes of the employees. For the most part, all the front-line employees would leave the front door of The Bubble unlocked and ajar – by turning the bolt outwards so that the door could not fully close – when leaving it for a short period of time (this allowed them easy re-entry without having to use their keys to unlock the door, a sign of laziness, some even admitting so). This, however, ran blatantly in the face of the type of protection that management had envisaged and necessitated. Even more, it ran blatantly against the way management conceptualizes the shelter: as a place that is vio-lent, unpredictable, and dangerous. On one occasion, a member of the management team walked into The Bubble only to find the door unlocked in the ways described above. He immediately counselled the employees on duty, saying, "Keep it locked, boys. *That's why we built this for your safety and security*, so keep it locked" (emphasis added).

For all the exhortations, even admonishments, on the part of man-agement, the incompetence, even discourteousness, of the employees served to undo any potential advantage The Bubble could afford them (though, as I take up later, many saw it as giving rise to numerous dis-advantages, a product of the polysemic nature of security and its con-ceptualization). The blatant disregard of protocols was, unsurprisingly, not looked upon kindly by management. One supervisor, for example, excoriated the employees when discussing this matter:

> *If you use all the instruments properly*, while it might be a nuisance for them ... *that's what causes ... security*, because if you leave that door open, and this is what they do for ease, so they don't have to hear this guy asking all the time, they leave it open. So now people outside who know it's open can come inside, they can hide anywhere in the building, they can jump out at anyone, they can be rifling through people's things ... But if you ... just out of ease or laziness, you just want to keep it easy, you are going to find ... more problems ... (emphases added)

This passage is illuminating because the supervisor clearly and explic-itly connects security to material objects – in fact, makes a causal connec-tion between the two – and, yet, in the same breath, locates the absence or lack of security in the very laziness, perhaps incompetence, of the employees. This laziness, the supervisor opines, trumps the materials of security, and thus, places the shelter and its personnel at risk of vio-lence and bodily harm.

There is a "postscript" to the story of The Bubble, which aptly shines light on the polysemy of security. The male employee who was attacked and severely injured was not supposed to be at work that night. He had agreed to fill in for another employee so that employee could attend an important family function. Thus, had the shift not been switched, it could possibly have been the other employee who was attacked.

I raise this because I heard the story about this incident on numerous occasions during the time I spent in the shelter. On each occasion, the crux of the story remained the same, though several aspects were either omitted, glossed over, or embellished. While the emotionality of the story was certainly underscored by all parties, it was the employees and, in particular, the employee who had switched his shift with the employee who was stabbed, who spoke of this aspect of the incident. He spoke candidly about the threat of violence, but also about much more than bodily harm. In addition, he spoke of the emotionality of knowing that his co-worker was attacked in the way he was and, as well, having to bear the guilt and burden for indirectly being responsible for his predicament. I use this example to underscore the myriad faces of security, its polysemy, in other words, because, for him and his colleagues, the emotive aspects associated with this horrific incident are cast as issues of security but in ways that have little or nothing to do with the way management sees it – for management, the emotive aspect, which is separated from the physical violence, is not a security issue. Thus, the well-being of the employees is compromised precisely because management and employees view security differently. Such a disjuncture, as I take up in what follows, poses grave threats to the ordering of the shelter because one important plank of this order, security, and precisely what it entails, is unsettled.

## Contesting Security: The Bubble as Anti-Security

As a source and symbol of security, The Bubble is inextricably tied to an ethic of care. What complicates matters, however, is that the security-ethic of care nexus is conceptualized by the three major parties involved – management, employees (especially front-line employees), and clients – in very different ways. This poses serious problems to the order in the shelter. While The Bubble was heralded for its ability to provide unmitigated and uncompromised security, in practice, it posed more problems, both symbolically and instrumentally, than it seemingly resolved – in fact, as will become apparent, was even capable of resolving. Thus, The Bubble is a significant source of irritation, conflict, and acrimony for these parties and their interactions with one another.

From the perspective of management, the fundamental problem with The Bubble was that it shielded front-line employees from clients; in so doing, it essentially rendered the employees inconspicuous – a source of great concern for the clients as well, as I take up later. On one hand, such a concern appears counterintuitive. Recall, for example, that The Bubble was directly a product of an extremely violent incident and was designed and erected for the purposes of protecting the employees. Thus, if The Bubble shields employees from the clients, then it appears that The Bubble does precisely what it is tasked with; that is, where the employees are shielded from the clients, they are protected from them and, therefore, ostensibly at least, safe. This, however, is not what management had envisaged with The Bubble. As management saw it, The Bubble is the place where employees could retreat to if and when they believed that they were under imminent threats or danger; they could enter The Bubble, lock the door, and request help. During other times, management envisaged that the employees – or at least some employees – would interact with clients, both as a means of getting to know them, their lives, and their needs and, as well, use this as an opportunity to surveil and keep abreast of what is transpiring in the shelter. This, however, at least from the perspective of management, is not what has transpired.

Instead, as management sees it, The Bubble has bred and sustained an ethic of indolence at the expense of an ethic of care. Front-line employees, they believe, congregate in The Bubble and attend to myriad personal matters – from checking emails, making telephone calls, surfing the Internet to conversing with fellow employees, including gossiping about a variety of things and people, including the clients, all of which I (humorously) observed (and, in some cases, even partook in). As one supervisor put it: "The staff are all in … [The Bubble] and *they're chatting away and having a grand ole time* and everything is happening in the lobby and *they're not paying attention*" (emphases added). Another supervisor was equally blunt:

> We've hired adults, we've empowered them, we've told them that *they have a couple of duties to take care of* and then we leave them; we had left them to it thinking [that] as adults with a few limited duties and [being] empowered they would be able to handle that. But, what we have found is that not everybody has an equal work ethic [and] *some people are coming here to avoid work* … (emphases added)

Both these comments speak to the failure to undertake the work the employees are called upon, entrusted with, and expected to perform. There appear to be two related concerns, The Bubble and the recalcitrant and indolent employee: that is, The Bubble breeds indolence and recalcitrance in an already indolent and recalcitrant – not to mention incompetent – worker. Yet, the way the supervisors construct and narrate the problem locates responsibility solely with the employees, not The Bubble (recall, for example, the discussion of the incompetent employee and how The Bubble rectifies this problem). Thus, for example, in the latter supervisor's comments, the lack or absence of a work ethic is directly referenced, and the gravity of the problem is highlighted by juxtaposing the required work ("a couple of duties") to the failure to perform simple tasks ("some people ... avoid work"). In this picturing, the absence or deterioration of an ethic of care is tied directly to the aberrant employees. Regardless of how this problem is presented, the security-ethic of care nexus is at the forefront of the problem of order – in fact, it is what poses the problem in the first place. Thus, for example, when the other supervisor comments about the "grand ole time[s]" had by the employees while the lobby is simultaneously left in a precarious state, the supervisor is explicitly connecting the gravity of this security threat ("everything is happening") to the dereliction of duties ("they're not paying attention").

Interestingly, the two supervisors appear to be unmindful of the irony at hand: the need and desire to improve security – itself emanating because of the need to administer care on a daily basis, for example, attending to the request to be woken up – has contributed to, if not caused, the problems with the administration and the deployment of care. Even if, however, they are mindful of it, I suspect that blame would still be placed on the employees – as recalcitrant, indolent, and incompetent – rather than either on the need and desire for security or the material effects (e.g., The Bubble) that have arisen thereof. This is because, as they see it, care is best optimized and delivered in secure settings, and The Bubble epitomizes "perfect security" in the same ways that Jeremy Bentham spoke of the Panopticon, for example ([1811] 1962, 498–503). The problem, in other words, is not the structure, but the people; in fact, the very need for the former emanates because of the latter. Yet, for all this posturing, it must be recognized that it is not just a concern over security, but rather a rabid preoccupation with it and the concomitant desire to funnel most problems into a logic of security (and, in particular, that of primary safety), that is at least partly responsible for the precarious order in the shelter. The failure to recognize this, I suggest, is precisely why management and front-line employees clash, because both parties have very different views not just of security but of an ethic of care itself.

This can be illuminated by exploring The Bubble from the perspective of the front-line employees. There is little doubt that for the employees, just as it was for management, The Bubble has created a significant gulf between workers and clients. What supposedly was, for the most part, a cordial relationship between the two parties, has been made tepid and distant, a change that is palpably noticeable to all parties concerned. Unlike before, the newly erected physical barriers further enhanced and reinforced an "us versus them" mentality. The Bubble became symbolic of the trepidations the employees, supposedly, held towards clients. This only served to further enhance its infamy. As one client explained to a front-line employee: "To most of us, The Bubble is the place we don't know anything about. We know there is staff in there, but we don't know about it." His comments verged on – if not extended beyond – the hyperbolic. That is, it was not necessarily the visibility or lack thereof that he was speaking about. Rather, it was the distancing and separation, even if only symbolically, that clearly and vividly signalled that there were two different groups in the same space. Here, the difference is not one that hinges on the distinction between the deliverer and receiver of care. Rather, it is about humanity itself, based, that is, on worthiness: constructing the employees as in need of protection *from* the clients is problematic not simply because the clients are labelled as dangerous, but also because the employees' security is deemed more important than the clients'. This is best evinced in the comment of a supervisor: "My primary concern is the safety of my staff." It is precisely this gulf, both real and symbolic, that The Bubble represented to the clients and employees alike.

Examined in this light, the employees had numerous problems with the The Bubble. In what follows, I provide the counter-narrative of The Bubble in order to examine how the production of the polysemy of security negatively affects the administration and deployment of care.

## Structuring Insecurity

Most employees spoke disparagingly about The Bubble and its effects on their work lives. Elizabeth, for example, was blunt, claiming that The Bubble "is suffocating," while another employee was even more so, saying, "I hate The Bubble. *I really hate The Bubble*" (emphasis added).

Shedding further insights as to why the employees held such strong feelings, another employee opined: "This room is a prison. Everybody sits in here, then everybody gets miserable." Her comments hint at several pressing issues constitutive of The Bubble. First, The Bubble was viewed either as a prison or a prison-like room that led, therefore, to suffocation (and, by extension, suffering). This was largely, if not solely, because of its diminutive size, another and related problem. As one employee put it matter-of-factly, "There is not enough space to move around ... It was poorly designed, so it's just like everything ... feels trapped in there."

It is ironic that The Bubble was viewed as a prison that evoked feelings of suffocation and being trapped. First, both management and employees, in a rare instance of concordance, firmly believed that the strictures of the daily life of the shelter, including its architecture, (unwittingly) recreated a prison-like environment for the clients, who therefore felt trapped and suffocated – a feeling shared by many who have occupied time in shelters (e.g., Grunberg and Eagle, 1990, 523; Marcus, 2003, 137–8; DeWard and Moe, 2010). For many clients who had previously served prison or jail sentences – the shelter houses numerous such individuals – the shelter was a rather seamless and fluid transition from one institution to another. For the rest of the clients, as well, this prison-like experience was reinforced in the shelter or, at least, such was the view. Thus, one employee believed that a "kind of ... prison mentality" pervades the shelter because, as a supervisor put it, the shelter is "one step from being in a prison." The latter statement hints at the fluidity discussed above, especially for those who had experienced prisons or jails. In large part, the processes by which clients are admitted into and then governed while in the shelter play a significant role in spawning this mentality (again, perhaps, unwittingly). A striking aspect of this is that when clients book a bed they are provided with a bed number. From that moment until they exit the shelter, this number becomes a significant part of their lives; indeed, it constitutes them as clients of the shelter, so much so that when confirming their beds, something that must be done on a daily basis, or when lining up for meals, they provide as an identifier their bed numbers, not their names. Even though employees know the names of the clients and address them by their first names, the identity of the client, institutionally at least, is based on this number, just as it is in prison. In addition, the daily routine of the shelter is quite like a prison. As one caseworker explained, clients, just like prisoners, lose their autonomy because virtually every aspect of their lives, ranging from when they must wake up, go to bed, eat, shower, watch television, or apply for aid, is institutionally regulated – one aspect of this, discussed in chapter 3, is the evisceration of privacy that further mimics prison-like conditions (see Marcus, 2003; Desjarlais, 1997, 76–9). Even the morning wake-up calls, which are performed daily at 7 a.m., supposedly remind some clients of their experiences in prison and, thus, employees were told by a supervisor during a staff meeting, "You gotta be diligent in wake-ups." Unsurprisingly, employees firmly believe that clients "think it is like they are in jail."

The irony is that the employees, who are called upon to provide care for the clients, themselves feel trapped and suffocated; this feeling is not simply a reflection of the work they perform (as will be discussed in chapters 7 and 8), but is also directly related to – in some ways caused by – The Bubble and its effects. The diminutive size of The Bubble mimics a prison cell that houses two or three prisoners; in The Bubble, two to three (sometimes more) employees are cramped into small quarters and tasked with attending to myriad chores. The same employee who said that she hates The Bubble also mentioned that "at times there is like eight people [sic] in … [The Bubble] which drives me crazy because it gets really claustrophobic." At least spatially, the daily work lives of the employees are reduced to a prison-like setting. The near-total institution (de Lint, 1998, 266, 281n1; Goffman, 1961) that constitutes the shelter and the experiences of the clients, in some ways at least, also extends towards, and appears to structure the lives of, the employees. What is most ironic is that this feeling of suffocation is directly a product of an attempt to alleviate such a feeling in the first place. That is, the desire to securitize the space, and with it, encase the employees in The Bubble, is what leads to a sense of suffering, suffocation, and insecurity. It is the logic of security, an important part of the ordering of the shelter, which has created numerous dire effects: most directly, it severely affects the daily work lives of the employees and their ability to deploy care.

The diminutive size of The Bubble also posed an array of other related problems. A recurring one was that The Bubble was often untidy, unclean, and littered with trash, this, despite the daily cleaning it is subjected to by the housekeeping staff. The diminutive size does not make The Bubble easily amenable to cleaning and, to make matters worse, the size magnifies its aesthetically unpleasant nature given that there is little room to "hide" unsightly elements such as garbage (see Figure 5.2). On one occasion during an overnight shift an employee caught attention of the garbage and paper that littered the space below

Figure 5.2. The inside of The Bubble littered with garbage and other items. (Photo credit: Author)

his chair. "What the hell is all this stuff under here?" he queried his colleague and then commented, "It's like a garbage can!" After spending considerable time cleaning the place, he commented to another colleague that The Bubble is "pretty gross." His relatively small work area was, more often than not, "like a garbage can," one that carried with it serious health consequences.

Looked upon as such, the space in which front-line employees work contains some parity with respect to the aesthetics and conditions throughout the shelter. As discussed in chapter 3, the aesthetics of the shelter, especially in relation to garbage bags that litter the floors, tables, and chairs in the lobby, paint the area as slovenly and chaotic. While the inside of The Bubble is not easily visible as the lobby is, it is, nevertheless, aesthetically unpleasant; indeed, it can resemble a "garbage can," which in some ways is perhaps more slovenly, disorderly, and chaotic than the lobby itself.

Also of major concern was the air ventilation in The Bubble, about which one employee said, "There is not enough air circulating." Whether this problem was directly related to the diminutive size of The Bubble or not mattered little: what mattered was that the employees had made such a connection. On some days, especially in the winter, it was unbearably warm and many male employees were reduced to wearing T-shirts. The one fan in The Bubble was looked upon to provide some solace, though inevitably it failed to consistently do so. "We were cooking, man," an employee once commented to a colleague about an exceptionally warm and humid night that he and I endured in The Bubble. On other days, it was extremely cold and some employees would wear sweaters over their sweatshirts, or two sweatshirts, to keep warm. The inconsistent temperature made working conditions far from pleasant. Much more than pleasantness, however, was at stake. Many employees complained that this inconsistency was making them sick. One employee went as far as requesting, even demanding, that management either instal a window in The Bubble, which would provide fresh air from the outside, or provide an air purifier. In explaining what transpired, a caseworker commented that "in the front desk, the air in there was very poor [and] we had someone try it out and that's when we got that air purifier." The air purifier made things somewhat better. However, in an effort to find reprieve from the extreme heat and discomfort that pervaded The Bubble, employees would often leave one of the front doors ajar to facilitate better air circulation. This meant that the attempt to alleviate the potential health risks caused by The Bubble literally opened up the opportunity for violence and bodily harm, thereby nullifying its purpose.

The winter months brought additional challenges because of the influenza (hereinafter flu) season as highlighted in the following example. One cold and wintry night, an employee walked into The Bubble to begin his shift. He had been battling a severe cold and flu for about a week and was clearly showing signs of fatigue – he was at the point where he had "lost" his voice. He blamed his predicament on another employee whom he believed originally contracted the flu but failed to take precautionary measures, such as seeing a doctor. He had become despondent because of what he saw as inevitable, that is, the spreading of the flu from one to another, which would only prolong his agony. His colleagues sympathized with him because they clearly understood the gravity of working in such close quarters and the near certain result, that is, sickness, that awaited them. During the "flu season," one employee noted, anyone "who comes in [to The Bubble] coughing, you know, or has whatever, it is so easy to infect the colleagues around them." Similarly, the same employee who spoke about feeling trapped, commented, "If somebody sneeze[s], trust me, it is going to be circulating for a good couple [of] seconds before it evaporates." Her comments hint at how easy it is to fall sick while working in the shelter, a large part because of The Bubble. The foregoing example and comments speak to much more than the tensions among employees. While the spread of the flu in the workplace is quite common during the winter, in the shelter, it is magnified and exacerbated because of the very small space the employees find themselves in. The Bubble, perhaps unexpectedly, also posed great strife in the life of the employees, in this case, relating to health and well-being.

These examples highlight specific problems with (and in) The Bubble. These problems are a product of the rabid preoccupation with, even paranoia over, security, specifically pertaining to violence and bodily harm. Yet, as the foregoing suggests, many of these problems, such as aesthetics, have little or nothing to do with violence (in the sense of bodily harm). They, therefore, do not receive the type of traction they would if they were problems of violence. The foregoing, then, alludes to the different ways that security is constructed by different parties; that is, security is a site of a discursive struggle to lay claim to what it is and ought to be. I have hinted at this through the discussion of health concerns. Next, I discuss the problem of health in greater detail by exploring how it is constructed by the employees as a security issue. In so doing, I seek to underscore the production of the polysemy of security and its implications for the order in the shelter.

## The Security of Health

For the employees, health issues such as the common flu are direct threats to their security. First, and most obviously, sickness is a sign that the body is not secure: it is ill, weak, and compromised. There is also the possibility of infecting fellow family members, a concern especially for those who have young children. As Kim Hopper (2003) writes of his observations in a shelter: "Almost without exception, employees were fearful, not only of falling victim to some random act of violence by a client, but also of catching some dreaded disease from the men and bringing it home to their families" (96). In addition, being sick means that employees would miss work; this is particularly concerning to part-time employees or those still on probation because their absences are not compensated monetarily. Their health, in other words, is their (ticket to) security, in this case, the ability to earn a living and provide for their families. As many commentators do (e.g., Burris, 2006), employees see health and security as going hand in hand. One employee explained his trepidations as such:

> Health issues ... you know, the clients, they [are] touching the [door] handle all the time and we have no gloves [and] we also go there, you know, so the doors [are also] just pushed [read, touched] by the same clients ... So I know we wash our hands but, you know, before we wash our hands, you don't know what you got, right? I always wash my hands whenever I touch something.

This employee's fear is about becoming sick should he pick up something from touching surfaces, such as a door handle. If the health-security nexus is only implicit in his comments, it is explicit and unequivocal in the comments of another employee:

> I will stand off to the side because if you spit and you have hepatitis or whatever, it is coming at me, so [as] I already talked about those kinds of safety [issues] ... so as he [a client] comes to talk, I will be pulling off to the side. They don't know why, but for me *that's my personal safety*. Because, if you get angry enough to start spitting, then it's going to come at me. Then I am going to have to worry about getting some health check or something ... (emphasis added)

Her fear about getting sick ("getting some health check") is directly constructed as an issue of security affecting her "personal safety." At another time, after discussing various problems in The Bubble, including the lack of space, she explained:

> If they [management] wanted to *enhance my safety* they would have made it [The Bubble] on the side with more breathing space. They make The Bubble, but they block out the sunshine which [gives] you ... low energy. I mean personally, when I come to work, I don't need to feel like I am going to bed; you come [to work, and] the light is off, you have no sunshine, and it's like everybody is [feeling] blah. When it is the middle of the day, you should have sunshine and energy to do your work ... I don't have it there. (emphasis added)

Here, the employee links the lack of energy directly to the absence of natural light, which is constructed as a health issue. However, she goes further and connects the problem of health to a concern over safety, so that even things such as employee morale, energy, and sunlight are all constructed as issues of, and about, security.

In a similar vein, aesthetics, briefly discussed above, are also constructed as health issues and then translated into concerns about security. Despite the daily cleaning the shelter is subjected to, it is, as I have discussed in chapter 3, more so than not, not just aesthetically unsightly, but hygienically disgraceful (cf., Hopper, 2003, 98). There are numerous reasons for this, but, in the main, the clients and their practices make it virtually impossible to keep the place clean, tidy, and hygienic. This is best evinced in a front-line employee's sympathetic comment and sobering realization: "Our housekeeping staff ... *they got a wild job trying to keep this place clean*" (emphasis added). In explaining the problematic nature of the space, this employee bluntly said:

> The one thing that stands out ... is the cleanliness here. This place has never been clean since I've been here ... and that's an opinion, I guess. I mean, clean to the point where I think it is acceptable for people to be living in it. I certainly would never sleep in a place like this ... I just wouldn't live here ... I would not live in a place this [run] down, this filthy ...

As problematic – and sad – as this situation is, the employee does not limit his analysis to aesthetics, hygiene, or cleanliness, but goes on to fuse and conflate them into an issue of security:

> Well, if you look at safety issues ... there's stuff that [is] just run down [and] literally falling apart in this place. This washroom to our left here, it's flooded every single day. I mean we've had spills come out as far down as the caseworkers' desks ... Our fourth-floor ceiling leaks every time it rains and it doesn't leak a little bit, it leaks, like, we change buckets ...

Thus, the leaking washroom is a health risk, but that risk is immediately turned into a security risk, for example, over the concern about slipping and falling; similarly, the leaking roof is presented as a dual problem, one of health, one of security, so that the two come to be one and the same. The shelter, which is, as he sees it, "falling apart," poses grave threats to *his* security.

This employee's comments also reveal how security (inclusive of health concerns) directly impacts an ethic of care. In stating that the uncleanly nature of the space makes it inhabitable – it is not "clean to the point where I think it is acceptable for people to be living in it" and "I would not live in a place this [run] down, this filthy" – he is explicitly and unequivocally claiming that the type of care provided is below standard and, thus, grossly unethical.

I do not claim that management is unaware of the problems with, and in, The Bubble. It certainly is (despite still blaming matters on the incompetence and indolence of employees). A senior manager, for example, acknowledged the poor air quality and diminutive size of The Bubble: "We actually had a company come in and test the air and I know they're going to be doing something with that ... That was pretty much the only drawback that I saw. Yes, I could [also] use more room." As well, I do not claim that health concerns are not taken seriously by management. They certainly are, evinced, for example, in promptly furnishing The Bubble with an air purifier. Rather, I contend that health concerns are not constructed as a security issue by management, because, as I have noted, for management, security is about violence and bodily harm. Sickness, while having numerous repercussions that can harm the body, is not equated with the type of harm that is occasioned through violence. Take, as one example, a supervisor's comments – some facetious, some humorous, and the others conveying annoyance – about ways the supervisor perceived how employees behaved during a particularly heightened flu outbreak:

> When the H1N1 thing was going on, in spite of the fact that everyone was provided with the appropriate information and education ... about how it was transmitted ... good Lord, I had a whole team of staff wearing gloves, masks, gowns at the front desk, and people threatening to go home. And I could not tell them to take those darn things off because you know [wearing them is] kind of helping the clients ... [So, we said] let them wear those things. [However,] it affects the clients, it affects the mood and you might have one person who's panicking or something like that, over here another person ... is saying "That's crazy. We have the information," and then ... they're not going to be able to get along because their looking at things differently.

According to this narrative, there is no doubt that management and employees view particular events – here, a pandemic – very differently. It is not, however, that the supervisor (and management more generally) is unsympathetic towards the plight of the employees: the supervisor clearly understands that front-line workers, because of their face-to-face contact with clients, are more susceptible to contracting the flu and other diseases. In that sense as well, the supervisor understands that front-line workers would possibly be more fearful than others of such contraction and, therefore, is willing to tolerate this fear as rational. Yet the supervisor is also mindful that such fear – whether rational or not – makes the daily governance of the shelter very difficult because it unnecessarily creates panic and alarm and this negatively affects the mood in the shelter. As I have discussed in chapters 3 and 4, the mood of the shelter – from aesthetics and smell to noise – is critical to its sound ordering. Even more to the point, this health concern is not constructed as a security concern by management; in fact, there is an explicit recognition that it is not a security issue. Rather, the flu is annoying and the overreaction on the part of the employees aggravates this annoyance. Thus, the flu becomes a site of struggle because one group, the employees, seeks to turn it into a security issue, while the other, management, vehemently opposes this. In what follows, I further explicate the struggles between management and employees over the discursive production of security and the ordering of the shelter, focusing on the problem of bed bugs.

### Bed Bugs and the Signs of Insecurity

On a cold wintry night, a client rather sleepily approached the front desk and told the employees that he had found a bed bug in his bed. The immediate reaction of the employees – from "panic mode" to "action mode" – aptly shines light on the place of bed bugs in the shelter. I followed a female employee as she jumped out of her chair and ran upstairs to the sleeping quarters. With the aid of a flashlight – she did not wish to awaken the clients who were asleep nor cause panic – she carefully examined the mattress. She spotted a dead bed bug and communicated what she had found to the supervisor, who, by now, had also come upstairs. The two quickly shifted into "action mode." The sheet and the mattress on the bed were immediately removed from the room. The supervisor proceeded to spray the mattress with insecticides – itself humorous because it took the supervisor some fifteen minutes to find the insecticides, only to discover that there was barely enough to spray the mattress. While this was unfolding, the female employee awakened the client who was sleeping on the bed above the bed where the bed bug was found – this was a bunk bed – and told him that he needed to vacate the bed and then shower and change his clothes. He was in such a deep sleep and daze – possibly from medication or heavy drug use, or both – that it took him some ten minutes to register that he needed to get up. In the process of "jumping" down from the bed he hit his leg on one of the bed poles, which not only caused him great pain but disturbed several clients, most of whom were by now not only awake because of the whole commotion but annoyed and agitated as well. It took a further twenty minutes to get the client into the shower and, while he was there, a new set of clothes was found for him. During this time, the employee stripped the bed sheets on his bed and, along with his clothes and the sheets from the other bed, bagged them and took them to be put in the washing machine. The other mattress was then sprayed by the supervisor using what looked to be a cleaning product. Slowly, order was restored in the shelter: the clients tried to settle back into their beds, and the employee and the supervisor proceeded downstairs to continue their shifts.

Though the dramatics of what unfolded might be aberrant, bed bugs are, without a doubt, part and parcel of shelter life. In explaining this, an employee compared his work to other occupations to underscore, in a rather blunt and matter-of-fact manner, the different concerns that are present: "If you're a nurse, you're going to have to deal with poop sometimes, and if you're a police officer, you're going to have to deal with violence sometimes, and if you work in a shelter, you are going to have to deal with smelly people and you're going to have to deal with bed bugs." His comments should not be read to mean that bed bugs are of little or no concern to those who work in the shelter. This is far from the case. In fact, the same employee commented that bed bugs are "part of the risk. When you come into work, you're acknowledging that you know that [it] is a risk, and I accept that risk." In using the word risk – thrice, in what is a rather terse statement – the employee contextualizes the frequency and gravity of the problem in a particular manner, one which, as will become apparent, concerns not just health but security as well. In other words, the well-being of the employee and his surroundings – his security, that is – is risked in this environment where bed bugs are a commonality.

What the foregoing does not fully reveal, however, is the fear and panic, verging on paranoia, that wholly consumes the thinking and being of employees. There are two particular concerns at hand. First, the physical health concerns emanating from a bed bug bite. One female employee, for example, was bitten by a bed bug, or two, though she is unsure as to how and where this happened. She explains that the marks remained on her body for nearly two weeks and the itching was incessant (even when describing the incident she slightly quivers and mimics scratching her hand). "I got [a] bite [on] my butt and I am not supposed to get it there," she told her colleague. She then quipped, "Now they owe me a coat because my coat shrunk" – presumably when she had it dry cleaned. Her paranoia was revealed to me when she – with the best of intentions – would gently admonish me for leaving my bag on the floor and pick it up and move it to higher ground; this happened virtually every time our paths crossed. Often, she would use a flashlight to check her coat for bed bugs. She is, however, more than mindful of her paranoia and how unhealthy and consuming it has become. Another employee described the effects in this way:

> I mean, some guys [clients] react worse than others. So some guys will come out with a couple red dots but some guys will come out with welts … and that trickles down to us [and] we've had some staff … with bed bug bites and it's not pretty, and it's scary because if you bring that stuff home, not only is it … a health issue, but … you're getting rid of your stuff if you don't catch it in time; you're not saving the couch, you know what I'm saying [*laughs*].

While the foregoing speaks specifically about the physical health concerns and the resulting pain and suffering – bite marks, red dots, or welts – it also explicitly raises the second, broader, concern, namely, the well-being of the employees' lives as a whole: family, home, and material goods, such as the ruined coat or ruined couch. Here, it is easy to appreciate the way the health concern of the bed bug is turned into an issue of security, visible, for example, in the following employee's comments:

> Bed bugs, yeah, you could bring that home [and] that would be a big safety issue and here it is a big paranoia … When I go home, I'm paranoid to the point where I do take off my clothes at the front entrance. That's paranoia. Who comes into their front entrance and strips down? Like, that's decontamination; that would be a safety issue for me and that's the thing …

What might seem like rather outlandish behaviour – verging on the hyperbolic – is, in fact, not so. Rather, what on the face of it appears as paranoia is, in fact, very rational thinking and behaving, and this is because bed bugs and the concerns emanating as such are constructed very differently, both symbolically and instrumentally, by the employees and management. I do not claim that management either does not take this problem very seriously or is lackadaisical in its approach. In fact, management has been extremely proactive in addressing this problem, this especially after a significant outbreak in the shelter just about the time when I began my research (recall the discussion of the policy implemented regarding emptying lockers and its resultant fall-out, discussed in chapter 3). On each of the floors, the points where the walls and floors meet are sprayed every week with insecticides. Management also embarked on a major renovation of the lockers to address this problem. Prior to the renovation, the lockers were some six feet in height and, more problematically, situated from the ground up. New, smaller lockers, about three feet in height, were installed about six inches above the ground to ensure that bed bugs would not be able to "hide" in the crevices between where the wall and lockers meet (see Figure 5.3). This change also provided easier access when spraying was undertaken. Management also purchased new mattresses, which did not contain creases, an important change because it was believed that bed bugs could "hide" in the creases (see Figures 5.4 and 5.5).

The issue is neither the efforts of management nor the protocols that have been put in place. Rather, the issue is that the problem is

Figure 5.3. The new lockers, raised above the floor. (Photo credit: Author)

Figure 5.4. The new mattresses without creases. (Photo credit: Author)

conceptualized very differently by the two parties: where the employees construct it as a problem of security, management does not. I draw on an interaction between a front-line employee and a supervisor during a staff meeting to illustrate this. The employee had recently "carried" home a bed bug – at least, he had only spotted one – and he spent considerable time "combing" his home for more and cleaning it. He was worried not only about being bitten by bed bugs but also of the damage to the property that would be incurred, along with the great inconveniences this would pose to him and his wife, and their pets. He was unclear, however, of the exact procedures in place to compensate staff affected by such incidents. In seeking clarification, what became plainly obvious is that for him – and many other employees – the concern about bed bugs was not just a concern about health; it was also concern about security: the security of life and body (in this case, being bitten by a bed bug and the effects of the bite), the security of property (damaged property that would have to be discarded), and the security of well-being and quality of life (his and his wife's mental health and

Figure 5.5. The older mattresses with creases. (Photo credit: Author)

happiness – he once remarked to me that his wife was unhappy that he was working at a shelter largely because of the concerns about bed bugs, which it appeared, was a mild strain on their relationship). Bed bugs, in other words, became a powerful symbol of the insecurity that pervaded his work and *home* life. The bed bug was a security threat.

The supervisor who listened to the queries of the employee appeared to be sympathetic to the situation. The supervisor explained that the shelter had instituted immediate measures (e.g., facilities to take a shower and be provided with "fresh clothes") and more long-term measures (e.g., paying the cost of fumigating the home, if deemed necessary) to address this problem. These measures and sympathies, however, were insufficient to assuage the employee's concerns, largely because, conceptually, he and the supervisor were on different "pages." While bed bugs were a significant concern for management, this concern was quite narrow in construction, relating to physical bodily harm and, to a lesser extent, damage to property. In the most significant sense, bed bugs were a threat to the good order and governance of the shelter: the absence of bed bugs, in other words, meant that the shelter operated with less hassles. The employee, however, was less concerned with the order and governance of the shelter; rather, he was concerned about *his* well-being both at work and at home. Yet he found little reprieve because of how management made sense of the problem, which tended to take the particular, in this case, the employee, and abstract his concerns to broader concerns about the shelter. His security, to a large extent, only mattered insofar as what it signified about the shelter; even more problematic, his security, as he broadly conceived it, was largely irrelevant to the issues at hand. The supervisor admitted to me that from the perspective of the employees, "the bed bugs ... [are] a safety issue of mental strife ..." While this statement appears to construct the problem as one about security, it actually locates it as a problem of mental health, which, by extension, removes it from the realm of security. This was made clear in the supervisor's additional comments: "Until they [presumably scientific studies] tell us that the bugs are transferring communicable diseases ... then I don't consider it [a problem]. I just think of them as pests. They're like fireflies." Equating bed bugs to pests – that is, as something that is, at most, a nuisance – is significant. In the most obvious sense, something which is a nuisance is just that, and cannot be anything more: it is problematic, a hassle – something that is, perhaps, a recurring issue – but, its gravity is not one that is constructed along the same lines as violence and bodily harm. It is not, in other words, a matter of security.

Similarly, another supervisor was equally explicit that bed bugs and other health concerns are not matters of security:

> I don't think it's considered a safety issue. I think it's more considered a challenge in terms of the staff. I'm always warning them ... to make sure ... the stuff they are bringing home is either cleaned or bagged before ... they put it in their house ... because ... we leave our stuff lying around and it doesn't take very long for a bug to climb into it ... and bringing that home you just don't want to deal with that ... [*laughs*].

Thus, while this supervisor, like the previously quoted supervisor, recognizes the problems associated with bed bugs and is sympathetic to the plight of the employees, the supervisor is explicit that this problem is not a matter of security. This is clear in the supervisor's conceptualization of security:

> It's kind of easy to get complacent on any type of security or safety, so I usually try to ... keep people's eyes open and try to ... wake them up

and it's easy to just leave your pendant [panic button] on the counter, just cause it's, you know, a little bit awkward on your belt; but if you're upstairs doing a round and somebody jumps out of their bed crazy … you are going to wish you had it.

In exhorting the employees to be proactive, the supervisor is reminding them to use the tools they are given, such as the panic button; these tools would allow an employee to easily contact others for help. Here, the specific reason for why help is necessary is also spelled out, that is, violence and bodily harm (in this instance, occasioned by a "crazy" client). This, for the supervisor, is what constitutes a problem of security, that is, primary safety relating to violence and bodily harm, and the two are conflated and used interchangeably. In this spirit of exhortation, it is true that the supervisor also urges the employees to be vigilant and proactive about bed bugs, for example, by bagging and cleaning their clothes. However, this proactivity is necessitated not because of a security concern, but because of an immense inconvenience posed by bed bugs. This is evinced in the seriousness that characterized the supervisor's discussion of violence and the way the supervisor laughed about the damage to property. In other words, while harm to the body or damage to property occasioned by bed bug is serious, it is not considered as grave or dire as violence and bodily harm. Therefore, it is not conceptualized as a problem of security. This is also evident in the additional comments of the other supervisor – who was present at the staff meeting discussed above – about what security entails. Here, the supervisor juxtaposed physical violence and bodily harm to emotional or psychological stress:

I really try I keep it [the conceptualization of security] physical in the physical sense of the context. I can see where one can make an argument that if I'm drained, I can't think straight, or if I'm about to leave, I'm not thinking correctly. I'm not thinking coherently about the consequences of this decision. I think there is an element there, there is an element to that. I could recognize that, I could acknowledge it, but I don't usually think of it in that sense.

The example of bed bugs is just one among many in the incessant and acrimonious struggle between the employees and management to define what security is and ought to be – the discussion about aesthetics, hygiene, and cleanliness, among others, illustrates the plenitude of such issues. These struggles illuminate not only the polysemy of security, but the site of struggle that constitutes security. These struggles have serious implications for the ordering of the shelter, particularly in regards to the conceptualization and administration of an ethic of care. In the foregoing, I explicated one aspect of the security-ethic of care relationship through the example of The Bubble. The Bubble, recall, was product of the paranoia concerning violence and bodily harm, and it not only shielded the employees from the clients but, ironically as well, from the entire workings of the shelter itself. This resulted in the front-line employees tending to work strictly inside The Bubble without much thought of, or cognizance or concern about, what was happening outside its four walls. I will return to the way the logic of security affects the administration of care in the next chapter. In the final section of this chapter, however, I explicate why it is that the employees are so eager to translate their myriad concerns into issues about security, how they so do, and the implications that follow therein.

**The Fetishism of Security**

It is now well documented that late-modern life unfolds, among others, in what is referred to as a "security society" (Zedner, 2003b, 156) or a "security state" (Hallsworth and Lea, 2011). These descriptors capture the prevalence over the concerns about myriad issues that are translated into concerns about security – for example, food or cyber security. What has resulted is an "obsession with security" (Zedner, 2009, 1). In other words, security is becoming – or has already become – the framework within which social life is conceptualized, organized, and administered. This phenomenon is referred to as "governing through security," by which I mean that virtually all of social life is subsumed under the banner of security (see Valverde, 2001, 89–90).[3]

As I have explored and explicated, this is precisely what is unfolding in the shelter, where the logic of security, in particular, that of primary safety relating to violence and bodily harm, is heavily drawn and relied upon to order and manage daily life. To a large extent, the rabid preoccupation – tantamount to paranoia – over violence and bodily harm is directly a product of the legality of the collective agreement that orders the relations between management and the unionized employees (as will become apparent in chapters 7 and 8). Thus, it is not simply that management is bound by particular legal obligations, duties, and responsibilities, but that it has translated these into an almost schizophrenic concern and seeks, therefore, to hyperactively meet them.[4] A good example is the way the use of personal or communal computers is not constructed as a nuisance or dereliction of duty but, rather, as a problem about the potential bodily harm that may violently befall an employee. In other words, the logic of security and the tactic of governing through security infuse the thinking and being of management, so that everything in the shelter – including the ethic of care itself – becomes a matter of security, one that is conceptualized specifically as primary safety.

Given the foregoing, it makes perfect sense why the employees seek to translate a variety of concerns – for example, poor pay, bed bugs, and other health concerns – into issues of, and about, security. Such a translation provides them with traction not only to have their voices heard but also have them recognized as (and in) a commensurable form. It is precisely in this act of translation that security becomes – and is – a site of struggle and exists not simply as a commodity (see Spitzer, 1987), or even as set of practices or techniques (see Valverde, 2011), but as a reality extant in discursive spaces (see Ranasinghe, 2013c).

It is important to recognize that it is through – and because of – legality that the employees can find a sympathetic space within which to broadly construct and conceptualize their vast concerns in this way. In other words, given that it is legality which necessitates that management organize the shelter in a particular manner, then, it is precisely in response to such organization – and what unfolds as a result – that the employees not only find ground to translate a panoply of concerns into issues about security, but also see such need in the first place. This is ironic because these needs lead to struggles over the definition of security, further fuelling its polysemy. This, in turn, makes the ordering of the shelter that much more difficult, not to mention acrimonious.

A good example of the way legality shapes and produces security and thinking about it, is found in the Occupational Health and Safety Act of the Province of Ontario (R.S.O 1990, c. 1). Its title shines light on one way health and security are linked in law. To further illustrate this I draw from what transpired at a mandatory workshop for all employees conducted by a member of human resources (hereinafter, the presenter). At the very outset, the presence of legality was plainly evident. It was not, however, evident in the overt sense of the force of law often visible and equated with sovereignty. Rather, it was evident in the quotidian and humdrum (see Ranasinghe, 2014; Valverde, 1996); that is, if not in anything else, then at least in the mandatory nature of the meeting, a product of legality, here, evinced in the power of the office of human resources. Thus, even while the presenter sought to set a rather casual tone and mood, there was, nonetheless, an air of formality and propriety. The presenter explained that the meeting was prompted by recent amendments to the Occupational Health and Safety Act on 15 June 2010 (Ontario, Bill 168, 2009). Here, again, the direct relation of the workshop to legality, in this case, the law of the province, should not be neglected. These amendments required that every employer review its policies regarding violence in the workplace – a direct concern about security for management. According to the presenter, this required that additional material regarding harassment be covered, because, under the shelter's policy on workplace violence, "workplace harassment" is given a prominent role. In order to discuss "workplace harassment," however, it was supposedly necessary to introduce several other topics, namely, diversity and discrimination, which, *prima facie*, appear to have little to do with violence. In fact, during the entire session, very little was said or discussed about violence itself. Rather, the session began with a lengthy discussion about diversity, from which focus was cast upon respect, and finally, harassment. What was consistent about the workshop is that it was constituted by a sense of ambiguity and ambivalence – even convolutedness – because it was difficult to decipher exactly what was being discussed and why this was important.

Under the banner of health and safety a variety of tangential issues, such as diversity, respect, and harassment, became the focus of inquiry and were given prominence. I do not contend that these issues are unimportant. Rather, I underscore that the relation between these matters and violence is not so easily appreciable. However, because of the law, they were – in fact, had to be – funnelled into a discourse of violence, an act that aptly illustrates the polysemy of security. Thus, given that both health and safety – already conflated in law – are open ended, other concepts can be, and were, seamlessly brought into the discussion. In other words, the overly broad constructions of "health" and "safety," both in the policies of the shelter and in various legislation, pave the way for the employees to translate a variety of issues into concerns about security – it must be remembered that the employees are reacting to management who constructs security narrowly. Thus, issues such as poor pay, bed bugs, work-related stress, and health, which, at least from the perspective of management, have nothing to do with security, are translated and funnelled into a narrative of security via the same logic relied upon by management, that is, "governing through security." Given that "governing through security" receives the blessing of legal sanction, security becomes polysemic, thereby creating a virtually never-ending chain of struggle to define what security is and should be. This essentially leads to the "fetishism of security" (Spitzer, 1987), which speaks not only to the commodification of security, but also, and more importantly, to the overarching narrative that frames and constitutes the shelter and its daily operations. The logic of security, as I have indicated, and will discuss in greater detail in the final two chapters, is a product of, and simultaneously exists alongside, legality, the other important and powerful logic that orders the meanings of the shelter.

## On the Security-Ethic of Care Nexus: A Final Comment

The daily life of the shelter, I have explicated, is governed by the logic and discourse of security. Security, in other words, occupies an important place in the narrative of the shelter.

Facially, the place of this occupation appears rather innocuous until that precise moment when light is shone on the polysemy of security, that is, that what security is and ought to be is vigorously and bitterly contested. This revelation of security as a site of struggle illuminates the grave implications to the daily ordering of the shelter, in particular, the dire impacts that it has both on the conceptualization and administration of an ethic of care. The result is that an ethic of care is essentially diluted and turned into a securitized form, one which further fuels the fetishism of security.

Equally powerful in this unfolding is the place of legality, the other important logic that shapes the order of the shelter. What is important to underscore for present purposes is the contiguous relationship between security and legality. To a large extent, security – in particular, primary safety – is at the forefront of the organization of the shelter precisely because of legal precepts which behoove administrators to think and act in a particular manner. In so doing, it is not just that security occupies an important place in the shelter but, rather, that it essentially effaces a taken for granted assumption about an ethic of care, so that even the conceptualization of an ethic of care is now turned into an acrimonious site of struggle. This struggle, as I explain in the final two chapters is, not just between management and the employees, but among the employees themselves. The results are deleterious to the order in the shelter and its ethic of care.

# 6 Gendered Security and a Gendered an Ethic of Care

Chapter 5 examined the *place* of security vis-à-vis the daily ordering of the shelter, underscoring the way security constitutes the administration and deployment of an ethic of care. Light was also shone on how the place of security is buttressed through – and largely because of – legality. In so doing, I examined the production of security and the inherent struggles that constitute it. I explored the struggles between management and employees to define what security is and ought to be – a struggle between, on the one hand, the quest to locate the importance of primary safety to the well-being of the shelter and, on the other, a desire, even need, to turn virtually every foreseeable issue (e.g., aesthetics, concerns over poor remuneration, and myriad health concerns) into a logic of security. These conflicts aptly illuminate the discursive production of security, one highlighting security as polysemic and a site of struggle. The struggles surrounding security drastically affect the order in the shelter, one characterized by administrative chaos. To make matters worse, these struggles profoundly affect not only the conceptualization of an ethic of care, but its administration and deployment as well.

Thus far – and quite consciously – I have narrated the conflicts between management and employees in a particular manner: I have suggested that, more so than not, unity, harmony, and concordance characterize the employees. There certainly is veracity to such a claim, but it extends only as far as the employees are uniformly united against management. Although there is little doubt that the employees are in a collective struggle with management, as a whole, there are profound disagreements and conflicts between employees that lead to disharmony, even acrimony. In other words, there is a great deal of diversity that characterizes and constitutes the shelter's employees, which the earlier discussion tended to conceal. This diversity pertains to the different ways employees perceive the shelter and its daily operations. The conflict that is a product of this diversity is found not only between frontline employees and caseworkers (as discussed in chapter 4), but among front-line employees as well. Thus, this diversity contributes to and exacerbates the chaos in the shelter by weakening an already tenuous order.

In this chapter, I return to the production of security, casting my attention on primary safety, that is, concerns over violence and bodily harm. In so doing, I explore and explicate the reciprocal relationship between gender and security: gender shapes and produces security, which concomitantly reshapes and reproduces gender. This reciprocity is paramount to understanding the order in the shelter. The order in the shelter is a product of the gendered nature of security, which, by extension, leads to and sustains an ethic of care, itself gendered.

Given that I have already paid detailed attention to the production of security in the previous chapter, the means by which I explore the gender-security nexus in this chapter is through the production of gender. In discussing the production of gender, I focus on particular types of performances and performativities, often referred to as "doing gender" (West and Zimmerman, 1987, 2009; Butler, 1990, 2004) and "undoing gender" (Deutsch, 2007).[1] "Doing gender," according to Candace West and Don Zimmerman (1987), "involves a complex of socially guided perceptual, interactional, and micropolitical activities that cast particular pursuits as expressions of masculine and feminine 'natures'" (126). In other words, gender is discursively produced through practices and speech, some of which are "rapid … directional (linear), time bound, and informed by liminal awareness and non-reflexivity," and others, "intentionally and reflexively" (Martin, 2003, 361; see also Wittig, 1985). Similarly, Judith Butler (1990) notes that "gender is always a doing" (24–5), and adds: "Gender is the repeated stylization of the body, a set of repeated acts within a highly rigid regulatory frame that congeal over time to produce the appearance of substance, of a natural sort of being" (33). Building upon this way of thinking, and in an effort to refine the propositions put forward as such, Francine Deutsch (2007) uses the term "undoing gender" to highlight a potential limitation of the former, namely, its supposed disinclination towards social change, a somewhat unfair charge to begin with. "Doing gender," Deutsch claims, is a useful term insofar as it describes "social interactions that *reproduce* gender difference[s]" (122, emphasis added). Yet, she claims, focus should be cast on eradicating or minimizing such differences (see also Wittig, 1985), and where this occurs, the term "doing gender" fails to adequately capture what unfolds. Hence, "undoing gender," which "refer[s] to social interactions that *reduce* gender differences" (122, emphasis added), supposedly, better captures not just the result, but also the processes(es) that produced it. Drawing upon these ways of thinking, I use the term "(un)doing gender" in a very specific sense, that is, as an analytical and descriptive "tool" to explore and explicate the ways that gender practices and the ways of practising gender (Martin, 2003), both reflexive and non-reflexive, blur traditional conceptions of what masculinity and femininity convey and mean (see also Butler, 1990, 2004).[2] In so doing, I explore and explicate the ways that gender is inextricably linked to concerns over primary safety.

The production of the gender-security nexus cannot be extricated from its space and place. That is, the site in question shapes the production of gender and security, which, in turn, discursively underwrite the nature of that site. There is, then, a reciprocal relationship between gender, security, and space and place. It is now a taken-for-granted fact that space should not be "treated as dead, ... fixed, ... undialectical, [and] ... immobile," as Michel Foucault ([1976] 1980, 70) famously put it to his critics. Yet, given the reciprocity of this relationship, it is necessary to treat space both as lively, pliable, and dialectical, and as well, rigid, dead, and undialectical. This is because although many of the personnel working in the shelter appear to understand the pliability of space and place and the ways that both affect gender and security, there is at least one group – young female employees, who occupy the centre of this discussion – that does not appear to grasp this. To capture the inability of these women to see the reciprocity of these elements, it is also necessary that I narrate their vision of the site as fixed and dead. In so doing, I turn to a particular intellectual terrain that, although seeking to capture the richness of space, also appears to cast it in *a priori* terms. This is evinced, for example, in Gaston Bachelard's ([1958] 1994) influential and provocative *The Poetics of Space*, which beautifully fuses the image with the imagination (see also Ranasinghe, 2015) and, with it, the rather dual and contradictory aspects of space and place:

> Indeed, the images I want to examine are the quite simple images of *felicitous space* ... They seek to determine the human value of the sorts of space that may be grasped, that may be defended against adverse

forces, the space we love. For diverse reasons, and with the differences entailed by poetic shadings, this is eulogized space. Attached to its protective value, which can be a positive one, are also imagined values, which soon become dominant. Space that has been seized upon by the imagination cannot remain indifferent space subject to the measures and estimates of the surveyor. It has been lived in, not in its positivity, but with all the partiality of the imagination. (Bachelard, [1958] 1994, xxxv–xxxvi, emphasis in original)

The primary characters in this narrative are the young female employees of the shelter. It is through – and largely because of – them that the gendered nature of the securitized space and ethic of care will be brought to light. What emerges from their words and deeds is a profoundly interesting puzzle: why is it that while most of the employees find the shelter unsafe and dangerous, these young women find it extremely safe? In attending to this, my intention is not necessarily to provide a clear answer (see Ranasinghe, 2013b, where I seek to attend to this). Instead, I use this puzzle as a framework to narrate the production of this site as one that is highly gendered and securitized, which, by extension, deeply and significantly affects both the order in the shelter and the administration and deployment of an ethic of care. To this end, I begin by examining the way primary safety is conceptualized by the male staff – management and employees – which, rather ironically, unites these personnel and concomitantly distances them from the young women.

### Volatility, Unpredictability, and Danger: Masculinity and the Production of (In)Security and Fear

In the preceding chapter, I explored and explicated the way management is consumed, even to the point of paranoia, with primary safety, that is, concerns over violence and bodily harm. It, therefore, comes as no surprise that it conceptualizes the shelter as dangerous. One supervisor described the shelter and its clientele in this way:

I'm working and dealing with young volatile clients [and] that's ... what I'm most concerned of ... These are clients who have *substance abuse problems* or *mental health issues* [and] they are *very volatile* and *unpredictable* and I always try to portray that to my staff ... Nobody here is predictable so you kind of have to prepare all the time, always prepare no matter what you're doing, you prepare; so if you're going on a round, be prepared for somebody to jump out of their bed and try to attack you. (emphases added)

As the supervisor describes it, the potential problems are manifold and these are a direct product of the disposition (i.e., character) of the clients pertaining specifically to extreme volatility and unpredictability; these dispositions are, it appears, if not a product of, then certainly exacerbated because of, substance abuse, mental illnesses, or a combination thereof. It is worth noting that the supervisor specifically uses the word "prepare(d)" on four separate occasions, presumably, to underscore the necessity and importance of being ready for the unexpected and unpredictable. What is interesting is that while the supervisor is mindful of the grave dangers that exist, the supervisor appears to be unmindful that there is virtually nothing that can be done; this is because, if it is unpredictable, an event cannot be foreseen and, thus, cannot be attended to beforehand. There is, in other words, effectually no way to prepare for such an event. Yet the rationality of the statement, one laden with fear, is this: the supervisor is exhorting the employees to be prepared, that is, cognizant, that, more so than not, there is little that can be done to enhance their safety. What little could be done, however, ought to be taken very seriously and implemented. This is exactly the point raised by another supervisor, who similarly used the word "prepared" to implore the employees to be mindful of the dangerous space and people that make up their work lives: "If you're *prepared* to deal with the guys ... then ... you'll have *less problems, less issues* and it will be secure and safe" (emphases added). This supervisor's comment speaks to the capacity to lessen the gravity of the problem, not the capacity to completely eliminate it, a conclusion that is directly a product of the perceived dangers in, and of, the shelter.

In addition, what also makes the space dangerous is the belief that many clients are armed with weapons, especially knives. The same supervisor who spoke of the unpredictable and volatile nature of the clients, said:

[Safety] is almost always on the forefront of my mind ... I just don't want anyone to get hurt while ... they're just trying to make a living and *I don't want them to end up ... being stabbed* ... There's police officers [sic] who have, you know, stab-proof vests and bulletproof vests and we're walking around in T-shirts, so we're dealing with the same risky clients ... [and]

those people are equipped that way for a reason and we're walking around in T-shirts, so ... you got to keep your ... mind open. (emphases added)

The concern over knives and the even greater concern over being stabbed come directly from experience: recall, for example, the horrific stabbing that led to The Bubble being built and the panic and paranoia that enveloped the shelter. Here, the exhortations of this – and another – supervisor are a product of directly witnessing the horrors of violence in the work environment.

If this supervisor's advice, that "you got to keep your mind open," is read as a warning to the employees, the way this warning is received and understood departs markedly between the male and female employees, especially those women who are young. In fact, with respect to the male employees, the problem is not that they are unmindful of the potential dangers. Rather, the problem is that they are overly cognizant of it, often to the point of paranoia, so that virtually everyone and everything in and around the shelter is constructed as a threat to their safety. What is interesting is that these employees rely on essentially the same reasoning used by managers and supervisors to construct the shelter as dangerous. This, rather ironically, brings them much closer in thought and practice than either party would be willing to admit – assuming they are even capable of recognizing this similarity. One employee, for example, bluntly said, "*We are not safe here*" (emphasis added) because "anything can happen at any time." This statement recognizes the volatility and unpredictability that characterize the clients and, thus, the shelter as a whole. In fact, that "anything can happen at any time" is best evinced in the following (in what can only be chalked up as a rather humorous) incident that the employee endured: "Somebody even peed in my plate when I was eating!" It is precisely this type of unpredictable episode – whether fabricated or not, embellished or not – that captures the dangerous space that the shelter is said to be. Similarly, another employee echoed the problems of mental illness and substance abuse raised by a supervisor when he noted that "we have a high risk work environment ... where you have people who have mental health issues, people who are under the influence [and] people who might have their judgments impaired."

I draw on the words of a front-line employee – the one whose plate was (supposedly) urinated upon while eating – to give further colour to the construction of the shelter as dangerous and the particular rationalizations involved in it. This employee described his concerns in this way:

> I [have] always said it's a tough job … People, they want to pick on and fight the staff here. I would say that is a tough job; in the past somebody throws a chair [at] me and I had to take off … a few weeks … As you know, those guys, maybe half of them or most of them, are criminals … Some of them [will] lift a knife, you don't know what … [they] have … So it's kind of a risking of a life … so we really have no protection for [that] kind of stuff; that's why I'm saying it's … tough.

This description paints a picture of the space laden with specific threats – the physical dangers associated with knives and other material objects, such as chairs, which are used as, or turned into, weapons (on one occasion, I saw a large, though rusted, knife – the blade was about twelve inches in length – that this employee found in, and removed from, the locker of a client). Although there is little doubt that this employee believes the shelter is dangerous, in some ways, this belief borders on paranoia. For example, during my interview with this employee, the conversation turned to the subject of guns, as the following exchange illustrates:

> PR: Has anyone ever found guns in this place?
> EMPLOYEE: I would say I never heard [about] that since I start[ed] working here, but before I start[ed] working here I heard it's happened three times. Yeah, they find people with guns, but since [I've been] here, I never heard that.
> PR: I'm asking because you continuously refer to guns.
> EMPLOYEE: *That was just an example.* (emphasis added)
> PR: I see.
> EMPLOYEE: Yeah, because it was in the past, [so] it can … [happen] anytime.

The foregoing was thoroughly confusing to me at the time because the employee had repeatedly used the example of guns to convince me, or perhaps himself, of how dangerous the shelter is. I, therefore, had thought that many clients were so armed, even though other employees had made no such claims. Thus, this exchange represents my attempt to bring some clarity to this confusing discussion. What it revealed, however, is quite illuminating and captures his fear, even paranoia.

The statement that the discussion about guns "was just an example" reveals not just an embellishment or hyperbole, but fiction. It was fictional because the threat of guns in the shelter was non-existent – never once had any employee found a client so armed. Yet, it was seamlessly woven into *this employee's* reality so that the two existed side by side. He had taken the call for alertness that the supervisor had exhorted and expected to the very extreme that it tended to verge on paranoia. In fact, how far his paranoia had reached is evinced in the following when he assessed the chances of death: "You have to talk [to the clients]; they start yelling. They are being aggressive. They might jump on you. I'll call for backup but by the time they [come to me]... *I might be dead at that time*" (emphasis added)! Here, the simple and routine act of communication – not just part and parcel of the job, but one paramount to an ethic of care – is constructed in such dire terms that its potential end result could be death. It is this sense of paranoia, I suggest, that seamlessly unites the fears of the male employees and management.

In claiming that this employee's fears verged on paranoia, I do not intend to minimize the dangers associated with the shelter – concerns over knives and chairs and the usage of these as weapons clearly illustrate the potential dangers that are part and parcel of the shelter; the episode which led to The Bubble is perhaps an even better example. Rather, I underscore that the danger is said to be at such an extreme level that all employees are expected not only to see and appreciate what they face on a daily basis, but also to take proactive measures to secure themselves and others. Such a heightened state of alarm is meant to be of utmost concern to the women in the shelter who are believed to be more at risk than their male colleagues, and it is they, more so than the men, who need to be extremely vigilant. This, for example, was the position of a member of the management team:

> I feel safe ... I think, more because of my size. Usually when I'm walking in the shelter, I'm thinking, "Okay, if somebody was to jump me right now, at least ... I'd have a shot," whereas [with] some of our female staff members ... I'm a little bit more concerned about [them], but ... I trust that they ... know that ... *there's a risk there* and that they are equipping themselves with their pendants and radios and ... not taking *unnecessary risks* ... (emphases added)

According to this member, the female employees, because of their generally diminutive stature – at least in juxtaposition to men – are at more risk and, thus, need to be overly cautious; accordingly, if there is a group that ought to be paranoid, it is the women. A male employee echoed the same sentiments. He began by admitting that the shelter is dangerous: "A lot of things could go wrong in the job; a lot of things could go bad … so the potential is there." After discussing his physical stature and how this safeguards him from the potential threat of violence, he added: "*I can see how women working in this field may feel more threatened and intimidated*" (emphasis added). His position is quite simple and straightforward: the shelter is a dangerous place and it is more so for female employees.

To some extent, this type of thinking – and, as will be apparent, *being* – is a product of a male-centred norm that prioritizes, in fact, valorizes, masculinity. Robert Connell (1987) refers to this as 'hegemonic masculinity' (see also Goodey, 1997, 402, who speaks of the "hegemonic masculine biography"). Hegemonic masculinity refers to notions and images of masculinity that are constructed explicitly in juxtaposition to notions and images of femininity and, as well, other forms of subordinated masculinities such as homosexuality (Connell, 1987, 183). Here, the stature of the virile body, a sign of strength and power, is, facially at least, visualized as a source of security. Before, however, the positions of the member of the management team and the employee – and, other male employees more generally – are somehow construed as patriarchal, condescending, even, oppressive, I underscore that these men are extremely fearful of the shelter and its clientele. That is, at least in some ways, they represent the antithesis of the masculine norm where men are either said to be unfearful, unable to fear, or unwilling to disclose their fears (see Goodey, 1997; Stanko, 1990, 5; Stanko and Hobdell, 1993, 403). In this sense, there is a remarkable nuance and sophistication that threads the thinking and being of these men; they are cognizant that the site they work in is a "masculine space" where "violence is … [its] very life blood" (Lefebvre, [1974] 1991, 277). On the one hand, the masculine body is raised and highlighted as a marker of strength, power, and security – and this is done in contradistinction to, and at the expense of, the feminine body, which is constructed as weak and vulnerable; on the other hand, there is acknowledgment that this same body is unable to fully protect itself. That is, something other than – and outside of – this body is needed to safeguard and protect it. Thus, the very body which is constructed as strong and powerful is simultaneously constructed as weak and vulnerable. It is this realization that spawns fear in these men. The dialecticism of the body vis-à-vis its space and place – as both simultaneously strong and weak – is revealed in the comments of another male employee:

> I'm a big guy ... and I do a lot of the one on one ... going up and talking to people [and] sometimes that backfires on me ... because they just see a big guy and the other guy is agitated ... he's been in a lot of fights or ... is just pissed off at the world type of thing and they see that or [they have] just com[e] ... out of jail and there's big correctional officers and things like that and that's a problem.

Here, being male carries with it particular disadvantages, something that most male employees recognize and understand. What concerns these men – and, as will be apparent later, many of the older female employees – is that the young female employees do not seem to, perhaps are unable to, appreciate the dangerousness that is part and parcel of the shelter. This, they believe, puts everyone at risk of violence and bodily harm. It is from such a position of concern that they opine about the place of the masculine and feminine bodies vis-à-vis the shelter.

Thus, although it would be fatuous to claim that patriarchal norms do not influence the way these men think about safety and security, it does not make sense to reduce their thinking strictly to such norms. Rather, I suggest that particular exigencies surrounding the practices of security influence the way they think about the production of gender vis-à-vis security, which they are simultaneously conscious and unconscious of. Such a reading, in fact, appears to be validated by the many elderly female employees who take a position akin to that of their male counterparts. I draw in detail on the words of one such employee to illuminate this.

This employee, like many of her male colleagues, spoke rather matter-of-factly about the volatility and unpredictability that pervades the shelter: "Well, the shelters are never safe ... because you never know what could happen from ... minute to ... minute." Like her colleagues, she too located this unpredictability in the problematic dispositions of the clients, whom she described in this manner:

PR: So are some of the clients ... dangerous people?
EMPLOYEE: Yes, a lot are dangerous.
PR: And [do] you fear them?
EMPLOYEE: Oh yeah, and you can tell just the way they are, you can
  tell how their anger is. Some, a lot of them, are, they don't have that

respect [for] a woman, you know, they ... find women degrading [read, despicable] and they will treat you like a degraded woman.

Her inability to clearly convey her thoughts detracts from the importance and significance of what she wants to say, namely, that because the clients view the female employees – and, perhaps, women in general – as inferior to them, they are disrespectful towards them. This can lead to serious problems, including violence and bodily harm. In fact, just how dangerous the site is considered, and how fearful she is, is aptly revealed in this employee's response to my question about potential dangers in the shelter: "Getting raped, that could be happening. Get stabbed ... You know, one day if I do a round and I'm not alert *someone can come ... and corner me and rape ... and kill me*" (emphasis added).

There is, in this reflection, a certain invocation of the visceral that immediately grabs attention: the daily routine of a female employee at an emergency shelter – one premised upon an ethic of care as well, it should be underscored – could possibly result not only in violence and bodily harm, including sexual assault, but also culminate in death. This itself speaks to a particular irony, even paradox: that the act of care – and caring – itself is in need of supervision (in fact, care), lest the caregiver be subjected to a most extreme form of physical violence; as well, that the receiver of this care is unable to differentiate the hand that feeds him from others, which, thus, paints him as callous, uncaring, and, above all, dangerous – certainly traits which the words of the employees quoted thus far illustrate. What is equally powerful about these remarks, when juxtaposed to those of the male employee – whose plate was urinated upon while he was eating – is that both employees invoke the possibility of death in their work lives. That is, this possibility is one that appears to transcend gender so that, regardless of whether one is male or female, death is a possibility, albeit not a probability. This would suggest, then, that neither this employee, nor her male colleague – for that matter, any employee – is necessarily paranoid when drawing attention to such a possibility (though this possibility appears to be underlined for effect rather than fact).

It is noteworthy that for both the male and female employees, it is the routine act of care that puts them in this predicament. What is interesting, however, are the different paths towards death. For the male employee, it is his masculinized body – read as a sign of strength and power by the client who needs to be made weak and vulnerable – that precipitates violence; this, it should be added, while the employee is conducting one of the most routine and ubiquitous acts in the site, namely, communicating with a client. For the female employee, it is her body, constructed as feminine, weak, and vulnerable, that eventually could culminate in death, but its precipitator is, first, the reading of this body, still weak and vulnerable, in a highly sexualized form: it is in the quest to make (more) vulnerable the woman and her body that the threat and force of physical and sexual violence is applied.

I am aware that this analysis itself is an embellishment upon an embellishment, verging on the poetic rather than the "factual." However, I narrate the possibility of a particular form of danger as such to mirror the narratives of these two employees that hinge on fabrications or embellishments; it is one that is consciously deployed to underscore how dangerous the site in question is *perceived* to be. This much is without ambiguity: whether male or female, these employees see the shelter and its clients as dangerous and, thus, their well-being is said to be precarious.

To return once more to the female employee, this is precisely why she is constantly vigilant about what unfolds in the shelter. Thus, after admitting – unsurprisingly given the foregoing – that the shelter can be "dangerous if you put yourself in a dangerous situation," she explained that one should "be aware of your surroundings." "I never let anyone walk behind me, never!" she exclaimed and added, "And I follow my gut feeling." In further explicating this she commented: "I'm always watching everything, my eyes are everywhere and … I believe in, just always be alert, that's just my experience … And I listen to everything and I watch the body language around everybody." The two supervisors who exhorted the employees to be prepared for anything would laud this employee; she not only understands how dangerous the shelter is and can be, but also makes every conceivable effort to minimize these dangers.

While the dangers and risks of – and in – the shelter are clear to her and others, what deeply troubles her and many other employees and members of the management team as well is the apparently nonchalant attitude of the young female employees. Her rather detailed and vivid comments reveal how problematic she finds the young female employees and their actions to be:

> The young ones … they are naive, they are fresh off of school, they think they know everything, [but there is a] lack of experience. Just because you have an education doesn't mean you have life experience … You have the tools and the communication, the words to say, "Oh, you know,

I understand what it's like to be an addict," [but] if you don't, having [n]ever lived it, do you really understand that person? And then there's an older person like me ... So when I see the young ones coming out ... fresh out of school and they think they can save the world, they are going to have another ... [thing] coming; that's why they get very doubt[ful] in the middle of it, and they get disappointed, and you see their ... [pep] go down.

In admonishing these young women, this employee is drawing attention to their lack of experience and what this entails and, as well, how and why this is crucial to the well-being of not just the employees, but the clients as well – this means it is important to know and understand what the shelter is about, who the clients are, and how one ought to comport oneself. Her excoriation of the younger women, however, is not directed at their lack of experience. Rather, it is directed at their ignorance or apathy – or perhaps both – to recognize the very lack of experience that constitutes their work lives. This, she fears, not only puts them in jeopardy, but the rest of the employees as well. As she put it:

They think ... [they're] safe and that ... [violence] won't happen to them because they're comfortable. Once you get very comfortable in the shelter then there is something wrong, that's when something happens ... But they will be the first one[s], if something happens, it's going to be that one person that is not scared and comfortable, it's gonna happen.

The foregoing discussion narrates an important commonality that unites almost all of the employees of the shelter: the shelter is dangerous and every precaution ought to be taken to ensure safety. This unity comes at the expense of the younger women who are the *bête noire* of this group. In the next section, I look at the words and deeds of two young women to give colour to this problem in an effort to lay the platform to explore what the order in the shelter looks and feels like.

**Counter Narratives of Danger**

The following interaction with Elizabeth, a young woman in her mid-twenties, serves well to introduce the many points of conflict and tension between the young female employees and their colleagues:

PR: Do you feel safe working here?
ELIZABETH: *I can walk through here in the dark in the basement and do my runs and not feel an ounce of fear!*

PR: At all?

ELIZABETH: *At all!*

PR: And what is the reason for that?

ELIZABETH: *Ignorance [laughs]. I don't know, I really don't know.* Maybe it's because ... I've had so many people scream in my face and get in my face, and my heart rate never goes up.

PR: Here?

ELIZABETH: Yeah. I'm never anxious. I just, *I think I have a belief in me that is naive that I can talk my way out of anything* ... I think that my lack ... of fear is ... I don't know where it comes from, I have no explanation for it, maybe it's *cockiness* ...

PR: So this is a very secure place for you?

ELIZABETH: Oh yes. For me it is very secure. I feel more safe in this building than I do [i]n [The Square] (emphases added).

Elizabeth's views and feelings about the shelter – and the clients as well – are drastically different from any of the employees introduced thus far. Even though there is ambiguity in her responses, one thing is clear: she feels, even knows, the shelter is "very secure," so much so that she does "not feel an ounce of fear." This much, at least, is an undisputable fact – and it is worth underscoring the sharp contrast of her confidence to the fear, even paranoia, that consumes many of her colleagues. Partly, it appears, this feeling arises because she knows the place well, that is, she has a mental map of sorts, so that she "can walk in the dark and do [her] runs." Much more than the physical layout, however, is intimated. There is also reference to the clients who are constructed as safe or, at least, will not pose a danger to *her*; thus, she does not need light, because she completely trusts the clients.

What is equally interesting is how reflexive she is of her own position. That is, interspersed within this aura of confidence – "cockiness" as she admits – is also a profound sense of insecurity and doubt. It is a sense of doubt about her and herself that she might be reading this situation incorrectly – that she is "naive" and her beliefs are constituted by "ignorance." Interestingly, however, this reflexivity stops short at that precise point where she is, perhaps, able to appreciate the perceived dangers of the shelter and the clients. Yet she is unable – or unwilling, again a sign of "cockiness" – to recognize the potential dangers and admit them, which even by her own experiences appear to be a reality: "I've had so many people scream in my face and get in my face." Here, however, she fails – or refuses – to conceptualize this abuse as such because her "heart rate never goes up." This, however, probably speaks to how her body has acclimatized itself to such abuse, which also speaks to the frequency with which she endures it. Whether consciously or unconsciously, then, Elizabeth, as a young woman, is caught in a complex battle to define the shelter and its clients. Despite the reflexivity and nuances, her conclusion remains staunchly unchanged from where she began: the shelter is not only "very secure," but even "more safe" than the downtown core, and she simply does not – and need not – "feel an ounce of fear."

This is a powerful and remarkable description of the shelter and its clients. Where the rest of the employees are panicky and paranoid, Elizabeth, in stark contrast, is calm, collected, and able to easily navigate the daily demands and exigencies of the shelter. This position, however, and unsurprisingly, is not well received by many of her colleagues. To a large extent, they are simply unable to fathom how and why Elizabeth – and others like her – can possibly see the shelter and its clients as secure, especially given that she admits that she is not entirely clear herself: "I don't know, I really don't know." To make matters worse, Elizabeth readily admits to the potential dangers in the shelter. One example, noted above, is that she has been repeatedly screamed at. At another time, she admitted, "There are people who spit at us sometimes." Given the acknowledgment of such abuse, her colleagues are flummoxed as to why she cannot – or refuses to – admit that there are many dangers in the shelter, most, if not all, a product of the volatility and unpredictability of the clients. It is such an inability or refusal that greatly frustrates her colleagues, evinced, for example, in the excoriation by an older woman, who claims that these young women are naive: "The young ones think that they can use their looks and their little eyes … [batting their] eye [lashes] and they think the men will listen. *Naive, very naive! Very naive! That* [is] *naivety*" (emphasis added). This label of naivety, it should be recalled, Elizabeth gives to herself, only serving to further fuel the anger, frustration, and confusion that envelops the shelter.

Elizabeth's ways of thinking and being are far from aberrant: many young women think in exactly the same ways she does, and this only serves to exacerbate the problem of order in the shelter. The words of another employee, also in her mid-twenties, are similarly illuminating. What her reflections reveal is that she, unlike Elizabeth, is quite capable of seeing and appreciating the shelter's dangers. For example, in describing the course that she must navigate to enter the shelter, she explained: "Just walking on the streets, there's constantly people out-side with needles. I've had to ... dodge needles so I wouldn't step on [them] ... *It can be really scary at times*. In terms of ... safety ... *sometimes I'm spooked to come to work*" (emphases added). These descriptions, how-ever, pale in comparison to this employee's revelations, which vividly detail her direct experiences with violence:

> You never know if someone's had a bad night and based on ... [that] they may just lash out on you. I had a stalker, who's followed me and chased me down the street, and we had to call the police. I've had a man who was a known rapist run after me, and I shut the door just in time to get away from him, and I had to call the police ... I've been hit. I've been punched in the ribs. I've had a co-worker punched in the face ... It's unsafe, the environment, the clientele you're serving, it's a hard-to-serve environment, so, yeah, there's danger.

Her description of the dangers of the shelter closely mirrors the rationale many other employees rely on to explicate their concerns, an important one being that the clients they serve are volatile and unpredictable. In fact, she raises the same concerns as her colleagues, for example, in relation to physical violence and sexual assault. What sets her apart, however, is that she is not simply speaking about the possibilities of such dangers, as, for example, the elderly female employee who spoke about rape and death. She is narrating myriad incidents she experi-enced first-hand, from physical assaults to being chased by a known rapist. In other words, she represents the fine line where what exists in the realm of possibility (the possibility of violence and bodily harm) is turned into a likely probability (the probability of being subjected to violence and bodily harm) – she represents the blurring, even confla-tion, of the two where they become one and the same.

Given the foregoing, it comes as no surprise that she believes the shelter is dangerous – she has every right to think so and her experi-ences validate this. Yet, what is surprising, and what puzzles and frus-trates her colleagues, is that despite all the incidents of violence she has been subjected to, she is still unable to fully appreciate how dangerous the space is. In fact, she described the space as relatively safe. "*I feel safe*," she said, "but I wouldn't say a hundred per cent safe" (emphasis added). Exactly how safe she feels can be gleaned from the following comment: "I wouldn't say it [the shelter] [i]s really super dangerous. I would just say it's, if you want to say like, mild, moderate, and severe,

I would say below moderate, just slightly below." Thus, as she sees it, the shelter can be dangerous, but its dangers lie somewhere between "mild" – it is not dangerous – and "moderate" – it is somewhat dangerous, but nothing necessarily to be alarmed about, because it is not "super dangerous." For this reason, she reiterated, "Yeah, *I feel safe*" (emphasis added).

There are myriad ways to read this employee's reflections, from sheer naivety as many of her colleagues do, to a more nuanced and sophisticated view of the dangers in the shelter that do not fall victim to irrationality, which many women in her age group would countenance. I rely on the different ways danger is constructed to underscore an important conflict between the young female employees and their colleagues. Here, this employee appears to be very much like Elizabeth, concluding that the space is safe. Her views, however, frustrate and anger the employees more than Elizabeth's: while Elizabeth can be accused of naivety (she has not experienced the types of violence that this employee has), this employee, conversely, has experienced such violence in a direct manner. Yet she is unable to perceive how dangerous the space is. This is an important disagreement between the young female employees and the other employees, one which creates conflict and poses numerous problems to the ordering of the shelter. In the next section, I explore and explicate these problems by discussing how the failure to see and appreciate the shelter as dangerous leads to problems with boundaries.

## Compassion, Comfort, and Approachability: Sexuality, Femininity, and the Production of Safety

An important aspect of the everyday order in the shelter, as alluded to, is a product of a mutually reinforcing or reciprocal relationship between three major parties: first, the clients, second, the younger female employees, and third, the male and elderly female employees. The ways that each party feels about the others significantly impacts the interactions between them. Thus, it is not simply that the young women feel safe in the shelter and see the clients as such that is important. Rather, what partly contributes to such a feeling is the tepid, distant, and sometimes hostile relationship between the clients and male employees (and, in some instances, the elderly female employees). In other words, the relationship between the clients and the male employees not only distances the two parties, but brings the clients and the young female employees closer, which in turn further distances and strains the relationship between the clients and male employees.

Thus far, while speaking directly about the *place* of gender vis-à-vis the production of security, I have underscored the importance of age, that is, that young women feel safer than others. This, however, should not be read as though gender is unimportant and that it is age that explains the production of security. Gender matters profoundly. In what follows, I discuss the reasons offered by employees as to why the clients have a (more) cordial relationship with female employees than male employees. Some of these explanations find their roots in biology.

One straightforward explanation for the warm and affable relationship between the clients and young women is visceral, that is, a connection involving sex appeal. Although this appeal and attraction can be mutual, more often it is the men, especially those who are middle-aged, who are drawn to, and fascinated by, the young women, their beauty, charm, and sexiness. A supervisor, well aware of this – as are the rest of the supervisors and managers – explained this appeal as such:

> I think ... a lot of these clients are lonely males; they've been cast away from their families or whatever relationships they had ... So they are probably just looking for some sort of interaction with somebody who is of the opposite sex, so ... a lot of them ... do *attach* themselves better to females ... Especially if they are just there to shoot the shit with someone, I think they would probably choose the females over males ... (emphasis added)

In this particular narration, sex appeal appears to be downplayed by the supervisor, especially when speaking of "shoot[ing] the shit"; that is, the men simply want to talk nonsense and they prefer to so do with women. Yet there is a particular reason the men want to so communicate with these women, and only with them. The reason is an attachment, one premised on sex and sex appeal. In that sense, there appears to be little agency involved, which the supervisor fails to appreciate, when, for example, the supervisor claims the clients "choose" the women over the men. In other words, these young women, both wittingly and unwittingly, impart such a strong sexual appeal – akin to a magnetic force – that the clients, especially those who are middle aged, are powerfully drawn to them, almost unconsciously and without choice (recall the example narrated in chapter 4 of the young man who took a keen liking to one employee and found every opportunity to converse and flirt with her). This aspect of this relationship is not lost on another male employee who put it straightforwardly: "I think *a big part is due to just sex appeal*. If you have a middle-aged man ... talking to ... a young, attractive female ... [it] would probably be more alluring than talking to me. So I think that's a big part of it ... They find them [the women] sexy" (emphasis added). Here, what is noteworthy is not simply the recognition of sex appeal, but the reduction of the entire relationship to it.

The significance of sex appeal, however, can only be stretched to a point. Over and beyond – but in a complementary manner to – sex appeal, is another (socio)biological trait that has important explanatory value, namely, compassion. In the shelter, it is widely believed that women are born with the capacity to be compassionate – certainly far more than men (see Gilligan, 1982; Noddings, 1984; cf. Slote, 2007). The clients, therefore, are drawn to the compassion of women, essentially the clients' only source for it. A male employee, for example, stated that "they [the clients] feel that ... women are more compassionate than men and, therefore, they may end up getting their way more with women than with the men ... It's a game in some ways." Another male employee stated that the "female staff tend to have a more approachable personality ... So that's one of the big differences I see with [the] client and staff interaction[s] between females and males." Taken together, these comments provide important revelations into what the male employees think about the ways clients supposedly think and behave. The comment of the second employee, for example, shines light on a – perhaps *the* – basic difference between men and women: women are approachable and their approachability is responsible for the cordial relationship they have with clients. To a large extent, the approachability of women is directly related to their compassion, and this makes them warm and welcoming. An ethic of care, in other words, is visibly represented in these women (see Gilligan, 1982; Noddings, 1984). This, in itself, explains why the clients would have a more genial relationship with the female employees. There is, of course, more to this narrative. The comments of the first employee reveal that the employees are cognizant that the clients are consciously drawing upon the approachability and compassion of the women to their own advantage, for example, to garner favours. Given the men are not perceived as compassionate and, therefore, as unapproachable, they are also not seen as readily willing to provide such favours. This, in the end, drastically affects the ways that male employees are viewed by the clients, certainly far less favourably than female employees. All this significantly affects the relationship between the male employees and the clients, one characterized by tepidity rather than geniality.

The female employees are certainly mindful of what is unfolding. Elizabeth, for example, freely admitted that the "clients, for some reason, are *always approaching me and asking me things … They are drawn to me …*" (emphases added). At times she struggled with making sense of such supplications, even explicitly stating, "I don't know why really, I've never really figured that one [out]." Yet, for the most part, she was unable to recognize that her approachability is perhaps a disadvantage to her. Other female employees – and those older than her – understood what was happening, evinced in the following:

> They [young female employees] are more vulnerable, easier to manipulate. Women, all women, are like mothers, they want to take care, they want to save, and, you know guys, they all have, no matter what, boys will always be mama's babies, so when they see a female it's like they see that nurturing that they missed … So the guys here in the shelter, they're looking for that nurturing, that nurture, cause women are a lot for nurturing than men.

This female employee believes that women are, naturally, more compassionate and caring than men. Such a perception, she admits, works – or, at least, can work – to the detriment of women, because they are (or can be) manipulated. Yet, even such a recognition, it appears, is unable to free her from what is essentially a rather deterministic view of life given that it is nature that underwrites the relationships between men and women, those occurring in the shelter being no exception. The women, in other words, are naturally caregivers, epitomizing an ethic of care; the men, by contrast, prey upon this compassion. Yet, even her wisdom is unable to furnish an escape from this basic truth authored in nature: "To tell you the truth, we do get attached to certain people … It's just human. *We're human, right?*" (emphasis added). The latter question is most poignant because, even in the very cognition of a highly gendered relationship that structures the life in the shelter, she is seeking at least some justification or, perhaps even, clarification that the life she lives – and her explanations and explications of it – is rational.

It is worth underscoring that the gendered relationship between clients and employees, and between the employees themselves, is a product of an ethic of care. The naturalistic explanations of what women and men are capable of doing and not doing is important to this story.

In this context, nature, it appears, heavily influences the ways men and women think about themselves and each other, and this way of thinking heavily influences perceptions of safety. In other words, the young women believe the shelter is very safe because their relationship with the clients is genial and amicable; this relationship is a product of taken-for-granted assumptions about what it means to be male and female. Such a way of thinking, conversely, influences the ways male employees think about the shelter and the clients; this is a product of the tepid, distant, and acrimonious relationship between the two groups, one exacerbated because the young women have a warmer relationship with the clients. In what follows, I examine the ways that the amicable nature of the relationship between the clients and young female employees – in fact, with the women more generally – significantly affects the everyday order in the shelter.

## A Gendered Space and Gendered Care: (Dis)Ordering the Shelter

The (dis)ordering of the shelter, partly at least, is a product of the almost unconscious disregard or circumvention of the established rules, which itself is a product of the security-gender-care triad.[3] This issue, deemed critical by many personnel, is on the minds of management. During a staff meeting, a supervisor cautioned the employees, "*Be very, very, aware* of [the] boundaries" (emphasis added), flagging that the boundaries were frequently being (un)consciously disregarded.[4] As another supervisor put it to me:

> *There's been an ongoing issue* with boundaries ... *there's always been a boundaries issue* for as long as I can remember. I do my part and I try to inform people [of] what's *appropriate* [and] what's not, but there are some staff members, in particular the ones who have been here for a while, who continue to kind of push that boundary issue and ... it's unfortunate because it's probably going to get them in trouble at some point if it hasn't already. (emphases added)

The supervisor's narration of the problem explains why the other supervisor needed to counsel the employees to be aware of the rules. Beyond concerns over the knowledge of the rules (a crucial matter that I deal with in chapter 8), there is a related matter concerning their application. The comments of the supervisor who provided a lengthy explication speak to two important issues. First, although only inti-mated, the supervisor is referencing the young female employees when speaking of those who are "probably going to get ... in trouble." The supervisor is locating the disordering of the shelter, in this particular aspect at least, directly with the young female employees. Second, and related, is the issue of appropriate and inappropriate behaviour. Here, this supervisor – and management more generally – is well aware of the fine line between professionalism and friendship, one which must be strictly observed if the shelter is to function effectively and efficiently. What is disconcerting to management is the inability of the young female employees – and, in some cases, the women in general – to deci-pher what is, and is not, appropriate, especially after being notified in this regard (cf. Connolly, 2000, 26, 113). A male employee, for example, made a distinction between being friendly and being a friend, stating that while the latter is frowned upon because it breaches profession-alism, the former is essential to implement an ethic of care. Thus, he concluded: "I don't go past [the] boundaries, because if you pass the boundaries for one client, it is favouritism in my eyes, and every client is to be treated the same." What he is suggesting – essentially outlin-ing what is appropriate – is that the relationship he can (legally, that is) and should (practically, that is) have with the clients is undergirded by the principle of cordiality, but never friendship. This, another male employee echoed as well: "There are certain lines that you don't want to cross." The fact that the young female employees "cross certain lines," many believe, is partly responsible for the disordering of the shelter.

One aspect of this disorder, alluded to above, is the provision of particular services, essentially favours, to (some) clients, a ubiquitous practice well known among clients, employees, and management. When I inquired about it, one employee immediately said: "Oh defi-nitely, some staff like to do favours for clients and ... it's *understand-able* ... because we do have clients that are better, they comply with the rules more, so a staff member may do a favour for them ... But, in reality, we should be doing ... the same ... for all clients" (empha-sis added). What is interesting is not necessarily the acknowledgment that favours form an important part of the relationship between clients and employees or that this is highly unethical. Rather, it is the particu-lar paradox that underpins this relationship that is interesting, one the employee does not appear to be fully mindful of at least in terms of its gravity. The provision of a favour amounts to breaking or circumvent-ing a rule. However, in claiming that, more so than not, this provision is "understandable" (and, therefore, perhaps reasonable as well), the employee invokes the clients' obedience to the rules as the necessary justification for the very breaking of the rules the employees engage in. In so doing, the employee appears unmindful that it is in the very request of a client that the seeds for rule violation are sowed, so that, in many ways, the manipulation that virtually all employees speak of is represented in the very favour provided to the client. Rather strangely, and sadly, this is rendered "understandable" by this employee.

How deep-seated this manipulation is, is evinced in the provision of favours that are premised upon, and spawned by, a desire to help, the essence of an ethic of care. Take, for example, the explanation provided by a front-line employee:

> Some of the female staff here, maybe they give in a little sometimes to clients and ... we all have those ... *blind spots* where you see a client and you want to help them as much as you can, and, some of the female ... [employees], they'll see ... really young people ... like eighteen year-olds or something, and *they'll have some story*, and they'll go ahead and ... give them a lunch when they're not supposed to ... [or] give them extra bedding when they're not supposed to. (emphases added)

The employee is suggesting that although it appears that help is the primary motivation that explains a favour, that motivation is confounded by the manipulation that takes place. Thus, in invoking a story – "they'll have some story" – he is suggesting that the story, whether true, embellished, or simply false, is the manipulative tool that is wielded widely and wildly by clients who are most adroit at such storytelling. What makes matters worse is that the desire to help, the "blind spot" as he calls it, makes the employees unable to clearly see and realize that it is not just a provision of a favour that is at stake, but the entire relationship between the employee and client, one weighted in the clients' favour.

Daily, therefore, a particular drama involving the clients and employees unfolds rather (un)consciously. This drama, as its name suggests, is laden with problems to the order of the shelter. It involves clients asking – in some cases begging – for favours from any employee who is willing to lend a sympathetic ear, essentially akin to a beautifully choreographed performance. I draw on several vignettes to give "colour" to this drama and the ways it disorders the shelter.

The first involved an elderly man who approached The Bubble. He wished to collect his bedding for the night, as all clients do, but was explicit that he only wanted to communicate with Elizabeth because, he claimed, "she understands my problems." What precisely these problems were, is not clear; what is clear was that Elizabeth had agreed to make his bed, supposedly, "because of his problems." This is why, it appears, he only wished to speak with her – it also appears that this practice had been ongoing for a short time, though the exact time frame is unclear. A female employee listened to him and then denied his demands. She explained that if she made such an exception for him, she would have to do so for others as well, and she was unwilling to do this. At this time, the man began a series of pleas with her. Partly annoyed with his whining, partly to placate him, she spoke with Elizabeth. Elizabeth confirmed that she had, in fact, been making his bed and had agreed to do so on this day as well. Elizabeth, who had been occupied during this time, then asked the employee to make the client's bed. She agreed, but did so telling the client, "Just this once." About ten minutes later, she returned and her mood had changed dramatically: she was elated and joyous. She told Elizabeth that she made his bed, sung him happy birthday, and hugged him.

That Elizabeth had taken it upon herself to grant this client this favour posed some problems to the ordering of the shelter. These problems included more than just the demands of the client: that his bed be made and that he would only speak with Elizabeth. The fallout of these demands was also problematic. The employee had to spend additional time attending to this matter, listening to his exhortations, verifying the situation with Elizabeth, and, finally, making his bed. There is no doubt that the employee was well "aware" – to draw on the word used by a supervisor – that she was, as she herself said, "crossing the boundaries." However, she justified her actions because the client supposedly was suicidal, and this act made him happy and, presumably, less suicidal. It is perhaps this that explains the palpable change in her mood: while she engaged in this act rather reluctantly – she was annoyed that she was incommoded – all this was put into perspective because, at least as she saw it, she was able to drastically alter the mood of the client, from thoughts of suicide to thoughts of a comfortable night in bed. What she perhaps fails to understand, however, is that this is precisely the type of manipulation that many of the employees speak about; that is, the clients, as one employee put it, will "have some story" to tell in order to get their way. Here, the thoughts of suicide, a significant problem woven into a sympathetic story, potentially changed her mind about this favour, which was provided with the stipulation, "Just this once."

What is equally interesting is the response Elizabeth provided to this employee's question. While the employee was still grappling with whether what she had done was correct or not, she asked Elizabeth whether the supervisor would be angry with her. Elizabeth immediately and emphatically said "No," and added: "*It's reasonable. It's the man's birthday*" (emphasis added). For Elizabeth, the suicidal thoughts were not what made the act reasonable, as it was for her colleague. Rather, what made this act reasonable, on this day, was that the client was celebrating his birthday – what explains the reasonableness of the other days, however, is unclear. Yet, assuming that such a practice only took place on this day, Elizabeth still fails to realize that this would create an expectation among clients that they too could have their beds made on their birthdays – and receive a birthday song and hug as well. All of this would only create more problems than not. That is, at least while Elizabeth's colleague was grappling with the reasonableness of this favour, Elizabeth simply was unable to comprehend how this one simple act could lead to profound problems – based upon the expectations it would create.

What the foregoing underscores is the ways that particular behaviours-*cum*-expectations become cemented in the life of the shelter, carrying with them profound implications for its daily ordering. This is especially so for male employees who find it harder to navigate the life and space of the shelter because of the close relationship between the clients and young female employees, especially those like Elizabeth. The following vignette highlights this.

One night, I accompanied a male and female employee upstairs where one section of the sleeping quarters is located. A dispute about the sleeping accommodations provided to two clients had arisen, and these employees were tasked with sorting it out. The details of this dispute are irrelevant for present purposes, save that the entire episode was marred by profound confusion. What is noteworthy, however, is that the male employee spoke very briefly during the entire time. In fact, while returning to The Bubble, he explained to the female employee that the male employees need to be extremely careful if they turn on the lights in the dormitory rooms in the night because it can provoke the clients – recall the belief that many clients see the shelter as mimicking prison-like conditions. Thus, and perhaps in an effort to explain his reticence, he said: "That's why I let you do all the talking," and then told me, "*They* [the clients] *respond to women*" (emphasis added).

The employee's remarks speak loudly to the fact that he was fearful and firmly believed the best course of action to take was to say little and allow his female colleague to take charge. Such a feeling illustrates how uncomfortable he feels with the clients, a feeling that is exacerbated because of the high level of comfort between the clients and female employees. In this instance, what worked in favour of the female employee was at the expense of the male employee's safety and feelings of it.

As noted, many elderly women speak disparagingly about the young women and their behaviour – recall, for example, the acerbic comments of the female employee who labelled these women as naive. Yet, in many ways, their own behaviour is partly responsible for the disordered state of the shelter. This is a product of the gendered space of the shelter: because women are viewed as compassionate and caring, the clients are drawn to them, thereby creating a cordial relationship between the two parties. In this sense, what unites both the older and younger women is their, almost unconsciously driven, behaviour, one aspect pertaining to granting favours (there is, however, an important difference with respect to the degree to which these are deployed, the younger women appearing to take more liberties with established protocols).

There is, then, an interesting paradox that unfolds daily in the shelter. Consider, for example, the comments of an elderly female employee who had this to say about the implications of the behaviour of these women (the same one, it should be noted, who castigated the young women as naive):

> Well, *it affects us* because the ones that ... don't give hugs or ... say "no" to plug[ging] in your cell phone, they [the clients] [will] say, "Well, this person let me do it." So *they manipulate* [us], *the clients here are very manipulative* and they know ... who to manipulate and how to manipulate, and they will manipulate you. So if you don't set those boundaries ... then, [when] the other staff is coming in on her shift, that client is going to scream at that staff and say ... "You're this, you're that," and start insulting that staff, and it's not fair for the other staff, and it's not fair to the client either. (emphases added)

These comments, powerful and penetrating, are unambiguous about the order in the shelter and aptly illuminate and capture the discussion thus far. The employee leaves no doubt that the words and deeds of the young female employees make it very difficult for her and others like her to perform their jobs. These comments also underline the ways the clients manipulate these women – a word she uses on five distinct occasions in the same sentence, presumably, to emphasize the gravity of the problem. As she sees it, the rules play an important role in setting standards in the shelter, and these ensure that order is present.

For all this posturing, however, her deeds simply do not correspond to her words. An example illustrates this. (It is worth noting that this is the same employee who said that women are compassionate and want to nurture the people around them while men, in turn, seek and desire such nurturing. This is how she rationalized the close connection between clients and female employees.) A severely intoxicated man entered the shelter one night. He was neither able to stand straight nor speak coherently. To my surprise, he was swiftly booked in by the employee. If there was any doubt as to whether he was intoxicated, this was allayed when the man returned to The Bubble to confirm his bed number, which he had forgotten. After a few minutes had passed, my confusion surrounding this situation disappeared when the employee, perhaps sensing that I was perplexed by what had transpired, explained that she knew the man well and was able to judge his level of intoxication. However, she also immediately added: *"He's my favourite. I don't know why"* (emphasis added). This acknowledgment suggests that it was favouritism, rather than the absence of severe intoxication, that determined how the situation was assessed. Perhaps still cognizant that I continued to be dumbfounded about what had transpired, she further rationalized her actions by saying that even though "you get attached" to some clients this does not prohibit her from treating everyone fairly and equitably. This, however, is just one among many examples I witnessed that confirmed the provision of favours in the shelter. For example, on another day when the shelter received some socks – a prized commodity, especially in the winter – this same employee earnestly urged her colleague: "Keep one for … ['James']," her favourite client. Whether she is able to see it or not, she clearly performed many favours for the clients she liked, despite her steadfast claim that favouritism is wrong and problematic and that she treats everyone equally. She too, then, is a product of the very manipulation that she counsels her colleagues against, manipulation that is part and parcel of the gendered space that the shelter is. This much, however, she appears unable to recognize precisely because it appears to function and sustain itself unconsciously – evinced, for example, in her comment, "I don't know why" the particular client is favoured; that is, she seems to recognize the favouritism on her part, but is unable to explicate why this is so.

Here, it is possible to appreciate the way even her actions also gravely disorder the shelter – the actions of a mature woman who is, supposedly, not naive. The gendered space of the shelter, then, not only affects safety and security, but the conceptualization and administration of an ethic of care as well, one that is evinced in the disordering of the shelter.

## On Gender, Security, and Ordering an Ethic of Care: A Final Word

In the foregoing, I have explored and explicated the administrative chaos that constitutes the daily ordering of the shelter, both the humdrum and significant. The administrative chaos is, in many ways, a response to a more informal, that is, unofficial, type of chaos that unfolds with, and because of, the daily happenings in the shelter, equally humdrum and significant. Ironically, there is a reciprocal relationship between these two types of chaos that only exacerbates the problem of order. It is in this sense that the production of security and its implications must be situated and understood. As detailed in chapter 5, the official response to violence and bodily harm, that is, the rabid concern over primary safety, only serves to create a sharp gulf between the employees and management. If this problem is not grave enough, as detailed in this chapter, there is further strife between the employees themselves regarding primary safety, only serving to strain an already tenuous order.

The space of the shelter – as a concept, site, and set of practices – is heavily gendered. It is, to put it another way, constituted by its gendered status and brought to light through the production of fear, equally underpinned through its relation to gender. That is, there is an important reciprocal relationship between space and place, gender and security, each affecting and influencing the other(s). Thus, the space of the shelter is ordered in a particular manner, traversing and cross-cutting the securitized and gendered aspects that constitute it. All this has profound implications for the conceptualization and delivery of an ethic of care that, unsurprisingly, is itself gendered and securitized, and this is so both administratively and informally. The end result is chaos, again, administratively and otherwise, that envelops and consumes the shelter, its employees, and clients.

# 7 The Logic of Legality and the Administration of Chaos

Throughout the preceding pages, I suggested that the logics and rationalities of security and legality play a significant role in shaping the daily order in the shelter. The preceding two chapters, to this end, explicated the *place* of security to this order. In so doing, I discussed how the polysemy of security – a product of security as a site of struggle between management and employees to lay claim to what security is and ought to be – is significant to this story. In addition, I examined how primary safety – one important aspect of security – is conceptualized and practised. Here, I underlined the gendered nature of security. I extended this line of inquiry to the ways the space and place of the site – as concepts, practices, and things – and, perhaps more importantly, an ethic of care itself, are gendered. What this means is that the order in the shelter is quite precarious and constituted by chaos. All this, unsurprisingly, bodes poorly for the administration of an ethic of care.

In particular, I suggested that the shelter is constituted by administrative chaos: a significant part of the chaos is a product of the efforts of administration to attend to the problem of order. A good example is The Bubble – designed specifically with primary safety in mind and, thereby, intended and believed to secure the shelter and its employees. The Bubble has only exacerbated the already tenuous order: the literal and figurative distancing and separating of the employees and clients leads to acrimony among the parties, especially between clients and male employees (further illuminating the gendered nature of the ordering of the site).

This, then, is a propitious occasion to examine the *place* of legality to the order in the shelter. In this chapter, I explore and explicate how legality exacerbates the problem of order, thereby seriously compounding the problems associated with the conceptualization and delivery of an ethic of care. Drawing upon and paying heed to an eclectic literature in the sociology of law, in particular the place of law vis-à-vis order (e.g., Galanter, 1974; Macaulay, 1963; Mnookin and Kornhauser, 1979; Engel, 1984; Ellickson, 1991) and legal consciousness (see below), I explicate the place of law – here rules – to the daily life of the shelter (I have elsewhere developed this as a theory of private ordering, see Ranasinghe, [2014]).

There is, much like the logic of security, an irony that pervades the place of legality: on the one hand, the conscious administrative effort to address and attend to the problem of order creates a climate and place for legality which gives rise to myriad rules, both formal and informal, that order and regulate virtually every word and deed. On the other hand, in practice, what transpires is not simply chaotic, but does significant harm to the overall tenor of the shelter, both conceptually and materially. In other words, the desire to structure creates additional problems. It is for this reason, I claim that the daily life of the shelter is constituted by administrative chaos.

Two related things comprise what I refer to as legality, both important in their own ways to its production. First, the official and (often) codified norms, evinced in legislation or rules, which clearly and unequivocally state the tenor of the shelter and are paramount to its daily ordering. Two types of norms govern the shelter: one is the myriad provincial legislation and municipal by-laws of the city. A good example is the city's *Emergency Shelter Standards* that explicitly detail a host of issues surrounding shelters, ranging from their scope and function, including the services to be provided, funding, and governance, as well as the rights accorded to clients. Another is the Occupational Health and Safety Act of the Province of Ontario (R.S.O 1990, c. 1), which regulates safety in the workplace (as detailed in chapter 5, this act is important to the production of security, including a preoccupation with primary safety). These legislation and by-laws, official and codified, unsurprisingly, are significant to the daily ordering of the shelter; indeed, they are the foundation upon which shelters and the provision of care are conceptualized and delivered. Second – especially germane to this work and the focus of what is to follow – are the myriad in-house rules and regulations, some codified and others not, that are equally, if not more, important to the daily ordering of the shelter.

These rules seek to capture, mimic, represent, and deliver an ethic of care, and it is here that light is shone on the place of legality in the ordering of the shelter and the inherent problems that constitute the conceptualization and provision of care. These rules are vast, diverse, and numerous but, for present purposes, can be distinguished along three lines (some have been subjected to detailed discussion in earlier chapters and others will be the subject of discussion later in this chapter). The first rule concerns the provision of care and deals with the following: the number of meals and the times they are served, the times clients can access and must leave their beds, the protocols for rebooking beds, and the times clients must check into the shelter for the night, along with a host of other protocols pertaining to their rights and duties. The second rule concerns appropriate conduct between clients and employees and concerns the following: being treated with respect and dignity, prohibiting relations between employees and clients (whether of an intimate or platonic nature), sharing personal information, and offering and accepting gifts, to name a few. The third rule outlines protocols regarding safety and security of the clients and employees, but particularly the latter, and this is of foremost concern to management (see chapters 5 and 6). Thus, clients are prohibited from entering the shelter with weapons, drugs, or alcohol. They are also prohibited from entry if they are intoxicated, under the influence of drugs, or appear to be overly angry or agitated and believed to pose a risk to staff and other clients. Safety is taken very seriously, and the employees are mandated to be vigilant while on duty and keep a fair distance from clients when conversing with them.

The second aspect of legality concerns the legal consciousness of the employed personnel of the shelter. As explicated in the introduction, legal consciousness can be understood as the way(s) the institutional power(s) of law is sustained over time and across space (Silbey, 2005; Ewick and Silbey, 2016; Sarat, 1990; see also Ranasinghe 2010b, 2014). The rules of the shelter cannot be understood apart from the ways they are thought about and made sense of by the stakeholders involved. The legal consciousness of stakeholders, in other words, is crucial to the ordering of the shelter, culminating in administrative chaos.[1]

I begin with a discussion of the place of rules in the shelter, outlining the concord that, for the most part, exists between management and employees. Despite this appearance, however, as I show next, the rules serve to fundamentally disorder the shelter. Here, I examine the ways a variety of ethics of care competes with the enforcement of rules, how this profoundly disorders the shelter and, by implication, how this disorder jeopardizes the delivery of care.

## The *Place* of Rules

In previous chapters, I suggested that problems of order are a significant concern to management because they disrupt life in the shelter. These problems range from the mundane (the lacklustre, even apathetic, performances of employees, one explanation being the sheer boredom of the job – recall, for example, the excessive use of the Internet for personal needs, including watching YouTube videos) to the more significant and disconcerting (the preoccupation with primary safety – recall, for example, the senior manager who admonished two employees for failing to lock a door of The Bubble). Given these recurring themes, it is not surprising that management has sought to attend to and address these issues, taking both the humdrum and significant as pressing matters. The primary means by which this has been attempted is through the rules, in particular through an attempt to have the rules enforced strictly and consistently.

The *place* of rules to the order in the shelter is impossible to overstate. The rules are, as Amir Marvasti (2002, 626) puts it, "living documents." As management sees it, the rules and their strict enforcement provide numerous benefits, one relating to consistency. As a supervisor said, "You have to have consistency; if you don't have consistency, it causes all kinds of problems … *All kinds of things happen when … [the] rules get broken*" (emphasis added). This supervisor speaks to the inherent order of consistency relating to "sameness" – a recurring issue is the provision of favours, which has been discussed previously and will be further discussed later. Consistency, it is believed, is immensely beneficial to ordering a space that is comprised of myriad people with a plenitude of needs. Another supervisor echoed these sentiments, but went further in explicitly underscoring the place of rules: "I think [that] most of the … rules … were created for a reason … *they are there for good reason* and they are there to either avoid a problem or … prevent a problem" (emphasis added). Here, the supervisor is overly abstract about the potential benefits, for example, avoiding or preventing a problem, where the problem alluded to is generic in form. Yet, it is precisely in the explicitly generic manner that the solution of rules is cast that highlights their importance to the shelter. That is, for this supervisor (and management more broadly) the rules serve a purpose – they were "created for a reason" – and this purpose, as the supervisor acknowledges, is "good." This reasoning, however, finds its logic *a priori*: that is, rules are good and they address something bad, that is, problems. Cast in this way, rules provide a simple solution to *any* problem. It is in this sense that I locate the importance of the place of rules not just to the ordering of the shelter, but to its very foundation, a commonality in many such institutions (e.g., Karabanow, 2002, 106–15; Desjarlais, 1996, 883–4).[2]

The foregoing appears to suggest that management has carved a rigid relationship between the shelter's rules and their strict and consistent enforcement. This is true, though it requires further refinement. A manager, for example, opined that the consistent enforcement of rules "is doable … [and] practical." Here, the practicality and capacity to *do* have already been extended to, and constructed as, an *expectation* to so do – that is, because it can be done, it should be done and vice versa. However, management is mindful that discretion is necessary; that is, the strict enforcement of the letter of the law is an impossibility (cf. Lipsky, [1980] 2010). Rather, as discussed in chapter 4, management believes that the need and, more importantly, *right*, to use discretion should rest with management – and, to some extent, caseworkers; most crucially, however, this right should not be accorded to front-line employees.[3] Thus, when I asked the same manager whether he was "sympathetic … that the rules might not always be followed," he emphatically responded, "No! *I don't want that kind of discretion*" (emphasis added). "The way I explained it to the supervisors," he continued, "is 'the front-line workers, *I want them black and white, following the rules, 'Yes' or 'No' kind of thing'* … I put the supervisors in the positions they are [in] so [that] they can use the grey area" (emphasis added). The rules, as he sees it, are only useful if they are practised as intended: consistently and according to the letter of the law. Thus, he summed his position up as follows: "Consistency is what I strive for." This desire stems from the steadfast belief that consistency provides – in fact, *is* – order (precisely the same sentiments the above quoted supervisor echoed).

From an administrative standpoint, it makes perfect sense that management has chosen the path it has. Beyond practicality and the optics of order also lies the symbolism of rules. The rules serve an important purpose: they unequivocally state the tenor of the shelter and how it will be ordered. Hence, the symbolic value of rules – or law (see Arnold, [1935] 1941; Edelman, 1964, 1971; Gusfield, 1963, 1981) – is significant for what it reveals: the ordering of the shelter is tied to the legality of the rules and nothing else. There is also a related issue. Discretionary practices by employees means that the rules of the shelter – and, hence, its tenor – are produced not at the administrative level but on the front lines in the same ways, for example, that Barbara Yngvesson's

(1993) study of a New England courthouse demonstrated how the law is "made" at its doorway by the court clerks who decided which cases were worthy of the court's time. From the standpoint of accountability, this bodes very poorly for the shelter because it receives a significant portion of its funding from the city and, thus, is accountable to it; yet its policies are a creation of the ad hoc and idiosyncratic practices of the employees – who are paid the minimum wage, a commonality in the social service field (see Loseke, 1992, 71; Ferrill, 1991, 85–6) – rather than the personnel who are responsible for its administration. Framed as such, it is not surprising that management has emphasized the importance of rules and seeks to eliminate or, at least, limit discretion in the hands of employees.

The foregoing appears to construct a disjuncture and highlight a disparity between the ways management and employees view the place of rules to the ordering of the shelter. This, however, is not precisely the case. Although perfect concordance between the two parties does not exist, there is, however, a remarkable similarity that needs mentioning. The employees, just like management, wholeheartedly believe that there is inherent value in (and to) the rules. For example, one caseworker explained that "order is ... if everyone is doing their work properly and effectively and in a way that will benefit themselves and [the] clients ... I mean, order is just *everybody doing what they are supposed to be doing*" (emphasis added). This statement simultaneously speaks to two things: first, that order is about doing – and doing well – what needs to be done; second, and related, order is about *not doing* things that should not be done. In constructing order as such, the caseworker, even though implicitly, underscores the importance of rules to the ordering of the shelter in precisely the same ways as management. If order is about performing effectively, then this can only be achieved by following the rules because following the rules ensures that what needs to be done is (and can be) done. Another employee, "Captain Delight," was somewhat poetic in constructing the order-rules nexus. "It is up to us," he stated, "the way we behave, the way we interact is how they [the clients] will behave ... *If you are crazy, they will be crazy*" (emphasis added). Here, the freedom to choose, which is bestowed upon the employee, is possible only because of, and through, the rules. By using the word "crazy," I claim that "Captain Delight" is not speaking about mental illness – a ubiquitous sight given the alarming rate of illness in the shelter – but, rather, of the craziness that envelops a disorderly space. In other words, he is stating that order is a product of the rules: when they are enforced, the behaviour of the clients is conducive to the deployment of care; when they are not, disorder prevails. This is precisely the point a female employee sought to make as well: "You're supposed to show by example: if that person is angry, you're supposed to show that you can be calm." The rules, in other words, are a representation of this calm: this is what order should look and feel like.

In reiterating the position of management, the employees wholeheartedly and firmly believe that the rules need to be consistently enforced if they are to be effective and efficient. According to one employee, "If more rules were followed here, it might be a little more efficient … It would be efficiency and consistency [be]cause consistency will lead to a more efficient[ly] run shelter." Another employee echoed this sentiment as well: "If everybody was following the rules, there is … consistenc[y] and then *we'll be okay, we'll be fine*" (emphasis added). These employees – and several others as well – explicitly use the word "consistency" in exactly the same way that it is used by management to underscore the value of rules, this value tied specifically to the emergent order. This is evinced, for example, in the comments of the latter employee who opines that the rules do not simply make things "okay" but "fine," a word that denotes wellness in relation to being. In fact, just how much the views of the two parties align is evinced in the comment of another employee who even more strongly underlined the inherent order in the consistent: "I think *order kind of falls in line with consistency*" (emphasis added). For him, as it is for his colleagues and management, consistency *is* order.

The legal consciousness of management and employees is very much the same: both venerate the place of rules to the order of the shelter. Yet, this congruence and harmony is more apparent than real because the employees firmly believe that the strict and consistent application of the rules will not – and cannot – provide the type of order and care *they* believe is necessary and just. This is so for several reasons, but the primary one, as I explicate below, concerns how the polysemy of an ethic of care is incongruent with the constitution of law, namely, its binary coding.

## The *Place* of Rules, the Polysemy of an Ethic of Care, and the Making of Administrative Chaos

Perhaps *the* fundamental problem plaguing the ordering of the shelter is the legality-ethic of care nexus, one constituted by, and further

contributing to, what I have called administrative chaos. This is a problem that is a product of the constitution of the law itself, namely, its
binary character. The law – and, in this case, rules – for all its purposes,
pomp, and glory functions in one way (in fact, it can only function in this
way), namely, it must be unequivocal about what it stands for: where it
does not, it is bereft of clarity, effectiveness, and efficiency, and is, thus,
in need of interpretation, revision, or, at the most extreme, abandon-
ment (in fact, where this binary logic does not constitute it, the question
of whether it is, in fact, law arises). In other words, and put simply,
the law can only operate upon a binary logic, namely, between what it
demarcates as legal and, by extension, illegal (cf. Luhmann, 1989; Teubner, 1989; Bourdieu, 1987).[4] Although the law is driven by particular
principles in relation, for example, to "right" and "wrong," "just" and
"unjust," or "moral" and "immoral," even in instances where these
principles guide the interpretation necessary to address these matters,
the resulting judgment only reinforces the binary logic between what is
legal and illegal. Yet many of the issues the law is called to address, for
example, the so-called hard cases (cf. Hart, [1961] 1967; Dworkin, 1986),
are complex, complicated, and often composed of, even confounded by,
numerous rationalities that cannot be neatly reduced to binary coding
(see Valverde, 1996). This is also the case with an ethic of care, which as
has already been elucidated though perhaps only briefly, is polysemic
rather than uniform and singular.

The polysemy of an ethic of care renders the place of rules important to understanding and making sense of the ordering of the shelter. This much, as elucidated above, is clearly visible in the words and
deeds of management, best evinced in the wholehearted endorsement
of the binary logic of the rules – recall the "black and white," "yes or
no" philosophy explicitly and unequivocally espoused by a member of
management, one laid down as the basis upon which the rules are to
be both thought about and applied. It is for this reason, as briefly explicated before, that discretionary practices are viewed by management
as extremely dangerous to the order of the shelter and why strict limits
about its use are put in place. Despite these efforts – counselling and
exhortations deployed *ad nauseam* – discretion is a common and important feature of daily life in (and of) the shelter, evinced most visibly on
the front lines.[5] Discretion, as I explicate below, must go hand in hand
with the administration of care.

This point, both management and employees understand and realize.
It is, however, from the struggle to control who may use discretion that

friction and acrimony between the two parties – and, as discussed in chapter 4, between the front-line employees and caseworkers as well – emerges, takes shape, and comes to a boiling point, so to speak. In explaining the import of discretion, a caseworker noted that "not every co-worker is like a robot that will obey everything; there is always leniency and discretion." In an effort to justify the violation or circumscription of rules, the caseworker added: "Every situation is different," and *"people are suffering from some discretion not being used"* (emphasis added). This is an important recognition on the part of the caseworker, because it clearly and unabashedly highlights that care cannot be delivered without discretion. The binary logic upon which care is to be delivered, as mandated by management, simply does not work. In other words, the strict enforcement of the rules, at least in some cases, does more harm than good. This same point was made in different ways by all the front-line employees. One, for example, commented that *"this is not a military base* ... so basically, with most of the rules, [although] it is great to follow them ... it is also better to reflect on some of the rules and add that *humane touch* to it" (emphases added). Here, notice that it is the site in question, an emergency shelter premised upon an ethic of care, that renders the "black and white" approach to the application of the rules, if not completely impossible, then almost impossible. In other words, this employee is not saying that the strict enforcement of the letter of the law, as a whole, is unfair or unpractical. Rather, he is saying that at this site, such an application would be both unfair and unpractical – as he put it, "this is not a military base," a site fraught with images of strict discipline and no-nonsense attitudes. On a deeper level, this employee is underscoring a problem with law: its binary coding renders it inappropriate for the delivery of care. This is precisely why he claims that it is necessary to reflect upon the rules, and where a more compassionate approach is deemed necessary – what he calls a "humane touch" – this should take precedence over the strict application of the rules. As he sees it, rule violation, not obedience, is likely to be an important feature in a space that is meaningfully interested in promoting care. This point was also made explicitly and unequivocally by his colleague: "I do what I can within the rules to get the best possible outcome for [the] clients ... and when that doesn't work, I essentially break the rules." As this employee sees it, the rules are only to be followed as long as they facilitate care; when they fail to so do, rule violation is necessary.

Discretion, thus, is an important feature in the daily ordering of the shelter. Discretion is not only important to the delivery of care, but it also shatters both the binary logic of the rules and the very order upon which the shelter professes to exist and function. Yet the key issue is not simply the important place that discretion occupies, but the rather convoluted, disorganized, and inconsistent, even idiosyncratic, manner in which it is practised. As I explicate below, this has to do precisely with the polysemy of an ethic of care. In what follows, I explore this polysemy, first documenting its existence through a detailed discussion of the words and deeds of two employees, and then explore its implications and ramifications.

*The Production of the Polysemy of an Ethic of Care*

To do full justice to the polysemy of an ethic of care and vividly illustrate how it comes to take shape, I draw upon the biographies of two front-line employees, "Captain Delight" and Elizabeth. I do not claim that they are representative of each other or the other employees. Although there are some points of overlap, there are also numerous points of departure and it is these differences that I focus upon. So doing permits me to document and illustrate the multiple ways an ethic of care is thought about and practised.

"Captain Delight" is a middle-aged man who was born in a poverty-stricken region in a lesser developed country. He moved to North America when he was a late-teenager, but was – and still has been – unable to escape poverty. His outlook on life, unsurprisingly, is shaped by this history and its experiences. So, too, is his work ethic. He recalls one job cleaning floors, work he recounts proudly and with fond memory. He is proud because cleaning floors requires patience, care, and precision to ensure they are clean, bright, and shiny – the work, he stated, "is like art" and cannot be rushed. Such a work ethic, according to him, hardly exists today. Reminiscent of the communitarian ethic advocated by Amitai Etzioni (1993, 1–11) – that rights presuppose responsibility – "Captain Delight" strongly believes that many people are lazy and think they are entitled to things they have neither earned nor deserve. This is his view about most of the clients who walk into the shelter, whom he must deal with daily.

Like other employees, "Captain Delight" believes the shelter serves an important function in addressing visible poverty. "I do believe," he claimed, "that ... this place is [there] to help the homeless ... and ... disadvantaged people." He is, however, consumed by the belief that most who enter the shelter are not in need of assistance. Similar to the social reformers of the eighteenth and nineteenth centuries who distinguished between the "deserving" and "undeserving" poor (see Himmelfarb, 1995, 124–42; Ranasinghe, 2010a, 59–61; Katz, 1986, 13–21),[6] "Captain Delight" also distinguishes between those he calls the "professional homeless" and the "working poor." The "working poor" are genuinely in need and, therefore, deserve assistance. "Captain Delight" describes the "working poor" in this way:

> People ... who [have] lost their job[s], people who have managed to go back to the workforce but they are not doing what they were doing before, at minimum wage, or something little to survive, and this amount of money doesn't allow them to support their families ... and they, [in order] to fill their basic needs, ... [are] forced to come to these places.

For him, these people deserve help because they are proactively seeking to make a better life for themselves, evinced in their willingness to (look for) work, even at a low wage – the title, the *working* poor, highlights this. In other words, a good work ethic is important to "Captain Delight" because such an ethic, supposedly, constitutes his history, one where he created "art" on the floors he cleaned.

Conversely, the "professional homeless" are men who "are making a business selling drugs." These men rely on a system designed to relieve vulnerability to advance their own agendas. "What I see," "Captain Delight" commented,

> is [that] most of the population here ... it is their home. Just because they live in the streets [does not mean that] they are ... homeless. We can see a big percentage of people staying here a long, long time [be]cause it's good for their business, their illegal business ... They use this place to hide ... They have money ... I don't know what it means to have money, but ... people [are] using laptops ... [and] you don't see them getting desperate or anxious to be here. For them, this is [a] life they have made ... a way of living. They are not homeless.

The "professional homeless," for him, are unworthy of assistance because they do not need it: "They are not poor. They don't know what being poor means." The proof, he claimed, can be found "if you check their pockets [and you will see that] they have more money than we do." This statement highlights his resentment towards these clients, especially when considering his earlier comment, "I don't know what it means to have money" (a view shared by several employees as well – recall the comments of an elderly female employee who, rather disgustingly, spoke of how many clients eat better meals than most "ordinary" people, including her). Unsurprisingly, "Captain Delight's" disdain for the "professional homeless" is palpable, and he boldly stated that "they need to be kicked out. There are people who deserve to be kicked out." For "Captain Delight," the problem is systemic. The institutionalization of poor relief (see Stark, 1994, 15; Ferrill, 1991, 44) and its numerous problems easily permit the "professional homeless" to thrive. At times, there is even a hint of respect for, and admiration of, their guile and sage, as when he readily admitted that "they are manipulating us ... They know to work the system ... [and] they know how to read us." This, however, is immediately followed by a scathing criticism of the system and the credulity of its employees, he of course being the one laudable exception.

The foregoing locates and contextualizes the ways "Captain Delight" thinks about and makes sense of an ethic of care. Although his ideological position represents an extreme end of the spectrum, it is far from anomalous. "Captain Delight's" beliefs cohere well with many in the social services. Perhaps the words of "Tom" – an employee in his twenties in a shelter which Jean Williams (2003) studied – best illustrate the similarities:

> Ninety per cent of homeless people don't want to work. Most shelters don't force people to work – they're like three-month vacations for people. You get your rent, your food paid for – it's great! Why wouldn't anyone want to live for free? I know people who go to Alaska, then, come here for three months and stay in a shelter for that time. I know there are a lot of people who go from shelter to shelter – they'd rather do drugs and drink than have to work. For some of them, they make more money from benefits than they do at work; why would they want to work? ... You can't just provide free shelter to these people and not force them to work. It's like giving a fat person who's on a diet lots of food – cake and candy bars – it's too tempting for them. These people have to be taught responsibility. (70)

The views of "Captain Delight" and "Tom" reflect two important issues concerning the provision of services to the visibly poor. The first is the deservedness of aid, which necessarily gives rise to – and is simultaneously a product of – labelling. As Michael Katz (1989) writes, "The preoccupation with classifying poor people persists" (10) and regardless of whether this is cast on grounds of morality or expediency (the effective and efficient provision of aid), or other grounds, such lines are constantly drawn. For example, Elizabeth Tracy and Randy Stoecker (1993, 44) examine how "bad people" versus "bad luck" explanations guided workers, and Donileen Loseke (1992, 75) speaks of how "workers were ... oriented to selecting 'appropriate' clients" (see also DeWard and Moe, 2010, 122–4; Williams, 2003, 4, 176–7; Lyon-Callo, 2004, 123–6, 140–6; Liebow, 1993, 126). The second aspect pertains to the effectiveness of the aid delivered, in particular the belief that indiscriminate charity breeds further dependency (see Desjarlais, 1997, 149; Liebow, 1993, 141; Williams, 2003, 70). These issues, deservedness and effective poor relief, are what "Captain Delight" grapples with, and they have important implications for an ethic of care and its delivery.

If "Captain Delight" is representative of one end of the spectrum, Elizabeth is representative of the other. Elizabeth is a young woman in her mid-twenties. She is polite and kind, and her time and efforts are spent attending to virtually every request she receives, so that by the end of each shift, she is exhausted. As she put it: "I love to help people. I have always loved to bring something to the people that I am around. I love to take care of people. I love to feed them. I love to give them clothing. I love to see people smile. I like to hear people's stories." As her comments indicate, she is full of love and compassion, and this can be further appreciated in the following: "Some people, I don't have compassion for, but I help them anyway ... It's a hard thing to do."

Born in Canada, Elizabeth grew up in poverty, in conditions that, though not necessarily identical to those of "Captain Delight's," contain the commonality of struggle. Elizabeth's mother was a drug addict, and from very early in her life, Elizabeth remembers being around addicts, alcoholics, and prostitutes. Her childhood was volatile and unstable: "I grew up a lot in this atmosphere and this community ... I have dealt with drugs in my family and in my friends [sic]; a lot of poverty and just building your life up basically from nothing." Her adult life is more stable even though it too is characterized by numerous difficulties and struggles, most relating to finances and personal relationships.

There is at least one aspect about her early childhood, however, that she is unable to extricate herself from. The same men who, in her presence, (ab)used drugs and alcohol with her mother, continue to be in her life as clients of the shelter. "A lot of these people," she explained, "used to know my mother, and ... she has addiction problems. She is still out there in the community, so a lot of these gentlemen are known to her and they know me." This familiarity with their struggles has spawned a desire to help. "I knew a lot of the people here," she stated, "and I knew the situations they were in, and I knew that I could help them because I knew a little bit about it." Yet this familiarity also poses numerous difficulties, especially in understanding and making sense of her life and work. "I have trouble," she reflected, "putting that boundary in ... [the] middle ... [that] this is not my friend, this is a client. This is ... not the guy who used to babysit me when I was five years old, he is a client now [and] he has addiction problems ... I'm still working on it every day."

Elizabeth believes that a shelter is purposed to help people who are in need (recall her belief that it "is a place where anyone can walk in for help"). Thus, she and "Captain Delight" are very much alike. Unlike him, however, she refuses to distinguish between the deserving and undeserving: such a distinction is meaningless because the very entrance into a shelter is itself evidence of need, if not desperation (cf. Hopper, 2003, 86, who writes of the employees in the shelter he studied, who believed that "only the desperate ... would willingly undergo the ordeal" of a shelter). Her experiences have taught her this lesson, and she resolutely holds to it despite the difficulties it creates. "Captain Delight," like Elizabeth, believes that the purpose of the shelter is to provide help. However, he views most clients differently: at best, they are negligent, irresponsible, and lazy; at worst, they are criminals. In both scenarios, they are undeserving of help. These differences, products of individual biographical histories, shine light on the ways these employees make sense of and conceptualize an ethic of care. What results is polysemy. This polysemy has grave implications to the ordering of the shelter. In what follows, I explore how different visions of an ethic of care lead to different implementations of them, visible in the ways the rules are thought about and implemented.

*The Delivery of Care and the Unwitting Results of Rule Violation*

Recall that, for management, the rules state unequivocally what is and is not accepted and, thus, establish boundaries within which action should be comported. The rules, in other words, breed consistency, and consistency is order. Quite often intentionally, sometimes unintentionally, the words and deeds of the employees breach these boundaries. At times, these infractions are minor – accepting "small" gifts, such as cards, drawings, or notes from clients or, where young female employees are concerned, lending a sympathetic ear to their flirtations; at other times, these infractions are more serious – sharing personal information with clients, doing personal favours for them and, in some instances where young female employees are concerned, commencing intimate relationships with them (the previous chapter explored some of the behavioural differences between the male and female employees vis-à-vis the clients and the problems they pose to the ordering of the shelter). These infractions are of serious concern to management for many reasons, the safety of the staff being paramount (cf. Connolly, 2000, 131–42; Ferrill, 1991, 172). I use the example of the rules surrounding a mundane, everyday activity, namely, communication between employees and clients, to illustrate how different ethics of care lead to different ways that boundaries are circumvented or disregarded and the problems that ensue as such. Again, the words and deeds of "Captain Delight" and Elizabeth are relied upon to give colour to this discussion.

Ostensibly, "Captain Delight" thinks about the rules and their application straightforwardly. In lamenting the absence of consistency, he stated, "They are very *simple* rules ... so I don't see the problem ... [as to] why we don't do it" (emphasis added). For all this posturing, however, the equation of the rules with their simplicity fails to accurately portray the complexities involved, something "Captain Delight" is mindful of. He admitted that "it is not ... all black and white, grey also exists for me." Here, he acknowledges that the binary logic of rules, so valued by management – recall the "black and white," "yes or no" philosophy – is problematic and impossible to follow. Thus, he explained how he makes sense of and applies this middle ground:

> I don't bend the rules just because I want to ... and this is what happen[s] with other people ... I will break the rules if the client is clear and sits there with me and says, "I need this because" and if there is nothing behind that [read, if he is being honest], I will break the rules. I will because, in my way and in my head, *I am rewarding his good behaviour*. (emphases added)

Thus, rule breaking itself is not problematic. Rather, the bases upon which they are broken is the problem. That is – as paradoxical as it is – there should be consistency to the inconsistent application of the rules. "Captain Delight" believes that, unlike him, his colleagues break rules without good reason – "just because [they] want to" – an accusation that connotes the inconsistencies associated with rule violation. For him, the justification for rule breaking is deservedness, and this is found not simply in "being" – being (apparently) poor – but, in "doing" – doing something that demonstrates worthwhileness, for example, by actively seeking employment. This is what deservedness looks and feels like, evinced, for example, in his earlier comment, "I am rewarding ... good behaviour." Thus, particular scenarios warrant the violation of rules because of the binary logic that constitutes them (recall, again, the "black and white" approach); the failure to do so, thus, will be tantamount to injustice. Hence, "Captain Delight's" description of the rules as "simple" – "They are very simple rules" – could also be read as a recognition of a problem with this very logic. That is, because the rules are constituted by rigidities, the provision of care is cumbersome. His response to (the enforcement of) the rules must be understood as such, as an exercise to set the scales of justice aright.

The way "Captain Delight" interacts with the "professional homeless" illustrates this. Given that he regards them as undeserving of care, he devotes virtually his entire work life to making (or trying to make) their lives as difficult and unpleasant as possible. He does this either by not attending to their requests for assistance or stalling as much as possible, either by pretending to be busy or not to have heard them, before finally conceding. Thus, when "the professional homeless" approach the front desk with a question or a request, "Captain Delight" pretends he has not heard them. About twenty seconds later – and after some probing on their part – he will abruptly ask, "What?" or "What do you want?" This is a powerful question since it vividly portrays annoyance, even disgust, especially because, more often than not, he is simply doing nothing more than sitting on a chair and, hence, his annoyance signifies that it is his very mundaneness that is disrupted. Such questions are often accompanied by a baffled look to further convey that he is unsure why the client is even standing in front of him. Thus, once when a client asked him, "Has 'Frank' [a supervisor] come back?" he, donning a look of puzzlement and while pointing to the supervisor's office, retorted, "Oh, he's not there?" Then, after a long pause, one meant to portray concern, he simply ended this "conversation" with the sound, "Hmmm." The client waited for a while and, realizing he was not going to receive a further response – even acknowledgment of his presence – left. Unsurprisingly, the clients are mindful of "Captain Delight's" beliefs and avoid interacting with him as much as possible. On one occasion, a client requested help from an employee who, because he was supervising the meal line, told the client to request assistance at the front desk. The client, however, was aware that "Captain Delight" was working at the front desk and, rather than risk hassling him and being hassled by him, told the employee, "Can't ask him to do anything," and added, "I'll wait for you. You'll make the call quicker than he will."

The latter example illustrates that it is not only the clients who are inconvenienced by "Captain Delight." His co-workers are also inconvenienced, and this leads to frustration. This is evinced, for example, in the comment of an employee, who, in speaking about "Captain Delight,'" stated, "He is a good guy, but working with him is … very hard and frustrating." To underscore this, he added: "It's even better when he's not here." These absences, however, are ephemeral when, for example, "Captain Delight" is on vacation or when this worker changes shifts, as he sometimes does. This recognition leads to a defeated and jaded attitude, evident in the answer the employee provided to his own question: "But, what you gonna do? Just take it easy, that's all." It is not just him, however, who disagrees with "Captain Delight." One morning, when I asked an employee – who generally works the overnight shift and who had switched shifts with the employee discussed above – how it is to work with "Captain Delight," he commented: "He's got a lot of support for his ideas," and then sarcastically added, "in his own mind, that is." This statement illustrates how different ways of thinking about and implementing an ethic of care can cause strife among employees.

"Captain Delight" is mindful that his actions appear unsympathetic, even callous, an appearance, however, he consciously propagates. Appearances aside, callousness or the lack of sympathy do not accurately represent his values because, for him, the "professional homeless" are undeserving of care. Therefore, not helping them is deploying justice. This is why, for example, he refused to seriously respond to the client who wanted to know whether the supervisor was in his office. As he sees it, the client could have walked another twenty feet to find out. For "Captain Delight," such an attitude, indeed laziness, is indicative of how clients consider themselves entitled to services that have been translated into rights through the extant rules (recall the discussion in chapter 2).

That it is, undoubtedly, an overwhelming sense of justice – not irrationality, callousness, nor the absence of sympathy or empathy – that constitutes "Captain Delight," his thinking and behaviour is further evinced in the way he interacts with clients whom he deems deserving of care, that is, the "working poor." One afternoon, a client who had an overly worried look on his face approached the front desk rather sheepishly and politely asked "Captain Delight" whether his bed was still assigned to him. The client was so inquiring because he had violated a rule by not vacating his bed in the morning by the stipulated time. He was additionally worried because it was "Captain Delight" who was on duty that morning, and "Captain Delight" has a reputation for vigorously enforcing particular rules, especially this one (in contrast to others who are somewhat lax in enforcing this rule). "Captain Delight" simply nodded his head to indicate that he still did. The client was shocked. Perhaps being caught up in the moment – perhaps to placate him or perhaps as gratitude – the client exclaimed, "Why does everyone misunderstand you? You are a hospitable guy and since the very first day I have been here, you have been very hospitable to me." "Captain Delight" nonchalantly turned to the client – an act laden with meaning because he wished to clearly reveal that he did not require this type of disingenuous gratitude – and explained that he was aware that several men had overslept that morning because of fatigue due to working late into the night. Thus, he decided that he would make an exception in this case. Given that he had made an exception for them, he explained that it would have been unfair to single out particular clients to be booked out. Therefore, he decided not to enforce the rule that morning. In so stating, "Captain Delight" was intimating that the reprieve he provided was specifically to the clients who worked late into the night, not to this client who was simply fortunate to have overslept on this particular morning, given these circumstances.

Here, concerns over justice drove "Captain Delight" to not apply a rule that would have required these clients to vacate their beds in the early morning despite having had very little sleep. It was not the rule itself that was deemed unjust. Rather, it was after accounting for the particular circumstances that "Captain Delight" concluded that its application would have been unjust. In arriving at this conclusion, it was a sense of deservedness – the clients deserved more sleep because they are hard-working men – that guided his actions. Thus, there is a great deal of thought behind "Captain Delight's" actions.

This example also illustrates that "Captain Delight's" actions are driven by *his* sense of justice, that is, his sense of right and wrong, which is highly personalized and based on his personal history. This personalized sense of justice, thus, cannot appeal or be reduced to, nor be rationalized within a broader, objective, even abstract, sense of it. This poses numerous problems to the ordering of the shelter. In addition, however, even accounting for "Captain Delight's" own sense of justice, this example reveals numerous and profound inconsistencies in the ways he thinks and behaves. Ostensibly, lumping the clients who were tired because of their night jobs with those who were, presumably, lazy is itself unjust because it does not distinguish between the deserving and undeserving – philosophically, the very opposite of what he believes in. Although such an argument might not be completely fair – he appears to distinguish the two groups, evidenced in how he labels the client who approached him as undeserving of his generosity – what is clear is that there is still some ambiguity with respect to the ways "Captain Delight" enforces the rules. Thus, this example shows that even taken on his own terms, "Captain Delight's" logic can be confusing and inconsistent, and it has the potential to pose problems to the governance of the shelter (recall the comment of the worker who facetiously lauded "Captain Delight's" ideas when he said that their value can only be appreciated by "Captain Delight" himself). Competing logics between employees clash and pose immense problems to the shelter, as the juxtaposition of Elizabeth to "Captain Delight" illustrates.

Like "Captain Delight," Elizabeth believes that in particular instances, namely, when the provision of care is jeopardized, rule violation is just and necessary. "I don't rationalize it," she said about rule violation and explained:

> What *I feel is good and bad is what I'm going to do.* Whether it has to do with the job or not ... if I am not allowed to give this person food before nine o'clock [in the night when clients receive a snack, the final "meal" provided for the day] and they're hungry, I will go to the back and get them some food ... *This place is there for stuff like that.* (emphases added)

That Elizabeth does not rationalize rule breaking, however, is untrue; there is a great deal of thought behind her actions. The supposed absence of rationality, rather, highlights that an ethic of care does not require justification because an ethic of care speaks for itself. The shelter exists to help clients – "This place is there for stuff like that," "a place where anyone can walk in for help" – and not doing so "is very inhumane." That is, not helping because of the rigidities of the rules is what is irrational, and she refuses to accept this, even if her actions are grounded upon, and driven by, her personal feelings of right and wrong – "What I feel is good and bad is what I'm going to do."

It is easy to appreciate that different ethics of care will compete and clash. For "Captain Delight," deservedness is not simply tied to "being" but "doing" as well. Conversely, for Elizabeth, it is tied directly to "being" – in fact, the notion of deservedness is foreign to her because the shelter is for anyone and, thus, everyone. Simply entering it is sufficient for the receipt of care: all other reasons are irrelevant and redundant.

I return to the "boundaries" involving communication with clients to illustrate the interplay between competing visions of justice, ethics of care, and what constitutes rule violation. For Elizabeth, boundaries detract from caring:

> There are boundaries ... [that] you cannot get close to the clients as much as you would like to. That is a boundary that I have always struggled with ... I do speak about my personal life ... because ... you have to give a little bit in order to get anything back ... They want to know how you feel about what you're hearing; they want to know about your life so they feel *comfortable* speaking to you. (emphasis added)

For Elizabeth, communication is an important precondition for the delivery of care. Communication functions as a means of knowledge production, a "vehicle" allowing employees to know and understand exactly what the clients need and how these needs can be effectively and efficiently provided. In addition, communication reveals compassion towards the clients. For Elizabeth, this presupposes that communication is natural, that is, organic, rather than artificial. The rules, she believes, steer conversations towards a contrived model, making caring unnecessarily difficult. Thus, even the ability to lend a sympathetic ear, she claims, requires not just listening to the personal and intimate stories of clients but also revealing one's similar experiences; not doing so shows both a lack of compassion and interest. For Elizabeth, creating a comfortable and comforting environment is paramount to providing care. What she sees, however, is the evisceration of comfort (recall the discussion in chapter 3 of the important place that comfort – or the lack thereof – occupies in the ordering of the shelter, for example, in relation to the making and unmaking of the shelter as a home).

Thus, Elizabeth feels she has little – or no – choice but to circumvent or break the rules. This view is in sync with the beliefs of "Captain Delight." The problem, however, is that given the reasons upon which their rule violations are grounded – that is, different ethics of care – the hitherto discursively extant congruence breaks down revealing the fissures and inconsistencies that constitute the deployment of care. "My problem," "Captain Delight" stated, "is when there is no respect for boundaries," which means, he added, "we don't have consistency." This, he continued, "creates conflict; [it] poses … big problem[s]" leading to "frustration." Similar to his colleagues – certainly, his supervisors – "Captain Delight" is lamenting the absence of order that is directly a product of the inconsistent enforcement of rules. This is one way his lamentations can be made sense of. They can also be understood as a reflection of the very inconsistencies associated with the ways rules are broken. That is, "Captain Delight" is not frustrated that the rules are broken – his own story reveals that sometimes rule violation is a precondition for justice. Rather, he is frustrated because the rules are not broken in ways approved by him, ways that are congruent with his views of the clients as deserving or undeserving.

It is frustration that explains "Captain Delight's" excoriations of his colleagues, especially those like Elizabeth, as "totally unprofessional." In the quest to promote what they see as care, he believes they have become too friendly with the clients. Thus, he explained that when many young women, though with good intentions, greet clients by saying, "Hey, sweetie" or, "Hi sweetheart," it "makes it difficult for us to deal with these guys." "I won't cross that *friendly line*," he added, because "that will destroy what we do" (emphasis added). This statement, a warning of sorts, shines light on "Captain Delight's" conceptualization of care, one devoid of emotions. That is, the provision of care is a professional obligation, not a friendship.

While Elizabeth would not necessarily acknowledge that her actions are unprofessional – she would not recognize them as such – there is evidence that she is mindful that she might be taking things too far: "I mean not everybody should be doing what I'm doing. *I don't think I should be doing half the stuff I am doing* sometimes, *but to me, it's right*" (emphases added). This is a powerful statement highlighting that she is capable of seeing the problem. More powerfully, this is exactly the "ammunition" that "Captain Delight" draws on in his excoriations of her and others like her. Yet – and a poignant "moment" in her reflections – for all these admonitions, even ridicule, she is steadfast, unflappable and indefatigable: she is "right" and seeks to champion her views (recall her position: "What I feel is good and bad is what

I'm going to do"). Thus, she and "Captain Delight" are very much the same; however, the different ways they make sense of an ethic of care and, by extension, justice, markedly separate them and their work lives. This much is evident in Elizabeth's words, which clearly capture the disorder that constitutes the shelter: "You're going to clash with a lot of people!"

As the foregoing suggests, the polysemy of an ethic of care is chiefly responsible for the disordering of the shelter, and the rules, meant as the antidote to this problem, are simply unable to counteract the extemporaneous order that constitutes the space – elsewhere I have theorized the system of "private ordering" that constitutes the site (see Ranasinghe, 2014). This ordering, often ad hoc and inconsistent, even idiosyncratic, gives rise to and sustains what I call administrative chaos. While I have focused in great detail upon the words and deeds of "Captain Delight" and Elizabeth to give colour to the discussion, this should not detract from the fact that practically every employee has his/her own way of doing things, based upon what he/she feels is right and just. This leads to a profound sense of disorganization and disorder. Thus, as one employee put it, "We're all front-line workers but a lot of people have their own way to work." This is directly a product of the polysemy of an ethic of care. This is illuminated in the detailed and nuanced reflections of another employee:

> We have the freedom to make a lot of our own decisions of what we think is best for the clients [and] they rarely ever line up with what everyone else is thinking because everyone has developed their own pattern or their own ... way of dealing with things; even between supervisors ... [there are] different styles. I mean everyone is kind of different and that's why it doesn't always line up ... [This] happens all the time and it's going to happen all the time because you're dealing with ... judgment calls, you're going to have a clash of interest[s] ... So how are we dealing with it? It's usually a quick conversation – it's both sides pleading their cases – and then trying to make the best decision for the client.

This employee's reflections unequivocally underline that in (almost) all the cases it is the best interests of the client that drives the decision-making process. From the standpoint of an ethic of care, this is refreshing. Yet, because different employees make sense of an ethic of care in different ways – the "clash of interests," as he put it – the type of care provided and the manner in which it is so provided will always (or at least mostly) be subject to disagreement. This is the problem, aptly highlighted by the employee who refers to the extant order of the shelter: order that is premised upon disorder, characterized by disorganization and disagreement both between the employees and management and between the employees themselves. The end result, I contend, is the paradox of administrative chaos that envelops the shelter acting as its constitutive feature. Elizabeth's words capture this paradox well: "I think that we are all trying to help ... but, I think, we are all getting different versions of them sometimes. And that is where the conflict ... comes from. I don't think we get angry at each other, we just get frustrated."

## Administrative Chaos in Action: The Example of the Bed-Booking Procedure

The foregoing paints a picture of a profound sense of disorder, one comprised of disorganization and discretionary practices that are ad hoc, inconsistent, even idiosyncratic. The shelter is constituted by its "internal turmoil ... and instability," to borrow Jeff Karabanow's (2002, 107) description of a shelter he studied, and is "a world of chaos and crisis ... an ongoing, emotionally riveting soap opera," to use Loseke's (1992, 170) description. In what follows, I use the example of the provision of beds to clients to give further colour to what this chaos looks and feels like. Each client who has a bed registered to his name – whether occupied for a single night or longer – is guaranteed a bed the next night. There is, however, one condition that must be continuously fulfilled. Daily, between 4 and 6 p.m., the client must reserve, that is, re-book, his bed. This, however, need not be done in person; rather, the client can telephone the shelter, an allowance many clients, especially those who work, find useful and, therefore, utilize. The failure to follow this policy should result in the loss of the bed, leaving the client to register anew for one, in person, beginning at 7 p.m., at which time beds are provided on a first-come, first-served basis. This rule is made known to all employees so that their cognizance of it is undisputed. However, it is not consistently nor even-handedly enforced.

The afternoon shift – between approximately 2 and 3 p.m. until approximately 10 or 11 p.m. – is often worked by about four different young female employees, one being Elizabeth (the shift itself is composed of three workers). While these women do not necessarily share a similar ethic of care, they appear to work well to ensure their work unfolds as smoothly as possible. They have developed a different – what they believe is a simpler – approach to this policy. When they begin their shift, they print the list of the beds that were assigned to clients the previous night and reserve beds for particular clients. They rely on their experiences with each client – allowing them to create an extensive knowledge profile of him from which they are able to "know" the client and predict him and his behaviour – to make this decision (recall, again, the importance that Elizabeth places on uncontrived communication and its resultant benefits). Once a client is well known, his bed is always reserved in this fashion. This, however, has profound implications for the ordering of the shelter. While it is unclear whether this practice makes the clients unaware of the foregoing rule, it is clear that even if they are aware of it, they do not pay heed to it because of an *expectation* that *their* beds will be reserved – "It conditions them" to think and behave as such, an employee who disagrees with this practice stated. This practice frustrates "Captain Delight" (and some others also) because it illuminates that the clients believe they are rightfully entitled to particular services. (To some extent, "Captain Delight's" views are grounded in fact. On numerous occasions, I overheard these women, especially Elizabeth, telling the clients whom they know that their beds have already been reserved, essentially intimating that the telephone call was wasteful and the clients can count on the future reservation of their beds.)

The women who "authored" this "policy" explicitly acknowledge that it lessens their workload by significantly reducing the number of calls that need to be answered. There is, however, much more than the workload that is relevant. For them, this approach is more compassionate than the shelter's because it delivers care in an effective and efficient manner. Such thinking is, if not a product of, then, at least aligned with, Elizabeth's rationales. Recall that she seeks to create a space that is comfortable, an important aspect to the provision of care. Thus, her modification of this rule removes pressure from the client to find time and a payphone to telephone the shelter – a difficulty in the age of high cellular phone usage, though it should be added that many clients have cellular phones. It also eliminates the client's anxiety about whether his bed would be guaranteed for him. Finally, the client can save the 50 cents that he needs for the call, a savings of about $15 a month. This policy, then, both instrumentally and symbolically, is an explicit renunciation of the binary logic of the rules which stipulates "black and white" conditions upon which the right to a bed is founded.

This approach generally works well when these women work in the afternoon: the clients are unsurprised when they arrive at the shelter in the late evening or night because, as they expected, their beds await them. Sometimes, however, things go horribly awry causing numerous problems to all the parties concerned: the client, the employees, and the supervisors. This happens when employees who do not regularly work the afternoon shift, or who do not necessarily subscribe to the views of these women, work this shift. In these instances, clients arrive to find out that because they failed to follow protocol, their beds were not reserved for them. After pleading their case, often claiming, perhaps truthfully, that they were unaware of the policy, further indignation ensues on those occasions when the shelter is filled to capacity and additional beds are unavailable. Tired and grumpy by this point, they turn their anger, frustration and misery towards the employees and the shelter system revealing the perils and fragility of the order in the shelter.

On one occasion, a client entered the shelter at about 3:30 p.m. and asked that his bed be reserved for him. A male employee – who worked on a part-time basis, a problem in its own right, already explored in chapter 4 – informed the client that because bed-bookings commence at 4 p.m. and that the man was one-half hour early, he should return later. The client informed the employee that on the preceding day he booked-in at the same time and the young female employee who so booked him – presumably one of the four women who authored the policy described above – gave him "no problem." The male employee reiterated that he was following the rules and asked the man to return at the appropriate time. At this point the client became annoyed, which prompted the employee, who by now could see that the situation might get out of control, to ask the man, "What's with the attitude, Sir?" The client, quickly realizing that he would not be able to convince the employee otherwise – as he could have with some of the female employees – responded, "I am not having attitude," and proceeded to leave the building but not before muttering in a low voice, "Thanks for being so accommodating." In this case, the accommodation permitted to him and others by the women who had authored their own policy was translated into a shelterwide policy, as a matter of right, by this client, so that when the male employee simply followed extant protocol, it was read as if he was uncaring and inconsiderate (this was especially so because the request was denied by a male employee, and the already tepid relations between the clients and male employees, as described in chapter 6, only served to translate this denial into an act of uncaring, certainly an apt illumination of the gendered nature of an ethic of care).

In many instances, however, the situation is not resolved in such a straightforward manner and, instead, leads to very serious problems. On one occasion, when several employees were facing precisely this situation, they provided an irate client with the bed that was reserved for another client whom they thought would not arrive at the shelter that night. This provided a modicum of respite, but within an hour or so, the client whose bed was given away arrived. He was incensed upon hearing what had transpired and turned his outrage and indignation towards the employees. Upon hearing the yelling, replete with profanity, a supervisor intervened and asked the client to provide the employees some time to examine what had transpired and explore possible solutions. After discussing this matter for about thirty minutes, the client was provided another bed. Exactly how this solution was brokered is somewhat unclear – some of this discussion took place away from my presence in the supervisor's office – though it appeared that a client who was to be booked out that evening for violating a rule, was promptly booked out, thereby opening up space for the client who had lost his bed.

While this solution resolved the conflict, it was not before a vast amount of confusion, frustration, and anger enveloped the shelter and its personnel. More poignantly, this situation is emblematic of the order that constitutes the shelter, often constituted by spontaneity leaving room for additional problems to arise. Perhaps recognizing this, that very night, prompted by this incident, the supervisor on duty created small pocket-sized sheets which had printed on them several of the rules of the shelter, including the one in question; the supervisor provided the sheets to employees and clearly instructed them to tell their colleagues that each client who books into the shelter is to be provided with one and that the rules of the shelter are to be clearly explained to each client prior to registration. This was the supervisor's effort to counteract not just the administrative chaos but the manner in which clients rely upon it to avoid following the rules by claiming that they are unaware of them. As this supervisor and management see it, the rules might be rigid, but rigidity prevents the frequently occurring problems in the shelter, many of which *they* have to address. As the employees see it, however, the rigidity of the rules prevent the deployment of care, even though this deployment is characterized by disorganization and disorder, something which they are most privy to. In the end, and rather ironically, even these attempts to attend to this only lead to significant problems with the ordering of the shelter, which further serves to hinder the delivery of care.

### The Place of Rules and the Administration of Chaos: A Final Word

The place of legality – both in relation to the rules of the shelter and the ways they are thought about by the personnel who work in it – is crucial to understanding the ordering of the shelter. The rules are viewed by both management and employees as having profound importance: rules provide consistency and consistency breeds order – in fact, is order. The rules, thus, as seen by management are necessary for order. Yet, despite this belief, the polysemy of an ethic of care renders the place of rules largely problematic – in fact, virtually impossible to implement. The rules – and law, in the broadest sense – operate on a binary coding which makes it incommensurate with an ethic of care that is polysemic and ephemeral. This means that care cannot be provided in the rigid fashion as mandated. What results, thus, is an immense amount of discretionary practices that are required, at least from the perspective of the employees, to ensure that care is administered in a meaningful manner.

This, however, is really the start of the problem. The polysemy of an ethic of care ensures that even when the rules are violated or circumscribed, they are done so in such a disorderly manner that it is not just the order in the shelter that is compromised, but the very provision of care itself. In other words, the disorganization, spontaneity, inconsistencies, and idiosyncrasies that constitute discretionary practices make the provision of care dysfunctional. Thus, even the provision of a bed – a basic symbol of care and comfort – is rendered (or possibly can be rendered) utterly confusing and disorganized because of the discretionary practices that form the constitution of rule implementation.

It is crucial, however, to underscore that the front-line employees are most cognizant of this disorganization and its implications; that it might adulterate the type of care they wish to deploy. Yet they tolerate – even celebrate – this type of administrative chaos because, as they see it, this system is much better suited to delivering care than a system that *a priori* lays out what care is, looks and feels like, and how it should be administered. This, they believe, will create more problems than not. Thus, as these employees see it, it is in this type of administrative chaos – which they are, just like management, partly responsible for creating and maintaining – that their freedom is to be found and their sense of being and belongingness is made worthwhile.

# 8 From the Laughable to the Ridiculous: The Example of "Zero-Tolerance"

In the previous chapter, I explicated the place of legality to the ordering of the shelter, examining the ways rules are thought about, made sense of, and practised. While there is some concordance between management and employees regarding the inherent value of rules – rules provide consistency which in turn provides order (in fact, consistency is order) – for the most part, a deep gulf separates the two parties: one calls for the strict enforcement of the letter of the law; the other relies on discretionary practices to circumvent what is seen as an inherent problem with the constitution of rules, namely, binary coding. Thus, as explicated, the polysemy of an ethic of care makes it virtually impossible to follow the letter of the law. What results is what I call administrative chaos leading to myriad problems regarding the delivery of care.

While the foregoing illustrated a problem that is systemic, namely, two issues colliding head-on and with full force – the binary logic of law and the polysemy of an ethic of care – in this chapter I further illustrate the place of legality vis-à-vis the chaos of the shelter. I focus on how even the humdrum contributes to chaos (cf. Valverde, 1996). To so do, I examine the ways rules are understood and deployed. Several key themes discussed in the previous chapter figure prominently here as well, particularly discretionary practices. I locate discretionary practices and the resulting disorganization and disorder in the mundane, in particular, in the ignorance about the law. In so doing, I illustrate how disorder and disorganization are also produced through incompetent practices – perhaps, people as well – the results of which are nothing short of ridiculousness and hilarity. My intention is not to minimize the types of problems prevalent but, rather, illustrate that even the ridiculous is part and parcel of the administration of the chaotic that constitutes the daily life of the shelter.

## On Discretion and the Ridiculous

In previous chapters, I explicated management's policy on discretion: supervisor's – and, to a lesser extent, caseworkers – may use discretion, while frontline employees may not. As a foray into the discussion on the ridiculous, I commence with an incident which transpired one evening, at about 7 p.m., when a man who had been banned from the shelter entered it to use the washroom. He was immediately and rudely denied access by a female employee. Her reason, which she later explained to me, was that after 7 p.m. the shelter does not serve as a "public site" and, thus, its facilities may only be used by clients, that is, those who have been booked in. The man then asked another employee whether he could use the washroom and received the same response. At this point, the man began walking towards the supervisor's office presumably to plead his case with the supervisor. Sensing that this was about to transpire, the employee who originally denied the man access "radioed" the supervisor to let the supervisor know what was happening. The supervisor came out of the office, met the man halfway and directed him to the washroom; while the man was proceeding to the washroom, the supervisor signalled to the female employee that everything was okay. About ten minutes later, when the supervisor entered The Bubble, the female employee, who was most annoyed by what had transpired, asked, "So you let buddy use the washroom?" Keenly aware that the employee was both annoyed and confused, the supervisor explained the rationale behind the decision: simply put, it was easier to let the man use the washroom than explain the rules to him and deal with the potential ramifications that may ensue if the man continued to press his case.

This incident, I claim, aptly illustrates the type of confusion that is part and parcel of the daily life of the shelter. The actions of the female employee – save perhaps for her insolence – were perfectly aligned with the protocols of the shelter; these protocols, it should be remembered, the employees are both counselled and exhorted to follow and implement strictly and consistently, without a trace of discretion. This is exactly what she did. Thus, and naturally, she expected that her decision would be supported by the supervisor. Precisely the opposite, of course, happened. Given this, it is easy to see why many employees will be confused, not just about the policies of the shelter, but about their implementation as well. In fact, this incident aptly illuminates why many employees enforce the rules as they see fit.

What is also illuminating is the explanation the supervisor provided. In one sense, what the supervisor did was not problematic, because it could be argued that while the female employee had no choice but to follow the rule because she does not have the right to discretion, the supervisor, conversely, does and, therefore, is permitted to bend the rules if the situation is deemed appropriate. This is what happened. Thus, permitting the man to use the washroom is not what was problematic; in fact, there is nothing problematic at all about the decision. Rather, what is problematic is that the supervisor simply bent the rule to lessen the supervisor's workload: it was easier to allow the man to use the washroom than spend time arguing with him. Even this rationale, it could be argued, is without problems. However, what it shows is that the front-line employees are not permitted such leeway and relief: they have no choice but to enforce the letter of the law and face the consequences that come with it – ranging from displeasure to verbal abuse replete with profanity to threats of physical abuse, including being spat on (and, in one outlandish incident, being urinated upon during a meal). The supervisors, on the other hand, have this luxury, best evinced in the comment of another supervisor who claimed that the supervisor will bend the rule "if it is going to make my life easier." Looked upon as such, it is, again, not shocking that most employees only follow the rules as they see fit. This is precisely what one employee said in explaining why she breaks the rules: "To be nice and also to avoid confrontation. You don't want to get into a fight over a T-shirt or something remedial [read, trivial] like that." Thus, for all the posturing on the part of management, that the letter of the law must be followed, for the most part, rules are bent for a variety of reasons, one important one being whether it lessens the burdens of the workday of these supervisors. This, it should be underscored, the employees are most privy to and disgusted by.

## From the Ridiculous to the Incompetent: The Place of Ignorance

Despite the almost reverential manner in which the rules are viewed by both management and employees, especially the former, the practicalities of ordering the shelter reveal a very different story about their application. In explaining one aspect of the problem, a supervisor explained: "*We have so many* [rules] *and they change a lot* and when they change, half the time, I don't hear [about them], I don't hear anything until I get back after being away for my three days off ... There's nothing written anywhere [and] the only way I know something has changed is if a front-line worker says ... [something]" (emphases added). This narrative is hyperbolic and embellished and, for the most part, does not (in fact, cannot) speak for the way management as a whole – including the supervisors – feels about the rules (this is especially so given that notifications about rules and rule changes emanate from management and, thus, it is difficult to fathom many situations where a supervisor will not be privy to what is taking place). Nevertheless, these words shine light on the place of rules in the ordering of the shelter. According to the supervisor, two related issues combine to render the rules problematic. First, there are too many rules. This means that *knowledge of* and *knowledgeability about* the rules is made difficult, if not impossible – the first refers to whether one knows of a rule in the sense of being aware of it; the second whether one is knowledgeable about what it means and stands for. This appears to be a commonality in the social services field evinced in the comments of Rebecca Kissane (2006), who notes that the "directors of non-profit agencies serving the poor are not much better informed than clients" and a only "few had comprehensive knowledge about the rules" (342, 331). Second, and related, these rules (supposedly) change so often further exacerbating the first problem (see Kissane, 2006, 332). The fact that the already too numerous rules change constantly and considerably makes it difficult to know of the rules and modifications to them and, as well, be knowledgeable about what these rules and their changes mean. Thus, the supervisor is highlighting a particular and grave problem associated with ordering the shelter.

This is also evident in the somewhat sardonic comments of an employee, who explained why he is largely ignorant of the rules: "The thing is ... these guys [management] kind of did it backwards in a way where they kind of gave me the [rule] book and *I skipped through it* because a lot of it is jargon until you understand what it is like to be on the front line" (emphasis added). It is almost certain that the employee means that he skimmed through the rules and regulations, but regardless of whether the word "skipped" is intentional or not, an important insight is revealed into how employees become aware of the rules. Here, the very process of skimming (or skipping through) a book – one, it should be underscored, that contains a litany of rules and regulations, and, therefore, dull and monotonous – necessarily means that it is impossible to study it. This also means that knowledge of and about it is superficial at best. Thus, more so than not, the means by which the employees are made aware of the rules, as this employee sees it, makes little sense and does not ensure that they learn them.

It is also important to highlight that the employee's comments speak not only to the problems associated with the execution of rules, but the rules themselves – that is, their pedigree and constitution, which is perhaps even more troubling than the problem of application. Thus, in using the word "jargon" to convey the constitution of rules, the employee shines light on an important problem with ordering the shelter: the inherent nature of the rules is made up of (and by) jargon. This leads him (and others) to skim the rules because careful perusal is meaningless given the obscurity and esotericism that constitute them (in similar ways, for example, that legalese constitutes legislation thereby eviscerating the possibility of lay persons understanding laws and legal decisions).

### "Zero-Tolerance" in Action

In what follows, I focus on the application of the rules, in particular, casting attention on the limits regarding the knowledge of and knowledgeability about a specific – and rather contentious – rule, commonly referred to as the "zero-tolerance" policy. In order to capture the lack of knowledge about the rules and how it affects the ordering of the shelter, I narrate my experiences with coming to know and learn about this rule as it unfolded.

The shelter, I was led to believe, has a "zero-tolerance" policy concerning alcohol and drugs. This policy comprises two stipulations: first, the usage of either alcohol or drugs inside the shelter is strictly prohibited; second, those who appear to have consumed either are prohibited entry. During virtually my entire duration at the shelter – about one year – this was how the rule was repeatedly explained to me by numerous personnel working in the shelter. One employee, for example, stated that "we have a 'zero-tolerance' rule in terms of ... using or hav[ing] [a] drink or whatever." Another employee commented that "technically, the policy says that this is 'zero-tolerance.'" Thus, during the time I spent in the shelter, I had no reason to think that the employees had somehow misconstrued the rule. This was not simply because they clearly stated it in unison but, as well – and, in hindsight, rather shockingly, if not appallingly – because several supervisors stated the same thing (the very persons, it should be remembered, who are chiefly responsible for ensuring the rules are enforced strictly and consistently). For example, one supervisor explained the rule straightforwardly in a manner meant to capture its rather simple and clear nature: "If you say 'zero-tolerance,' ultimately [it] should be a sip, a drink of beer, two beers, that's 'zero tolerance,' *you can't have any beers*" (emphasis added).

Yet what I observed daily was palpably different from the words used to define and describe the rule. I repeatedly witnessed the violation of this policy, which, it appeared, was purposive and conscious. Those who had consumed alcohol and were, in fact, inebriated – ranging from slightly to severely – were permitted entrance and allowed to access their beds for the night. Many employees explained that the violation of this rule was necessary, that the site in question, with the particular clientele it attracts, was simply not conducive to temperance. What they did, therefore, was manage drinking, rather than prohibit it, because the latter was simply impossible. As one employee put it:

> There's a lot of homeless people ... so you kind of have to make that judgment and kind of try to let some people pass, especially when ... they need to sleep and you get into the winter months and ... you don't want people freezing ... So ... if we were going ... work-to-rule type of thing [read, enforce the letter of the law], those guys would be screwed.

The employee's narrative locates the problem in the rule – "zero-tolerance" of drinking – not the population in question; in fact, his rationalization has it that given this population, not only is the rule meaningless, bordering on the fatuous, but it needs circumvention. The failure to so do, would, rather ironically, run counter to the very ethic of care that the shelter stands for and seeks to promote, especially if and when two basic necessities of life, warmth and sleep, are deprived. This is precisely why another employee commented, "Given the demographic that we serve, that, [following the rule], [i]s not possible."

In fact, such views were shared by several supervisors as well, only serving to further confound matters. One, for example, clearly noted that alcohol and drug consumption, even addiction, is virtually innate to the population:

> I think ... ultimately ... the population is so used to drinking and smoking ... When you're dealing with ... a disadvantaged group that

wake up and wonder what they are doing to make up ... their day or how they are going to get through their tough times, they're going to look to some of the vices that society has made available. So ... we say "zero-tolerance," but its "zero-tolerance," wink, wink.

As explained and made sense of by the supervisor – a source from which the rules emanate – the rule itself makes little sense given the population and, therefore, cannot be applied as intended. In this narration, the ordering of the shelter requires the circumvention of, even disobedience to, the rule. This type of thinking clashes with the calls for the strict and consistent enforcement of the letter of the law.

The foregoing provides important insights into the place of rules to the order in, and ordering of, the shelter. In particular, it appears that order is, rather counterintuitively, present when and where rule violation is extant. In fact, it appears that not only is rule violation necessary for order, but that rules might not necessarily be a requisite for order in the first place – rules, again rather counterintuitively, hinder order; rules equal disorder. This, then, appears to suggest that there is order in disorder, in the same ways, for example, that Richard Sennett (1970) speaks of the function(ality) of disorder. In what follows, I probe this possibility further by examining how the "zero-tolerance" rule is "disobeyed."

While conversing with two employees about the thought processes that occupy their minds when deciding whether or not to permit entry to a client who has consumed alcohol or is intoxicated, one stated that if the client "can walk in a straight line" – in the figurative sense of the term, as I have never witnessed the application of this test – or, is inclined to "sleep it off," she would permit him access. The decision-making process, it appears, is premised upon the degree of intoxication – as another employee, in a different situation, emphasized, "there's drunk, and then there's *drunk*" (emphasis in original). Thus, for example, if a client is able to walk straight, this would illustrate that he is either not drunk or only somewhat intoxicated and that he still has the wherewithal to function. Yet, even in those situations where the client is *"drunk,"* that is, in the most extreme sense of intoxication, it does not appear that this necessarily precludes entry – the explanation provided by the employee suggests that if the client is willing to sleep, he will be allowed entry.

In fact, it seems that the level of intoxication is not as important in the decision-making process as it appears – a recipe, as I show later, that poses numerous problems to the order of the shelter. One important factor, alluded to above, is simply whether the client is willing to go to bed. As one employee explained, "sometimes ... you'll have a guy who is only going to go straight to bed, but is really drunk ... [and] I just let them go to bed." On one occasion, for example, a client who was intoxicated entered the shelter sometime around 8 p.m. and the two employees on duty assessed him and the situation and decided that he was too drunk to be allowed entry. However, after conversing with the man for a while – both because of the prodding and pleading on the part of the client who wanted entry and, as well, one employee, who seemed very keen to allow the man entry, even telling her colleague to "humour me" – they struck a deal with the man: if he was willing to go straight upstairs and sleep, he would be permitted entry. He agreed and one employee escorted him upstairs. When the two employees were back together, I sought clarification on their decision, which one employee explained in this way:

> He's here a lot and never causes any trouble ... So it's kind of we just decided, if he's going to bed and not causing trouble, it's okay. But that's because we know him. We are just understanding of the situation to avoid all the drama ... we are looking out for him. It's a tricky thing and if we don't know them, we don't take the risk to let them sleep here. It's all judgment how drunk they are, etc.

The thought processes behind the decision reveal that several factors, including, as raised at the outset, the degree of intoxication, are considered. In addition, the employees are well aware that denying entry would mean the client would have to find alternative means for the night, something which would run counter to the notion of care – "we are looking out for him." Yet, at its core, there are two key factors that guide this situation. First, that the client was willing to go to bed, itself a sign that the man does not intend to pose trouble to the employees or other clients. In other words, regardless of whether the man was drunk or not, and regardless of the degree of intoxication, the client's desire for sleep is read as a sign of the impending order that looms regardless of the disorder that prevails momentarily. Second, and related, the sincerity of the client's words – that he will, in fact, go straight to bed – is gauged by the knowledge the employees have of the client. Thus, in this situation, these employees began their explication by explicitly noting that they are capable of speaking about the habits of the client – "He's here a lot and never causes any trouble" – and it is only this that led them to confidently rule that he will not pose any trouble – "But that's because we know him." This confidence, however, would be shattered within a span of some ten minutes when the client would return to The Bubble, a smile adorning his face and a handful of chocolates in hand for the employees. After providing them with the chocolates – perhaps as a sign of gratitude – which they accepted, itself a breach of the rules, the client made his way to bed.

The fact that decisions are based largely on the "intimate" knowledge of clients is troubling. Even with the intimate knowledge of the client in hand, these employees had decided that he was too drunk to be allowed entry. However, within a span of some ten minutes, the client – an intoxicated client, it should be remembered – was able to "convince" the employees that he should be permitted entry. It was not, however, a deep process of ratiocination that paved the way for this decision. In other words, it was not convincing that was required – the grounds for admission had already been laid *a priori* because the client was known to these employees and vice versa; indeed, it was this fact alone which led one employee to "convince" the other to listen to the pleas of the client. Thus, more often than not, these decisions are based on emotions, which have grave implications for the way the shelter is ordered (I have already discussed the ways that young female employees make decisions based on their attachments to the clients).

To give further colour to this, consider the following exchange with another employee:

PR: Okay, but often you will have people come in who are ... [interruption half way through the sentence].

RESPONDENT: Drunk, every day, and they let them in?

PR: Right. Now how does that play out, in other words why ... [interruption half way through the sentence].

RESPONDENT: I don't know, it depends. I guess ... if we know that [the] drunk person is not going to make trouble and is just going to go to bed, we usually let them go. But if we know someone is coming in and we know how they are, we're going to send them away. Which *in all honesty we should do* ... but I don't know, to tell you the truth, *we do get attached to certain people.* (emphases added)

This is a remarkable exchange because it illuminates what takes place on a daily basis, when, as the employee clearly understands and admits, it should not. At its core, her explanation suggests that the clients who are permitted entry are known to the employees and this knowledge foreshadows what is expected, that is, that the clients will proceed to bed – this is not, however, what necessarily transpires. What is most revealing is that she is also cognizant that this is not a rational decision, it is one based on emotions. That the employees "get attached to certain people," is what influences whether or not they permit these persons, intoxicated or not, and regardless of the level of intoxication, to enter the building. In other words, an emotional calculus, rather than a rational calculus, appears to guide this decision-making process, and many others as well – or, to put it another away, an emotional person, rather than a rational person, appears to be at the helm of the decision-making process. Unsurprisingly, then, the rules, as management sees it, are meant to eliminate emotion creeping into the decision-making process. This, management believes, produces – in fact, is – order. As the employees see it, however, the type of order that management envisages is quite disorderly. The emotional aspect associated with dealing with clients is paramount not just to the order in the shelter, but to promoting and safeguarding an ethic of care – recall, for example, the way the notion of comfort was discussed by many employees, especially Elizabeth, as crucial to the conceptualization and delivery of care.

As the foregoing suggests, there is a great deal of confusion in the application of the "zero-tolerance" policy. This is so for a variety of reasons, but an important one is that these decisions are made through an emotional calculus. In making this claim, I do not suggest that these women are unable to think rationality. The opposite is, indeed, the case (cf. Ranasinghe, 2013b). I also do not suggest that the male employees solely utilize a rational calculus when making decisions. They, too, I suggest, make their decisions through a particular emotional calculus – recall the discussion in chapter 6, where I explicated how fearful the male employees are of the clients, often verging on paranoia. Thus, it is quite plausible to assume that fear, rather than rationality, influences, even drives, their decisions. However, because it is the women who predominantly work the afternoon shift, it is they, more than not, who must decide whether to allow those who have been drinking or who are intoxicated to enter the shelter, especially during the reservation of beds, which takes place daily between 4 and 6 p.m. and again after 7 p.m. It is for this reason that I focus on their emotional calculus and the way their attachment to the clients shape the decisions they make. This way of thinking and doing, not surprisingly, will not be looked upon favourably by their male counterparts, who see these women as being emotionally swayed – despite their own irrationalities that constitute them and their behaviours. All this only enlarges and strengthens the gulf between the two.

It is safe to conclude, then, that a profound sense of confusion and disorder envelops – in fact, constitutes – the order in, and ordering of, the shelter. It is here, then, that I should reveal that I have been purposefully evasive about an important fact, which now must be disclosed, though this will unlikely be a surprise to the reader. This revelation is that I have not been fully forthcoming on the precise nature of the "zero-tolerance" policy. One aspect of it is precisely as I have narrated it – the use of alcohol or drugs inside the shelter is strictly prohibited. However, the other and, more important and contentious, aspect of it – "zero-tolerance" of drinking – is not the rule. The rule is "zero-tolerance" of *intoxication*, not drinking. In other words, whether a client has consumed alcohol or not is irrelevant. What is relevant is whether he is inebriated. Rather shockingly – in fact, sadly – for most of the year I spent in the shelter, I operated on an erroneous assumption because this is how the rule was conveyed to me by the employees and some supervisors. Ironically, it was a supervisor who first notified me of this error and shed light on the rule: "There is no such thing as 'zero-tolerance' here. I do know that people say that, they use that expression, but it's not true, and what it is, is that people shouldn't be intoxicated." Two senior managers later reiterated this as well, one stating: "It's 'zero-tolerance' of intoxication or behavioural issues related to intoxication."

There are, unsurprisingly, profound implications for what this means to the ordering of the shelter. An important one is that key actors who are charged with deploying care (namely, front-line workers) are either not knowledgeable of, or unclear about, the rules. In fact, it also appears that key actors in charge of ensuring the rules are applied (namely, supervisors) are themselves unclear of exactly what these rules are. In narrating this discussion as I have, I have chosen not to disclose the rule as it is in an effort to capture the type of confusion that is a daily feature of (and in) the shelter. What transpires daily is that these employees – and, as well, some supervisors – wholeheartedly believe in a rule that does not exist and, therefore, believe they need to disobey it to promote care. What they are not privy to, however, is that they are, in fact, not necessarily breaking the rule, but are, more so than not, enforcing it. Thus, while the employees believe that they must take a stance against management to ensure the deployment of care as they see fit, they are, more so than not, putting into practice what management envisages. Whether they like it or not or, believe it or not, they are, at least on this matter, quite similar in thinking and acting to management. Clearly, then, the moral of this tale is that the rules themselves are – or can be – problematic when two parties, believing they are operating on different planes, end up doing, ironically, mostly the same thing. What emerges, of course, is not order nor orderly, but a keen sense of disorder, because one party is always suspicious of the other. While the rule might actually be enforced as desired, that it is thought not to be so has symbolic ramifications to the ordering of the site – in the same ways, for example, that security is a site of struggle between the two parties.

In the instrumental sense, however, the application of the rule departs markedly from what management would countenance. The rule, as noted above, is that an intoxicated person is prohibited entry. Yet in practice, numerous factors – the level of intoxication, whether the client is willing to go to bed and, most importantly, whether he has an emotional attachment to one or more employee – are considered when the decision is made. The end result, of course, is that the rule – whether the letter of the law or its modified version – does not work and is a good example of the administrative chaos that constitutes the order in the shelter. On this matter, the same supervisor who correctly explained the rule stated:

> It does not work because … we've got too many people with too many different points of view. You have some people [who] are really good at detecting whether someone is intoxicated, you have some people who are not so good, you have some people who say, "I don't agree with any of these rules, so regardless of the fact that this guy is intoxicated, I'm going to let him go to bed." So there's all kinds of things … that are building up.

The supervisor's comments speak to two pertinent issues: the purposeful violation of the rules and the ability to gauge whether a client is drunk. It is important to underscore that the supervisor speaks specifically about an issue that is to be decided on black and white terms, that is, whether one is inebriated or not, not the degree of intoxication which is irrelevant to the application of the rule. The supervisor's comments show that even attempting to apply the letter of the law is virtually impossible because of the different ways decisions are made.

How problematic this situation is, is evinced in the reflections of the same supervisor, who discussed not just the gulf between the employees and management, but between the supervisors as well. The supervisor said,

> I'm a person who [believes] if there is a rule, you've got to follow it, and so if I were at the desk and somebody was intoxicated but quiet and someone was trying to book him in, I'd say, "We're not booking this guy in, we're not." I'm sure that ... the supervisors are all different ... so maybe another supervisor would be a little more lenient ... but not me.

While it is perhaps not shocking that perfect harmony between the supervisors does not exist, it is, nevertheless, worth underscoring what this means for the place of rules in relation to the order of the shelter. If the supervisors are the beacon of order – for example, the way consistency is lauded by management as a necessary virtue, inherently orderly in its own right – then the disagreements between the supervisors have important symbolic import for order because it illuminates that the letter of the law *cannot* be applied because what it is, itself, is unsettled. Thus, it would be unfair to expect the employees to apply the rules evenly when the authorities who are in charge of, if not writing them, then at least ensuring they are strictly enforced, cannot act in unison.

These comments do not reveal another pressing issue with the uneven application of the rule, one pertaining to bodily harm. Interestingly, if not ironically, this was what a client endured because of the decision taken by this very supervisor:

> I recall ... letting somebody upstairs. I talked to him, let him upstairs, thought, okay, obviously he's been drinking but I think he's okay and off he went ... He fell off of his bed, hurt his head, had to go to the hospital, [and it] turned out that he'd had like, a gigantic amount of beer that night, and so *I made a mistake.* (emphasis added)

Here, bodily harm was, if not caused, then at least contributed to because a severely intoxicated man was allowed to sleep on the top bunk of a bed, a mistake the supervisor accepts. The episode itself is a clear sign of the profound difficulties associated with gauging intoxication. This is precisely why the supervisor now champions the strict enforcement of the letter of the law. While this appears to go some distance in addressing the issue, because intoxication still needs to be gauged, it makes it difficult to even-handedly apply the rule. Also, because the employees are interested in gradations of intoxication, not intoxication itself, what is a simple rule – at least on paper – is made overly complex.

## On the Humdrum, the Ridiculous, and the Incompetent: A Final Word

In this chapter, I explicated how the humdrum plays an important role in the administrative chaos that constitutes the daily life of the shelter. That many employees (even supervisors) are ignorant about many rules – the "zero-tolerance" policy being one example – is quite problematic to the shelter. What results can verge on the hilarious: employees who have the best motives and intentions in mind seek to somehow circumvent what they see as the rigidity of the rules, which they believe preclude meaningful care; they are, however, unmindful that not only are such efforts unnecessary, but they are actually applying a rule as it is meant to be. Despite their keen sense that they are deploying care in a more meaningful manner, they are, sadly, not. In some cases, as the example of the client who needed hospitalization after falling from his bed shows, the care deployed is inimical to the well-being of the clients.

All this illustrates the ordering of the shelter: even the humdrum life that characterizes the shelter and its employees is constituted by the ridiculous and, even worse, incompetence. This is especially brought to light when considering that those in charge of ensuring the rules are implemented, that is, the supervisors, also seem utterly clueless as to exactly what the rules are. Thus, the rules, the beacon of hope and order as they are thought to be, flounder on their own terms because a rather simple and taken-for-granted fact about their effectiveness and efficiency, that is, knowledge, is absent. The administration of chaos is a product of legality, one which complicates and exacerbates the problem of order. Chaos, sadly, is the norm.

# 9 Conclusion

Throughout the preceding pages, I have detailed the ordering of the space of an emergency shelter. This ordering is constituted by an ethic of care, that is, an injunction, grounded upon moral principles, to serve and help those in need. The services offered run the gamut from the basic necessities of life to myriad other non-essential services. The ethic of care is manifested in the words and deeds of the employed personnel, as well as the materiality of the space. In this sense, this work can be considered a reading of space (see Bachelard, [1958] 1994, 14; cf. Lefebvre, [1974] 1991,142–3) undertaken through a tour of a typical day in the shelter to explore and explicate what an ethic of care looks and feels like both in thought and practice.

In narrating the daily life of the shelter, I have examined what happens to an ethic of care throughout its travels and travails as it is conceptualized and practised by myriad persons, from myriad backgrounds. There is little doubt that a desire to meaningfully serve and help encapsulates the ethic of the shelter, both in word and deed, and this is so with practically every employee, whether management, frontline worker, or caseworker. Despite the foregoing, this ethic is heavily contested and adulterated leading to problems in ordering the shelter.

The primary reason for this is because the logics of legality and security occupy a prominent role in the daily life of the shelter, leading to a space that is both heavily legalized (even bureaucratized) and securitized. Legality sets the tenor of the shelter: it unequivocally states that the shelter is (to be) constituted by an ethic of care and its mandate is to serve and help the needy. This explicit and unequivocal statement is only possible because the chief characteristic of law – binary coding – clearly spells out what is and is not condoned in its eyes, that is, what is legal and illegal. The binary logic, in other words, is characterized by a sense of simplicity, one of its paramount values: because the law is clear, it produces free subjects who can plan and live their lives accordingly. Despite this virtue – a virtue emanating from law's desire to simplify a concordance of voices into one – it is also problematic. The reductionism upon which the law is founded and works can only be manoeuvered to a point. Given that the ethic of care is polysemic, the binary coding of law is unable to fully capture and frame the myriad ways care is conceptualized and practised. The end result is a space that is disorderly, even dysfunctional, governed by administrative chaos.

This is particularly visible in the struggles around the conceptualization of security. The preoccupation with (and over) security consumes the time and efforts of management, a problem that is constructed strictly as a concern about primary safety, that is, violence and bodily harm. This concern (essentially paranoia) is, in some ways, a product of legality, because it is the law that spells out what safety ought to look and feel like in particular sites. Yet, while primary safety is taken very seriously by all parties, including the employees, it is management, again because of the heavily bureaucratized and legalized space of the shelter, that is preoccupied with it. For the employees, a host of other matters, ranging from health to remuneration, are conceptualized as concerns about security. This is done to make the language more palatable to management. Ironically, they are able to do this because of the presence of a heavily legalized and bureaucratized environment which permits such a translation. In this translation – the site of struggle that security is – the profound disjuncture between management and employees regarding how each conceptualizes security and the problems of order which crop up as such are plainly evident. In addition, the struggles over security also illuminate the gendered nature of the space which also leads to and sustains the gendering of an ethic of care. All this bodes poorly for the deployment of care.

The daily life of the shelter – what it looks, feels, sounds, and smells like – is constituted by administrative chaos. That is, the official efforts (both formally and informally) to implement a modicum of order and stability in(to) the shelter tend to do precisely the opposite, leading to a space that is disorderly and dysfunctional. Over and beyond the problem of order, the ethic of care is severely adulterated as well, because care is delivered on an ad hoc basis and is heavily idiosyncratic and inconsistent. Furthermore, the major issues which constitute and confound the shelter lie not simply in the struggles and disharmony between management and employees, but also between caseworkers and front-line employees and, among front-line employees as well. The cumulative effects of these relationships severely disorder the shelter. The ambiguities and ambivalences surrounding the "zero-tolerance" policy that push the limits of the binary logic of law into the ridiculous and laughable is an apt example. This, to some extent at least, is the tenor of the shelter, its flavour, in other words, if not ridiculous, then at least verging on it.

The daily disordering that is the shelter, then, negatively impacts the conceptualization and administration of an ethic of care. This is also seen in the materiality of the site which suggests that care cannot be anything other than uncomfortable: comfort and care, at least in this space, do not – and cannot – go hand in hand. Thus, from the moment a client enters the shelter (through the front doors, which only have an appearance of openness and being welcoming) to the services he receives (the poor quality and insufficient number of chairs; insipid and unhealthy food; poor accommodations for rest – the bed and mattress; the thin sheet that serves as a blanket) to the site itself (poorly lit; rampant with a nauseating stench; unhygienic and filthy washrooms), to name a few, point towards one conclusion: the care provided is minimal and marginal, a result of a space that is heavily legalized and securitized. This is the life in (and of) the shelter.

This narration has relied upon particular words or descriptors that carry powerful pejorative – or, at least, negative – connotations: "disorder," "dysfunction," "confusion," "inconsistency," and "idiosyncrasy," to name a few that repeatedly crop up. These words are intended to capture the state of the shelter as it is thought about and believed to be by the personnel working in it. That is, the participants were most privy to the disorder and dysfunction which pervades – in fact, constitutes – the shelter: their words captured these problems and their deeds reflected (and were reflected in) them.

This is visible through the travails of the three major "players" in the shelter: clients, management (managers and supervisors), and employees (front-line employees and caseworkers). While the clients did not form the primary lens through which the problem of order was narrated, there is little doubt that they are forced to deal with it on a daily basis, ranging from, for example, poor services, the perceived neglect and insolence they believe they experience, to racism. As they see it, what they receive is wholeheartedly insufficient to counteract the type of suffering they endure.

The problem of order is also powerfully illuminated in the difficult and acrimonious relationships between the paid personnel. From the standpoint of management, the shelter needs to be governed in a particular manner, this largely is based on bureaucratic principles that are all encompassing, running the gamut from remuneration and leave to security and health. The strict enforcement of the letter of the law, thus, is a taken-for-granted expectation, a presupposition based upon the inherent value of law. Yet despite this reverence to the black-letter law and the simplicity within which its application is thought possible, there is profound disagreement, even confusion, within the managerial circle. The example of discretion clearly reveals the different ways the managers and supervisors think about the place of, and need for, leeway in applying the rules. In addition, the "zero-tolerance" policy reveals that despite the importance placed on the strict enforcement of the law, incompetence and ignorance make its consistent application a near impossibility. Thus, even among managers and supervisors there is little recourse but to admit that profound problems – verging on dysfunction and confusion – constitute the daily life of the shelter. As management sees it, however, the law is not the problem; the employees are – problems ranging from incompetence and stubbornness to recalcitrance and laziness. All these problems, management further reiterates, can be redressed through the law. The law – like many other antidotes, for example, community (cf. Rose, 1996; Rose, 1999, 173) – functions as tautology. The circular logic which constitutes the views of management means that the shelter cannot be anything other than chaotic.

That the employees do not view the law as such exacerbates the problem of order. Given that the ethic of care is polysemic, the employees wholeheartedly believe that the binary logic of law and its strict enforcement will not provide meaningful care – despite, and somewhat ironically, acknowledging the inherent value of the law, which, however, they realize provides benefits to them at the expense of the clients. Thus, on the face of it, the marked disjuncture and disagreements between management and employees, premised upon the place of legality to the ordering of the shelter, lead to profound disorder and dysfunction and severely affect the deployment of care.

As problematic as these systemic issues are, profound disagreements between the employees make the problem of order even more acute. There are two such disagreements: first, between caseworkers and front-line employees, and second, among the front-line employees.

With respect to the former, the hierarchy that constitutes the ordering of employee relations – a product, partly at least, of the legalized and bureaucratized environment, which management both feeds off of and makes worse – serves to severely splinter the two parties. The result is animosity and suspicion among the two where both believe that each is better suited to understand the clients and their needs. What results is an incessant and bitter battle to lay claim to the deployment of care, which not only disorders the shelter but severely affects the administration of care.

Perhaps what aptly illuminates the disorder and dysfunction of the shelter is the acrimony and disharmony that constitutes the working relationship of the front-line employees, visible in word, deed, sound, and even gesture, and visible incessantly and without any pretensions. This problem, too, is systemic, a product of the polysemy of the ethic of care. This means that there is little or no agreement among front-line workers about what care is and ought to be, and how it should be administered – in fact, there is little agreement about who is deserving of care in the first place, a disagreement that has profound implications for the ordering of the shelter. What results, therefore, is profound disorder visible in the confusion which envelops the shelter: each employee, driven by what he/she believes care is and ought to be, applies or breaks the rules in ways that will meet his/her vision of this ethic. This way of thinking, being and acting is idiosyncratic. This creates animosity and distrust among the employees, where virtually each decision is questioned and often scoffed at. To make matters worse, the care deployed is not uniform – indeed, it *cannot* be. Rather, it is highly subjective and dependent upon which employee is at the helm on a particular day. The daily life of the shelter unfolds as such, cognizance of which every party in the shelter, from the clients to management to the employees, knows very well and understands even better. In fact, front-line employees relish the very disorder and dysfunction which they knowingly create – which they see as orderly and functional. This makes matters that much more difficult for management because without the support of front-line employees – in charge of enforcing the rules and deploying care – its views and visions will simply be thwarted and take a backseat to the desires of the employees. It is in this sense that I speak of the ordering of the shelter as administratively chaotic, constituted by disorder and dysfunction, amounting, simply put, to an utter mess.

Despite the sombre and sober – even damning – picture painted throughout these pages, I conclude with two points that are meant to be, somewhat strangely and obliquely, positive or, at least, reaffirming. Most of the problems outlined here are systemic. This is not to claim that the personnel working in the shelter – from management to employees – do not bear some responsibility. Rather, it is to claim that the bulk of the problems do not lie with the personnel but with the *structuring of care*. In other words, the removal of every employee, from the front lines to the caseworkers, will not necessarily solve the problems inherent in this shelter, and if there is improvement to be found through this technique, it would be marginal at best. This is even after the damning picture painted of the employees – issues ranging from incompetence to recalcitrance to apathy. Despite narrating the work lives of the employees as such, I note, as the first point, that a profound sense of nobleness constitutes their work. There is no doubt that all employees wholeheartedly want to help the clients: this is what constitutes their being and gives them a sense of worthwhileness. In addition, in this narration – and, what most likely will not be received well by some, if not many – the clients must also bear some of the burden for the plight of the shelter. This is not to claim that the clients are undeserving of aid – there is no need to traverse upon this debate. Rather, it is to suggest that one problem in the shelter is that the employees are, simply put, overworked: they are constantly bombarded, even harassed, by a never-ending litany of questions and requests, some valid, others verging on the impractical and ridiculous and illustrating the sheer gall and contempt the clients have for the workers. Thus, what these employees do on a daily basis is most noble (even heroic): they are tasked with performing an inordinate amount of, what is essentially, "dirty work," for which they are remunerated poorly. Many employees perform these tasks well and with admiration. Others, however, do not and might refuse to work. This reaction is less about their unwillingness to care and serve; it is more a sign of an inability to so do – an effort, that is, to structure some order, as ironic as it is, into what is essentially a severely disordered and dysfunctional system (the same can be said of the caseworkers who seek some reprieve behind closed doors or the supervisors who look to ease the burdens of their work which they find difficult to cope with). Thus, the systemic nature of the problem is shone through what looks like shoddy workmanship – which, in some cases, is precisely that. More so than not, however, what is revealed is a system that envelops and swallows the employees whole. Their dissension, even recalcitrance, is merely a reflection of the problems with the system.

The structuring of care, then, is *the* problem. In this light, even management faces the same battles as the employees. However, because it must, by law, implement an order that is legalized and bureaucratized, it simply fuels the problem of order which the employees seek to circumvent. In other words, *the problem of order is (in) the law*, that is, a legalized and bureaucratized environment which is unsuitable – and, therefore, unable – to order a site of care. This leads to the second point, one which might be shocking to some, even many: despite the foregoing, I contend that the system works. The functionality of the system is illuminated when it is understood that an emergency shelter is not meant to solve a problem, but manage it – many employees voiced this loudly. In this regard it functions as a Band-Aid and this it does quite well. It is only when the shelter is tasked with something that it is constitutively unable to perform that a problem arises. It is, in some ways, the institutionalization of care that is the problem, a point Lisa Ferrill (1991) makes: "When we institutionalize homelessness, we have lost the vision of a humane society" (118; see also Stark, 1994, 553).

I have painted a picture of what care looks and feels like, one that is not, and cannot be, comfortable: the care delivered in the shelter is uncomfortable and can only be so. Viewed as such, and with no other pretensions, the shelter works precisely as it is supposed to: it is only when it seeks to do something it cannot, that is, provide long-lasting comfort, that it becomes disorderly and dysfunctional. In other words, and to return once again to the front-line employees, it is only when they seek to promote their vision of care, one which they believe will promote comfort, that the system fails: here even their notions of care fall apart resulting in ad hoc and idiosyncratic ideas of what care is and should be. In many ways, then, if these employees are willing to do what they are tasked with, that is, follow the strict letter of the law, the system will not look as dysfunctional as it is.

Yet, and strangely, it is in the disobedience that the dignity of the clients and employees is found: in the circumvention of the rules, the employees are claiming that the clients deserve much more; in fact, they are claiming that they too, deserve much more. Ironically – and, tragically – it is this very quest and desire that makes matters worse. In other words, and put simply, this work illuminates what care, in an ideal world, should look and feel like, one which the real world of the shelter, however, simply cannot – and *should not* – meet. This, however, is the best that this site, in these conditions, can offer, one that is, as counterintuitive as it sounds, paramount to the well-being and dignity of the clients and employees. It is, in other words, in the very disorder and dysfunction of (and in) the shelter that care is – and can be – shone brightly. The picture is not bright. It is not meant to be. In fact, the history of the shelter suggests that it was never meant to be.

# Epilogue

The foregoing is not meant to be pessimistic or discouraging. Meaningful change is not only possible, but must be part of the mandate for those who wish to challenge orthodoxy. Thus, my intention is not to leave readers with a sense of hopelessness. Nor is it to undercut the profoundly important work performed by scores of people who devote their lives to make meaningful change for the indigent. Rather, I only intend to paint a vividly sobering picture. This is precisely as it should be in order to recognize the significant challenges ahead. This, however, does not foreclose on hope. Rather, it is from precisely such a place that meaningful change is not only possible, but must be conceptualized and administered.

# Appendix: A Note on Method

What is narrated is based on an ethnographic analysis of an emergency shelter for men in a large metropolitan city in the province of Ontario, Canada, undertaken over fifteen months, between September 2010 and December 2011. This involved approximately 300 hours of observation along with sixteen interviews with various personnel who worked in the shelter (namely, front-line workers, caseworkers, supervisors, and managers).

My initial request to observe the shelter was warmly welcomed by a senior member of management. Thereafter, I met with two senior members of management to further discuss my objectives and plans. These issues ranged from time frames, the types of access I desired, along with other issues such as security and confidentiality. In particular, management required assurance that the confidentiality of clients will not be jeopardized, especially for those young-adults between the ages of eighteen and twenty-one. Once these assurances were guaranteed, I was granted permission to commence my observations.

All personnel in the shelter – ranging from employees to clients – had already been informed of my presence when I commenced. This led to a keen sense of curiosity, of both employees and clients alike. Often, while I sat in the lobby during the early stages and sought to immerse and acclimatize myself with the culture of the space, I was approached by clients who wished to know more about who I was and what I was doing – they had either heard about my presence directly from management or indirectly from other clients. There were a few episodes where my presence, it seemed, was not welcomed – some believed that I was a police officer and held serious trepidations. Especially during the outset of the study, I tried to ensure that while I was conspicuous, I was, nevertheless, not obtrusive and obstructive. This helped allay concerns and suspicions. For the most part, however, I was well received by clients and employees. As time passed, fear began to fade and within about two weeks to one month of being in the shelter, I was received more warmly.

The observation phase began in September 2010 and comprised fifty-one visits to the shelter, each lasting, on average, five to six hours. I spent time during the mornings, afternoons, evenings as well as the overnight period and did so throughout the four seasons of the year. A significant part of my time was spent sitting and talking with, and observing, front-line employees, caseworkers, and supervisors in their respective offices (the former two groups occupying more time than the latter). In addition, I followed these persons as they were called to attend to various issues. This led me to other locations in the shelter, for example, upstairs where the sleeping quarters are located, the basement where meals are served and another sleeping quarter is located, and, as well, outside in the vicinity of the shelter. During these "walks" with these persons I was able to observe the way employees and supervisors responded to myriad issues and interacted with clients. Especially during the early stages of the study, as noted above, I spent considerable time sitting in the lobby observing employee and client interactions. During these times, when the opportunity presented itself, I engaged in conversations with clients and interacted with them (this opportunity presented itself quite frequently). I was fortunate to be provided with virtually unlimited access to, and in, the shelter. This allowed me to attend staff meetings and other information sessions, which provided further insights into the inner workings of the shelter.

The interviews were conducted post-observation, beginning in late September 2011. They were largely open-ended and lasted, on average, one hour. I used this opportunity to probe further into what I had observed during the year I spent at the shelter, posing questions and seeking clarification about the issues I had. While I directed the conversation in terms of the subjects I wished to discuss or the questions I required clarification about, I nevertheless encouraged each interviewee to discuss these and other matters as he/she wished.

My approach to this work both in its theoretical ambit and methodology is constituted by an eclecticism that permits a wide array of lenses to penetrate not simply the probing but the narration as well. Thus, while this work generally fits within the confines of an ethnography, its delivery, in several instances (notably in the discussion of the polysemy of an ethic of care, discussed in chapter 7) departs from conventional sociological and socio-legal enterprise.[1] In these instances, and to give full and vivid colour to the discussion, I focus upon the words and deeds of a few employees rather than many. Two individuals, namely, "Captain Delight" and Elizabeth, thus, serve as the primary characters in these narratives.[2] While this approach is not frequently employed, it does share a long and robust history, evinced, for example, in some of the classics of the Chicago School of Sociology, such as *The Jack-Roller* (Shaw, [1930] 1966) or *The Professional Thief* (Sutherland, [1937] 1956). However, rather than using "life history" of single subjects (see Becker, 1966), I situate my effort in the mould of *Street Corner Society* (Whyte, [1943] 1967), which draws on the stories of several characters to paint a picture of the order in, and of, the "Cornerville" neighbourhood.

Finally – and related – to ensure anonymity, there are several instances when I needed to be silent on particular traits about participants or not disclose pertinent information such as sex. Thus, for example, I do not mention the sex of the supervisors and caseworkers because their small numbers would easily lead to identification – three supervisors in total, of whom one is female; and four caseworkers in total, of whom one is male.[3] As well, while I treat supervisors and managers differently, when referring to management as a whole or the management team, I mean both managers and supervisors.

# Notes

## 1. Introduction

1 This phrase is intimately and inextricably intertwined with Charles Manson, who, readers will recall, spoke eerily about an impending apocalyptic war – one drawn on the lines of race and racial tensions between Caucasians and African Americans – prior to the brutal killings he ordered his followers to carry out (see Bugliosi and Gentry, 1974). There are, as well, other popular sites where this phrase is visible, notably in the title of a song – "Helter Skelter" – recorded and released by the Beatles in 1968.

2 It would be remiss not to mention that Deborah Stone (1994) also uses the phrase "helter-shelter" to title her review essay of two important works on homelessness that appeared between 1993 and 1994: Elliot Liebow's *Tell Them Who I Am: The Lives of Homeless Women* (1993) and *The Homeless* by Christopher Jencks (1994). Stone's usage of this phrase, however, has little or nothing to do with emergency shelters or the chaos and disorder in them.

3 A distinction is often drawn between the sociology of law – emanating from the tradition of Roscoe Pound (1910, 1911, 1912a, 1912b, 1931) and later Karl Llewellyn (1930, 1931) – and "law and society" scholarship. I do not wish to trammel upon this debate as it is not pertinent to the discussion to follow, though I am sensitive to this history (Adler and Simon, 2014; Simon, 1999; Friedman, 1986; and Constable, 1994 contain good histories of these scholarships).

## 2. Locating the Shelter, Locating an Ethic of Care

1 This section draws heavily from this interview and all uncited quotations are from it.

2 On the distinction between charity and care, see Held (2006, 44).
3 The name I will use to identify the area in which the shelter is located.

## 3. An Inside (and Closer) Look at the Shelter

1 It is unclear whether the lobby was part of the shelter itself – for example,
Desjarlais (1997) also writes that "residents often preferred to hang
'outside' – that is, in the lobby rather than in the shelter" (79).
2 I have consciously omitted the importance of odour, which is discussed in
detail in a future section.
3 Many have described the smells of a shelter as a mixture of things. For
example, Lisa Ferrill (1991) writes that "the air was stale, thick with odors
from old clothes, shoes, laundry detergent, and the overused dryer" (9),
and Irene Glasser (1988) writes of "a strong odor of cleaning materials,
perspiration, and old food [which] greets one at the entrance" (24).
Regardless of how it is described, the smell in a shelter is palpable and, if
"not unbearable," as Anthony Marcus (2003) writes of his experience, then
certainly "unpleasant and just nauseating enough to put one a little on
edge" (137).

## 4. From the Mundane to the Chaotic

1 This, I learned firsthand very early in my observations. One day, while
seated in the lobby observing what was transpiring, a client who was
seated next to me, and whom I recognized from before, muttered
something along the following lines: "Go home Paki, we don't want your
studies here; go home Paki." It was not so much that I was either startled
or fearful – such comments, and worse, are not so infrequently levelled
at me – but that for the fear of losing the ability to continue my study,
I reported this incident to a member of the management team, as I had
very clearly been instructed to do if such a situation arose. His reaction
was comical (though well intended) insofar as he treated this threat – if it,
indeed, could be termed one – as a serious security issue to my well-being
and the well-being of everyone in the shelter. In fact, for him, it was as if
I had already been physically assaulted. After profusely apologizing to
me, he asked a supervisor to counsel the client that such racial epithets
and derogatory comments will not be tolerated in the shelter and that he
would be denied services if he continued in such a manner. I, however,
persuaded the supervisor to take no further action, again, because I was
not necessarily put-off by the comment and was more concerned about

losing any credibility with the clients and employees which might hinder the rest of my project. The example is a vivid reminder not only of the racialized space of the shelter, but how this issue impacts the ordering of the shelter, so much that it is translated into an issue about safety, including the threat of violence and bodily harm.

2 I have altered the name to ensure anonymity.

3 In some instances, however, youth has been highlighted as an important characteristic that can aid in the provision of service and care largely because the very inexperience that comes with being young can also be beneficial in terms of keeping an open mind and attitude. This is what Scott Seider (2010) found during his observations of students at Harvard University who volunteered at and essentially ran the Harvard Square Homeless Shelter during the school term.

4 Poor remuneration is often responsible for these problems (see Ferrill, 1991, 85–6; Loseke, 1992, 71). Donileen Loseke (1992), for example, writes that she "once ... reemerged [after vacation] to find a totally new group of workers had replaced the ones ... [she] knew," and that "by the end of the third year of operation, it took a great deal of time, energy, and advertising to find *any* candidate for an open job" (6, 66, emphasis in original).

5 Towards the twilight of my observations, the union which represented the employees was contemplating a strike (the strike materialized just after I had finished the study). In preparation for the looming strike, numerous meetings between the representatives of the union and employees were held in order to convey the results of the negotiations and keep employees abreast of the next steps. Interestingly, from what I was told by the employees, the two sides were far apart, especially with respect to pay. The employees, it appears, were requesting an approximately $8 per hour raise (if true, a rather absurd amount given that it would have been an increase of close to 70 per cent of their current pay – though, given the events which transpired in many cities across the United States in September 2014, where workers from numerous fast- food chains requested a 50 percent pay increase, this might not seem so absurd). They were, however, offered an increase of $0.30 per hour, and later, again according to what the employees believed, $0.23 (that is, the offer had been reduced, another seemingly absurd claim). I am uninterested in the veracity of such claims. Rather, I simply underscore that the distance between the two sides, as narrated to me by the employees, is illustrative of how poorly they feel they were being treated, remuneration being one important consideration. As "Captain Delight" put it to me, management was "showing no respect" to the employees and their plight.

## 5. The Securitization of an Ethic of Care and the Administration of Chaos

1 As I explicate in the next chapter, the threat of physical violence and bodily harm is felt most acutely by the male employees and less so by the female employees, even to the point of being inexistent for them. This disjuncture further complicates the order in the shelter and the deployment of care.
2 As discussed in chapter 3, the glass pane facing the main entrance, over and beyond providing good visibility about the "comings and goings" in the shelter, also contains a small opening that allows clients who have been denied entry to plead their case or, query why they are unable to enter.
3 Conceptually, this is similar to what Jonathan Simon (2007) describes as "governing through crime," where a large part of life – for example, immigration, family, and health – are subsumed into discourses about crime. Crime and criminality, thus, become the guide by which daily life is organized and unfolds.
4 This much was plainly evident on the first day I began my observations, when a supervisor who was helping me acclimatize to the surroundings provided me with a copy of the collective agreement between management and the union. This act – virtually the first word and deed between us – was accompanied by a few cautionary words to the effect that management needs to be very careful about how it interacts with the employees; thus, the supervisor suggested that I too read through and familiarize myself with it.

## 6. Gendered Security and a Gendered an Ethic of Care

1 In an earlier iteration of this position (see Ranasinghe, 2013b), I was prohibited from bracketing the "un" in front of the "doing," so that rather than reading as "(un)doing," as it currently reads, it read as "undoing." In bracketing the "un," I am making the case that gender is, as will be apparent, simultaneously (un)done (un)consciously, something profoundly pertinent to the production of gender and security in the site under consideration (see Butler 1990, 2004).
2 I am aware that West and Zimmerman (2009) have distanced themselves from the "undoing gender" approach because it is thought to be theoretically untenable. "Gender" they write, "is not *undone* so much as *redone*" (118, emphasis in original). In using this term, I only mean the redoing of gender through practice and speech, rather than suggesting that gender can be *un*done (for a similar approach, see Chan, Doran, and Marel, 2010). Additionally, I also explicitly distance myself from the normative aspirations

that the term attaches itself to. It is worth noting, even if only in passing, that while "doing gender" limited itself, perhaps unintentionally, strictly to gender, "doing difference" (West and Fenstermaker, 1995; Fenstermaker and West, 2002) – an expanded and revised formulation in which West and Fenstermaker (1995) acknowledged that "doing gender" "is an incomplete framework for understanding social inequality" (9) – "provide[d] an understanding of how gender, race and class operate simultaneously with one another" (114). Though acknowledging the roles that race and class (can) play in constituting subjectivity, I nevertheless use the term "(un)doing gender" – rather than difference – because it is gender, more than others, that plays a role in producing concerns over primary safety.

3  In chapters 7 and 8, I examine how the rules are broken or circumvented through the conscious decisions the employees (both men and women) make. In this section, I focus on the ways feelings of safety and comfort, influenced by gender, *unconsciously* contribute to the circumvention of these rules.

4  I use the word (un)conscious because it is not entirely clear whether the supervisor is – and other supervisors are – aware of how, in this particular context, these actions are (or can be) unconscious. This would mean that the supervisor believed that these are deliberate choices.

## 7. The Logic of Legality and the Administration of Chaos

1  I have already explicated the ways that the legal consciousness of these employees vacillates between, on the one hand, ideology and, on the other, hegemony, and the active struggles along this continuum that shape thinking and acting (see Ranasinghe, 2014). I refrain from discussing this further for it is not pertinent to the argument developed here.

2  There is, however, evidence that some shelters were not rule-bound in the ways described above. Donileen Loseke (1992), for example, writes of the place she observed, "This was not a rule-bound organization … There were many rules on the record. But, formally, no rule carried any specific sanction and the primary rule was that all rules were negotiable" (68). Similarly, Jeff Karabanow (1999) speaks of a particular shelter he studied as "an open system that functions on flexible, innovative, nonbureaucratic, and nonhierarchical structures," and that "within the agency, there are few house rules" (343; see also Bridgman, 2003). Yet, in many of these discussions, not only does it appear that the rules were, in fact, implemented, but that they were implemented uniformly by the employees (see Loseke, 1992, 67; Spencer and McKinney, 1997, 197–8).

3 The right to discretion, as I have discussed previously, is significant to the ordering of the shelter because it hierarchically distinguishes caseworkers and front-line employees according more power to one group. This creates resentment leading to a tepid and distant relationship, only serving to render the deployment of care (more) difficult.

4 Niklas Luhmann (1989), for example, writes of his autopoietic theory that law, which is premised upon processing normative expectations "requires a binary code that contains a positive value (justice) and a negative value (injustice), and that artificially excludes both contradictions (justice is injustice, injustice is justice) and other values ..." (140). Such a view, which is starkly in contradistinction to the theory of Pierre Bourdieu (1987), for example, nevertheless finds at least some resonance in Bourdieu's own work who, though for the most part seeks to extricate himself from the binary logic of law (824–7), nevertheless admits that the law "need[s] to come to a decision – a decision relatively 'black or white,' for the plaintiff or for the defendant: guilty or not guilty, liable or not liable" (832). This is also visible in the exclusivity of law narrated by Boaventura De Sousa Santos (1987, 281–2). These are only a few examples of the many that can be mustered for law's binary character. I am not positioning my argument within these camps. Rather, I am simply stating that law can be read as constituted upon a binary code, which numerous narratives – even when in stark opposition to one another – countenance (see also Valverde, 1996, 207–11, who discusses the binary coding the law relies upon to filter and make sense of expert evidence in human rights cases, one example pertaining to the binary coding of sexuality the law creates between heterosexuality and homosexuality).

5 As Martin Lipsky ([1980] 2010) notes, "Situations [are] too complicated to [be] reduced to programmatic formats" and, thus, "the exercise of discretion" is a "critical dimension of ... [such] work ..." (15, xi).

6 This distinction stems from its historical predecessor found in early-modern England between the "sturdy" or "able-bodied" versus the "impotent" beggar (see Ranasinghe, 2010a, 59–61; Katz, 1989, 11–16).

## Appendix

1 I am mindful that some, even many, might not necessarily be comfortable with the use of the word "ethnography" to describe and characterize this inquiry, especially in anthropological circles, which rather narrowly permit the use of the term. Given that this work is based upon fieldwork, I hold no trepidations about which label to give it, and I am comfortable

replacing the word ethnography with fieldwork for those who might object to its use. My use of the term "ethnography," however, is strictly in the sociological sense, and this, too, in a very specific manner, as explicated in this section.

2 The names are fictitious. One day, while conversing with several employees, one employee used the name "Captain Delight" in a facetious manner to convey the morose attitude that constitutes "Captain Delight" and his outlook towards life, and I thought it perfectly captured everything he is not but what others wished he would – but, perhaps, could not – be.

3 I depart from this rule once when discussing an episode where the gender of the subject is essential to the story (see chapter 4); here, this departure does not pose any risk to the subject.

# Bibliography

Adler, Michael, and Jonathan Simon. 2014. "Stepwise Progression: The Past, Present, and Possible Future of Empirical Research on Law in the United States and the United Kingdom." *Journal of Law and Society* 41 (2): 173–202. http://dx.doi.org/10.1111/j.1467-6478.2014.00663.x.

Anderson, Isobel, and Julie Christian. 2003. "Causes of Homelessness in the UK: A Dynamic Analysis." *Journal of Community & Applied Social Psychology* 13 (2): 105–18. http://dx.doi.org/10.1002/casp.714.

Anderson, Nels. 1923. *The Hobo: The Sociology of the Homeless Man.* Chicago: University of Chicago Press.

Arnold, Thurman W. [1935] 1941. *The Symbols of Government.* New Haven, Connecticut: Yale University Press.

Bachelard, Gaston. [1958] 1994. *The Poetics of Space.* Translated by M. Jolas. Boston: Beacon Press.

Banfield, Edward C. [1970] 1974. *The Unheavenly City Revisited: A Revision of The Unheavenly City.* Boston: Little Brown and Co.

Bauman, Zygmunt. 2007. *Consuming Life.* Cambridge: Polity Press.

Becker, Howard S. 1966. "Introduction." In *The Jack-Roller: A Delinquent Boy's Own Story,* by Clifford R. Shaw, v–xviii. Chicago: University of Chicago Press.

Benbow, Sarah, Cheryl Forchuk, and Susan L. Ray. 2011. "Mothers with Mental Illness Experiencing Homelessness: A Critical Analysis." *Journal of Psychiatric and Mental Health Nursing* 18 (8): 687–95. http://dx.doi.org/10.1111/j.1365-2850.2011.01720.x.

Bentham, Jeremy. [1811] 1962. "Principles of Penal Law." *The Works of Jeremy Bentham.* Vol. 1, 365–580. New York: Russell and Russell.

Berry, Brent. 2007. "A Repeated Observation Approach for Estimating the Street Homeless Population." *Evaluation Review* 31 (2): 166–99. http://dx.doi.org/10.1177/0193841X06296947.

Bhabha, Homi. [1989] 1994. *The Location of Culture.* London: Routledge.

Bourdieu, Pierre. 1987. "The Force of Law: Toward a Sociology of the Juridical Field." Translated by Richard Terdiman. *Hastings Law Journal* 38 (5): 805–53.

Bourdieu, Pierre, and Loic Wacquant. 1992. *An Invitation to Reflexive Sociology.* Chicago: University of Chicago Press.

Bridgman, Rae. 2003. *Safe Haven: The Story of a Shelter for Homeless Women.* Toronto: University of Toronto Press. http://dx.doi.org/10.3138/9781442 679535.

Bugliosi, Vincent, and Curt Gentry. 1974. *Helter-Skelter: The True Story of the Manson Murders.* New York: W.W. Norton.

Burris, Scott. 2006. "From Security to Health." In *Democracy, Society and the Governance of Security,* Edited by Jennifer Wood and Benoit Dupont, 196–216. Cambridge: Cambridge University Press. http://dx.doi.org/10.1017/CBO9780511489358.010.

Burt, Martha R. 1995. "Critical Factors in Counting the Homeless: An Invited Commentary." *American Journal of Orthopsychiatry* 65 (3): 334–9. http://dx.doi.org/10.1037/h0085059.

Butler, Judith. 1990. *Gender Trouble: Feminism and the Subversion of Identity.* New York: Routledge.

–. 2004. *Undoing Gender.* New York: Routledge.

Casey, Rionach, Rosalind Goudie, and Kesia Reeve. 2008. "Homeless Women in Public Spaces: Strategies of Resistance." *Housing Studies* 23 (6): 899–916. http://dx.doi.org/10.1080/02673030802416627.

Chan, Janet, Sally Doran, and Christina Marel. 2010. "Doing and Undoing Gender in Policing." *Theoretical Criminology* 14 (4): 425–46. http://dx.doi.org/10.1177/1362480610376408.

Clark, Candace. 1987. "Sympathy Biography and Sympathy Margin." *American Journal of Sociology* 93 (2): 290–321. http://dx.doi.org/10.1086/228746.

Connell, Robert. 1987. *Gender and Power: Society, the Person and Sexual Politics.* Redwood City, CA: Stanford University Press.

Connolly, Deborah R. 2000. *Homeless Mothers: Face to Face with Women and Poverty.* Minneapolis: University of Minnesota Press.

Conradson, David. 2003. "Spaces of Care in the City: The Place of a Community Drop-in Centre." *Social & Cultural Geography* 4 (4): 507–25. http://dx.doi.org/10.1080/1464936032000137939.

Constable, Marianne. 1994. "Genealogy and Jurisprudence: Nietzsche, Nihilism, and the Social Scientification of Law." *Law & Social Inquiry* 19 (3): 551–90. http://dx.doi.org/10.1111/j.1747-4469.1994.tb00770.x.

Culhane, Dennis P. 1992. "The Quandaries of Shelter Reform: An Appraisal of Efforts to 'Manage' Homelessness." *Social Service Review* 66 (3): 428–40. http://dx.doi.org/10.1086/603931.

–. 1996. "The Homeless Shelter and the Nineteenth-Century Poorhouse: Comparing Notes from Two Eras of 'Indoor Relief.'" In *Myths about the Powerless*. Edited by B. Lykes, A. Banuazizi, R. Liem, and W. Morris, 50–71. Philadelphia: Temple University Press.

de Certeau, Michel. [1980] 1984. *The Practice of Everyday Life*. Translated by S. Rendall. Berkeley: University of California Press.

de Lint, Willem. 1998. "New Managerialism and Canadian Police Training Reform." *Social & Legal Studies* 7 (2): 261–85. http://dx.doi.org/10.1177/096466399800700206.

Dear, Michael J., and Jennifer R. Wolch 1987. *Landscapes of Despair: From Deinstitutionalization to Homelessness*. Cambridge: Polity Press.

Desjarlais, Robert. 1996. "The Office of Reason: On the Politics of Language and Agency in a Shelter for 'the Homeless Mentally Ill.'" *American Ethnologist* 23 (4): 880–900. http://dx.doi.org/10.1525/ae.1996.23.4.02a00110.

–. 1997. *Shelter Blues: Sanity and Selfhood among the Homeless*. Philadelphia: University of Pennsylvania Press. http://dx.doi.org/10.9783/9780812206432.

–. 1999. "The Makings of Personhood in a Shelter for People Considered Homeless and Mentally Ill." *Ethos* 27 (4): 466–89.

Deutsch, Francine M. 2007. "Undoing Gender." *Gender & Society* 21 (1): 106–27. http://dx.doi.org/10.1177/0891243206293577.

DeWard, Sarah L., and Angela M. Moe. 2010. "'Like a Prison!' Homeless Women's Narratives of Surviving Shelter." *Journal of Sociology and Social Welfare* 37 (1): 115–35.

Dezalay, Yves, and Mikael R. Madsen. 2012. "The Force of Law and Lawyers: Pierre Bourdieu and the Reflexive Sociology of Law." *Annual Review of Law and Social Science* 8 (1): 433–52. http://dx.doi.org/10.1146/annurev-lawsocsci-102811-173817.

Dordick, Gwendolyn A. 1996. "More than Refuge: The Social World of a Homeless Shelter." *Journal of Contemporary Ethnography* 24 (4): 373–404.

Dworkin, Ronald. 1986. *Law's Empire*. Cambridge, MA: Harvard University Press.

Edelman, Murray. 1964. *The Symbolic Uses of Politics*. Urbana: University of Illinois Press.

–. 1971. *Politics as Symbolic Action: Mass Arousal and Quiescence*. New York: Academic Press.

Elias, Christopher J., and Thomas S. Inui. 1993. "When a House Is Not a Home: Exploring the Meaning of Shelter among Chronically Homeless Older Men." *Gerontologist* 33 (3): 396–402. http://dx.doi.org/10.1093/geront/33.3.396.

Elias, Norbert. [1939] 1978. *The History of Manners*, Vol. 1. *The Civilizing Process*. Translated by Edmund Jephcott. New York: Urizen Books.

Ellickson, Robert. 1991. *Order without Law: How Neighbors Settle Disputes.* Cambridge, MA: Harvard University Press.

Engel, David M. 1984. "The Oven Bird's Song: Insiders, Outsiders and Personal Injuries in an American Community." *Law & Society Review* 18 (4): 551–81. http://dx.doi.org/10.2307/3053447.

Etzioni, Amitai. 1993. *The Spirit of the Community: Rights, Responsibilities, and the Communitarian Agenda.* New York: Crown Publishers Inc.

–. 1996. *The New Golden Rule: Community and Morality in a Democratic Society.* New York: Basic Books.

Ewick, Patricia, and Susan Silbey. 2016. "Looking for Hegemony in all the Wrong Places: Critique, Context and Collectivities in Studies of Legal Consciousness." Paper presented at the Working the Boundaries of Law Conference. Sponsored by the European Research Council. The International Institute for the Sociology of Law, Oñati, Spain, 10 March.

Fanon, Frantz. [1952] 1967. *Black Skin, White Masks.* New York: Grove Press.

–. [1961] 1968. *The Wretched of the Earth.* New York: Grove Press.

Featherstone, Mike. 2007. *Consumer Culture and Postmodernism.* 2nd ed. London: Sage.

Fenstermaker, Sarah, and Candace West, eds. 2002. *Doing Gender, Doing Difference: Inequality, Power and Institutional Change.* London: Routledge.

Ferrill, Lisa. 1991. *A Far Cry from Home: Life in a Shelter for Homeless Women.* Chicago: Noble Press.

Fischer, Sean N., Marybeth Shinn, Patrick Shrout, and Sam Tsemberis. 2008. "Homelessness, Mental Illness and Criminal Activity: Explaining Patterns over Time." *American Journal of Community Psychology* 42 (3–4): 251–65. http://dx.doi.org/10.1007/s10464-008-9210-z.

Foucault, Michel. [1976] 1980. "Questions on Geography." In *Power/Knowledge: Selected Interviews and Other Writings, 1972–1977.* Edited and translated by Colin Gordan, 63–77. New York: Pantheon Books.

–. 1984. "Space, Knowledge and Power." Interview by Paul Rabinow. Translated by Christian Hubert. In *The Foucault Reader.* Edited by Paul Rabinow, 239–56. New York: Pantheon Books.

Friedman, Bruce D. 1994. "No Place Like Home: A Study of two Homeless Shelters." *Journal of Social Distress and the Homeless* 3 (4): 321–40. http://dx.doi.org/10.1007/BF02091836.

Friedman, Lawrence M. 1986. "The Law and Society Movement." *Stanford Law Review* 38 (3): 763–80. http://dx.doi.org/10.2307/1228563.

Gaetz, Stephen. 2004. "Safe Streets for Whom? Homeless Youth, Social Exclusion and Criminal Victimization." *Canadian Journal of Criminology and Criminal Justice* 46 (4): 423–56. http://dx.doi.org/10.3138/cjccj.46.4.423.

Gaetz, Stephen, and Bill O'Grady. 2002. "Making Money: Exploring the Economy of Young Homeless Workers." *Work, Employment and Society* 16 (3): 433–56. http://dx.doi.org/10.1177/095001702762217425.

Galanter, Marc. 1974. "Why the 'Haves' Come Out Ahead: Speculations on the Limits of Legal Change." *Law & Society Review* 9 (1): 95–160. http://dx.doi.org/10.2307/3053023.

Gans, Herbert J. 1972. "The Positive Functions of Poverty." *American Journal of Sociology* 78 (2): 275–89. http://dx.doi.org/10.1086/225324.

Giddens, Anthony. 1984. *The Constitution of Society: Outline of the Theory of Structuration*. Cambridge: Polity Press.

–. 1991. *Modernity and Self-Identity in the Late Modern-Age*. Oxford: Polity Press.

Gilligan, Carol. 1982. *In a Different Voice: Psychological Theory and Women's Development*. Cambridge, MA: Harvard University Press.

Glasser, Irene. 1988. *More than Bread: Ethnography of a Soup Kitchen*. Tuscaloosa: University of Alabama Press.

Goffman, Erving. [1956] 1959. *The Presentation of Self in Everyday Life*. New York: Doubleday/Anchor Books.

–. 1961. *Asylums: Essays on the Social Situation of Mental Patients and Other Inmates*. New York: Doubleday and Company.

Goodey, Jo. 1997. "Boys Don't Cry: Masculinities, Fear of Crime and Fearlessness." *British Journal of Criminology* 37 (3): 401–18. http://dx.doi.org/10.1093/oxfordjournals.bjc.a014177.

Greenhous, Brereton. 1968. "Paupers and Poorhouses: The Development of Poor Relief in Early New Brunswick." *Histoire Social/Social History* 1: 103–26.

Greiffenhagen, Christiane. 2014. "The Materiality of Mathematics: Presenting Mathematics at the Blackboard." *British Journal of Sociology* 65 (3): 502–28. http://dx.doi.org/10.1111/1468-4446.12037.

Grunberg, Jeffrey, and Paula F. Eagle. 1990. "Shelterization: How the Homeless Adapt to Shelter Living." *Hospital & Community Psychiatry* 41 (5): 521–5.

Gusfield, Joseph R. 1963. *Symbolic Crusade: Status Politics and the American Temperance Movement*. Urbana: University of Illinois Press.

–. 1981. *The Culture of Public Problems: Drinking-Driving and the Symbolic Order*. Chicago: University of Chicago Press.

Habermas, Jurgen. [1962] 1989. *The Structural Transformation of the Public Sphere: An Inquiry into a Category of Bourgeois Society*. Translated by Thomas Burger. Cambridge, MA: MIT Press.

Hagan, John, and Bill McCarthy 1997. *Mean Streets: Youth Crime and Homelessness*. Cambridge: Cambridge University Press. http://dx.doi.org/10.1017/CBO9780511625497.

Hallsworth, Simon, and John Lea. 2011. "Reconstructing Leviathan: Emerging Contours of the Security State." *Theoretical Criminology* 15 (2): 141–57. http://dx.doi.org/10.1177/1362480610383451.

Hannigan, John. 1998. *Fantasy City: Pleasure and Profit in the Postmodern Metropolis*. London: Routledge.

Hart, Herbert. L.A. [1961] 1967. *The Concept of Law*. Oxford: Oxford University Press.

Held, Virginia. 2006. *The Ethics of Care: Personal, Political, and Global*. Oxford: Oxford University Press.

Himmelfarb, Gertrude. 1995. *The De-Moralization of Society: From Victorian Virtues to Modern Values*. New York: Alfred A. Knopf.

Hobbes, Thomas. [1651] 1985. *Leviathan, or The Matter, Forme, and Power of a Common-Wealth, Ecclesiasticall and Civill*. London: Penguin Books.

Hopper, Kim. 2003. *Reckoning with Homelessness*. Ithaca, NY: Cornell University Press.

Huey, Laura. 2007. *Negotiating Demands: The Politics of Skid Row Policing in Edinburgh, San Francisco and Vancouver*. Toronto: University of Toronto Press.

–. 2012. *Invisible Victims: Homelessness and the Growing Security Gap*. Toronto: University of Toronto Press.

Jameson, Fredric. 1984. "Postmodernism or the Cultural Logic of Late Capitalism." *New Left Review* 146: 53–92.

Jencks, Christopher. 1994. *The Homeless*. Cambridge, MA: Harvard University Press.

Karabanow, Jeffrey. 1999. "When Caring Is Not Enough: Emotional Labor and Youth Shelter Workers." *Social Service Review* 73 (3): 340–57. http://dx.doi.org/10.1086/514427.

–. 2002. "Open for Business: Exploring the Life Stages of Two Canadian Street Youth Shelters." *Journal of Sociology and Social Welfare* 29 (4): 99–116.

–. 2006. "Becoming a Street Kid: Exploring the Stages of Street Life." *Journal of Human Behavior in the Social Environment* 13 (2): 49–72. http://dx.doi.org/10.1300/J137v13n02_04.

Karabanow, Jeff, Jean Hughes, Jann Ticknor, Sean Kidd, and Dorothy Patterson. 2010. "The Economics of Being Young and Poor: How Homeless Youth Survive Neo-Liberal Times." *Journal of Sociology and Social Welfare* 37: 39–64.

Katz, Michael B. 1986. *In the Shadow of the Poorhouse: A Social History of Welfare in America*. New York: Basic Books.

–. 1989. *The Undeserving Poor: From the War on Poverty to the War on Welfare*. New York: Pantheon Books.

Kissane, Rebecca J. 2006. "Responsible but Uninformed? Nonprofit Executive and Program Directors' Knowledge of Welfare Reform." *Social Service Review* 80 (2): 322–45. http://dx.doi.org/10.1086/501490.

Klodawsky, Fran. 2006. "Landscapes on the Margins: Gender and Homelessness in Canada." *Gender, Place and Culture* 13 (4): 365–81. http://dx.doi.org/10.1080/09663690600808478.

Klodawsky, Fran, Tim Aubry, and Susan Farrell. 2006. "Care and the Lives of Homeless Youth in Neoliberal Times in Canada." *Gender, Place and Culture* 13 (4): 419–36. http://dx.doi.org/10.1080/09663690600808577.

Latour, Bruno. 1988. "Mixing Humans and Nonhumans Together: The Sociology of a Door-Closer." *Social Problems* 35 (3): 298–310. http://dx.doi.org/10.2307/800624.

Layton, Jack. 2000. *Homelessness: The Making and Unmaking of a Crisis*. Toronto: Penguin Books.

Lefebvre, Henri. [1974] 1991. *The Production of Space*. Translated by D. Nicholson-Smith. Oxford: Blackwell Publishing.

Levine, Kay, and Virginia Mellema. 2001. "Strategizing the Street: How Law Matters in the Lives of Women in the Street-Level Drug Economy." *Law & Social Inquiry* 26 (1): 169–207. http://dx.doi.org/10.1111/j.1747-4469.2001.tb00175.x.

Lewis, Oscar. 1966. "The Culture of Poverty." *Scientific American* 215 (4): 19–25. http://dx.doi.org/10.1038/scientificamerican1066-19.

Liebow, Elliot. 1993. *Tell Them Who I Am: The Lives of Homeless Women* New York: The Free Press.

Lindsey, Elizabeth W. 1998. "Service Providers' Perception of Factors that Help or Hinder Homeless Families." *Families in Society* 79 (2): 160–72. http://dx.doi.org/10.1606/1044-3894.1815.

Lipsky, Martin. [1980] 2010. *Street-Level Bureaucracy: Dilemmas of the Individual in Public Services*. New York: Russell Sage Foundation.

Llewellyn, Karl N. 1930. "A Realistic Jurisprudence – The Next Step." *Columbia Law Review* 30 (4): 431–65. http://dx.doi.org/10.2307/1114548.

–. 1931. "Some Realism about Realism – Responding to Dean Pound." *Harvard Law Review* 44 (8): 1222–64. http://dx.doi.org/10.2307/1332182.

Loader, Ian, and Neil Walker. 2007. *Civilizing Security*. Cambridge: Cambridge University Press. http://dx.doi.org/10.1017/CBO9780511611117.

Locke, John. [1689] 1982. *Second Treatise of Government: An Essay Concerning the True Original Extent and End of Civil Government*. Edited by R.H. Cox. Wheeling, IL: Harlem Davidson.

Loseke, Donileen R. 1992. *The Battered Woman and Shelters: The Social Construction of Wife Abuse*. Albany: State University of New York Press.

Luhmann, Niklas. 1989. "Law as a Social System." Translated by Shierry Weber Nicholson. *Northwestern University Law Review* 83 (1): 136–50.

Lyon-Callo, Vincent. 2004. *Inequality, Poverty, and Neoliberal Governance: Activist Ethnography in the Homeless Sheltering Industry.* Peterborough, ON: Broadview Press.

Macaulay, Stewart. 1963. "Non-Contractual Relations in Business: A Preliminary Study." *American Sociological Review* 28 (1): 55–67. http://dx.doi.org/10.2307/2090458.

Marcus, Anthony. 2003. "Shelterization Revisited: Some Methodological Dangers of Institutional Studies of the Homeless." *Human Organization* 62 (2): 134–42. http://dx.doi.org/10.17730/humo.62.2.1p2kehqeva66mt4p.

Martell, Daniel A. 1991. "Homeless Mentally Disordered Offenders and Violent Crime: Preliminary Research Findings." *Law and Human Behavior* 15 (4): 333–47. http://dx.doi.org/10.1007/BF02074075.

Martin, Patricia Y. 2003. "'Said and Done' Versus 'Saying and Doing': Gendering Practices, Practicing Gender at Work." *Gender & Society* 17 (3): 342–66. http://dx.doi.org/10.1177/0891243203017003002.

Marvasti, Amir B. 2002. "Constructing the Service-Worthy Homeless through Narrative Editing." *Journal of Contemporary Ethnography* 31 (5): 615–51. http://dx.doi.org/10.1177/089124102236544.

Mitchell, Don, and Nik Heynen. 2009. "The Geography of Survival and the Right to the City: Speculations on Surveillance, Legal Innovation, and the Criminalization of Intervention." *Urban Geography* 30 (6): 611–32. http://dx.doi.org/10.2747/0272-3638.30.6.611.

Mnookin, Robert, and Lewis Kornhauser. 1979. "Bargaining in the Shadow of Law: The Case of Divorce." *Yale Law Journal* 88 (5): 950–97. http://dx.doi.org/10.2307/795824.

Moore, Tim, Morag McArthur, and Debbie Noble-Carr. 2011. "Lessons Learned from Children Who Have Experienced Homelessness: What Services Need to Know." *Children & Society* 25 (2): 115–26. http://dx.doi.org/10.1111/j.1099-0860.2009.00270.x.

Moran, Leslie J. 2012. "Review Essay: Visual Justice." *International Journal of Law in Context* 8 (3): 431–46. http://dx.doi.org/10.1017/S1744552312000286.

Mulcahy, Linda. 2011. *Legal Architecture: Justice, Due Process and the Place of Law.* Oxford: Routledge.

Nielson, Laura Beth. 2000. "Situating Legal Consciousness: Experiences and Attitudes of Ordinary Citizens about Law and Street Harassment." *Law & Society Review* 34 (4): 1055–90. http://dx.doi.org/10.2307/3115131.

Noddings, Nel. 1984. *Caring: A Feminine Approach to Ethics and Moral Education.* Berkeley, CA: University of California Press.

O'Grady, Bill, and Stephen Gaetz. 2004. "Homelessness, Gender and Subsistence: The Case of Toronto Street Youth." *Journal of Youth Studies* 7 (4): 397–416. http://dx.doi.org/10.1080/1367626042000315194.

Occupational Health and Safety Act. 1990. Statutes of Ontario. *R.S.O* c:1.

Paris, Roland. 2001. "Human Security: Paradigm Shift or Hot Air?" *International Security* 26 (2): 87–102. http://dx.doi.org/10.1162/016228801753191141.

Pearson, Geraldine S., and Sheila Linz. 2011. "Editorial: Linking Homelessness with Mental Illness." *Perspectives in Psychiatric Care* 47 (4): 165–6. http://dx.doi.org/10.1111/j.1744-6163.2011.00317.x.

Ponce, Alison N., Ashley Clayton, Jenny Noia, Michael Rowe, and Maria J. O'Connell. 2012. "Making Meaning of Citizenship: Mental Illness, Forensic Involvement, and Homelessness." *Journal of Forensic Psychology Practice* 12 (4): 349–65. http://dx.doi.org/10.1080/15228932.2012.695660.

Pound, Roscoe. 1910. "Law in Books and Law in Action." *American Law Review* 44 (1): 12–36.

–. 1911. "The Scope and Purpose of Sociological Jurisprudence: I. Schools of Jurists and Methods of Jurisprudence." *Harvard Law Review* 24 (8): 591–619. http://dx.doi.org/10.2307/1324094.

–. 1912a. "The Scope and Purpose of Sociological Jurisprudence [Continued]." *Harvard Law Review* 25 (2): 140–68.

–. 1912b. "The Scope and Purpose of Sociological Jurisprudence [Concluded.] III. Sociological Jurisprudence." *Harvard Law Review* 25 (6): 489–516. http://dx.doi.org/10.2307/1324775.

–. 1931. "The Call for a Realist Jurisprudence." *Harvard Law Review* 44 (5): 697–711. http://dx.doi.org/10.2307/1331791.

Ranasinghe, Prashan. 2010a. "Re-conceptualizing Vagrancy and Reconstructing the Vagrant: A Socio-legal Analysis of Criminal Law Reform in Canada, 1953–1972." *Osgoode Hall Law Journal* 48 (1): 55–94.

–. 2010b. "Ambivalence towards Law: Business Improvement Associations, Public Disorder and Legal Consciousness." *International Journal of Law in Context* 6 (4): 323–42. http://dx.doi.org/10.1017/S1744552310000273.

–. 2011. "Public Disorder and its Relation to the Community-Civility-Consumption Triad: A Case Study on the Uses and Users of Contemporary Urban Public Space." *Urban Studies* 48 (9): 1925–43. http://dx.doi.org/10.1177/0042098010379275.

–. 2012a. "Jane Jacobs' Framing of Public Disorder and its Relation to the 'Broken Windows' Theory." *Theoretical Criminology* 16 (1): 63–84. http://dx.doi.org/10.1177/1362480611406947.

–. 2012b. "Vagrancy as a Penal Problem: The Logistics of Administering Punishment in Late-Nineteenth-Century Canada." *Journal of Historical Sociology* 25 (4): 531–51. http://dx.doi.org/10.1111/j.1467-6443.2012.01427.x.

–. 2013a. "Discourse, Practice and the Production of the Polysemy of Security." *Theoretical Criminology* 17 (1): 89–107. http://dx.doi.org/10.1177/1362480612 466564.

–. 2013b. "'Undoing' Gender and the Production of Insecurity and Fear." *British Journal of Criminology* 53 (5): 824–42. http://dx.doi.org/10.1093/bjc/ azt029.

–. 2013c. "Business Improvement Associations and the Presentation of the Business Voice." *Urban Geography* 34 (2): 242–60. http://dx.doi.org/10.1080/ 02723638.2013.778654.

–. 2014. "The Humdrum of Legality and the Ordering of an Ethic of Care." *Law & Society Review* 48 (4): 709–39. http://dx.doi.org/10.1111/lasr.12107.

–. 2015. "Refashioning Vagrancy: A Tale of Law's Narrative of its Imagination." *International Journal of Law in Context* 11 (3): 320–40. http:// dx.doi.org/10.1017/S1744552315000178.

Ranasinghe, Prashan, and Mariana Valverde. 2006. "Governing Homelessness through Land-use: A Socio-legal Study of the Toronto Shelter Zoning By-law." *Canadian Journal of Sociology* 31 (3): 325–49. http://dx.doi.org/10.2307/20058713.

Robinson, Fiona. 2011. *The Ethics of Care: A Feminist Approach to Human Security.* Philadelphia: Temple University Press.

Rose, Nikolas. 1996. "The Death of the Social? Refiguring the Territory of Government." *Economy and Society* (25) (3): 327–56.

–. 1999. *Powers of Freedom: Reframing Political Thought.* Cambridge: Cambridge University Press. http://dx.doi.org/10.1017/CBO9780511488856.

Rossi, Peter H. 1989. *Down and Out in America: The Origins of Homelessness.* Chicago: University of Chicago Press.

–. 1994. "Troubling Families: Family Homelessness in America." *American Behavioral Scientist* 37 (3): 342–95. http://dx.doi.org/10.1177/0002764294037 003003.

Santos, Boaventura de Sousa. 1987. "Law: A Map of Misreading. Toward a Postmodern Conception of Law." *Journal of Law and Society* 14 (3): 279–302. http://dx.doi.org/10.2307/1410186.

Sarat, Austin. 1990. "'The Law Is All Over': Power, Resistance and the Legal Consciousness of the Welfare Poor." *Yale Journal of Law & the Humanities* 2 (2): 323–79.

Sartre, Jean-Paul. [1961] 1968. "Preface." In *The Wretched of the Earth* by Frantz Fanon, 7–31. New York: Grove Press.

Scarry, Elaine. 1985. *The Body in Pain: The Making and Unmaking of the World.* New York: Oxford University Press.

Seider, Scott. 2010. *Shelter: Where Harvard Meets the Homeless*. New York: Continuum Publishing Group.

Sennett, Richard. 1970. *The Uses of Disorder: Personal Identity and City Life*. New York: Alfred A. Knopf.

–. 1990. *The Conscience of the Eye: The Design of Social Life in Cities*. New York: Alfred A. Knopf.

Shaw, Clifford R. [1930] 1966. *The Jack-Roller: A Delinquent Boy's Own Story*. Chicago: University of Chicago Press. http://dx.doi.org/10.7208/chicago/9780226074962.001.0001.

Shearing, Clifford, and Les Johnston. 2010. "Nodal Wars and Network Fallacies: A Genealogical Analysis of Global Insecurities." *Theoretical Criminology* 14 (4): 495–514. http://dx.doi.org/10.1177/1362480610378828.

Silbey, Susan. 2005. "After Legal Consciousness." *Annual Review of Law and Social Science* 1 (1): 323–68. http://dx.doi.org/10.1146/annurev.lawsocsci.1.041604.115938.

Simon, Jonathan. 1999. "Law after Society." *Law & Social Inquiry* 24 (1): 143–94. http://dx.doi.org/10.1111/j.1747-4469.1999.tb00795.x.

–. 2007. *Governing through Crime: How the War on Crime Transformed American Democracy and Created a Culture of Fear*. Oxford: Oxford University Press.

Slote, Michael. 2007. *The Ethics of Care and Empathy*. New York: Routledge.

Snow, David A., and Leon Anderson. 1987. "Identity Work among the Homeless: The Verbal Construction and Avowal of Personal Identities." *American Journal of Sociology* 92 (6): 1336–1371.

–. 1993. *Down on Their Luck: A Study of Homeless Street People*. Berkeley: University of California Press.

Spencer, J. William, and Jennifer L. McKinney. 1997. "'We Don't Pay for Bus Tickets, but We Can Help You Find Work': The Micropolitics of Trouble in Human Service Encounters." *Sociological Quarterly* 38 (1): 185–203. http://dx.doi.org/10.1111/j.1533-8525.1997.tb02344.x.

Spitzer, Steven. 1987. "Security and Control in Capitalist Societies: The Fetishism of Security and the Secret Thereof." In, *Transcarceration: Essays in the Sociology of Social Control*. Edited by John Lowman, Robert J. Menzies, and Ted. S. Palys, 43–58. Aldershot: Gower Publishing.

Stanko, Elizabeth. 1990. *Everyday Violence: How Women and Men Experience Sexual and Physical Danger*. London: Pandora Press.

Stanko, Elizabeth, and Kathy Hobdell. 1993. "Assault on Men: Masculinity and Male Victimization." *British Journal of Criminology* 33 (3): 400–15.

Stark, Lousia R. 1994. "The Shelter as 'Total Institution': An Organizational Barrier to Remedying Homelessness." *American Behavioral Scientist* 37 (4): 553–62. http://dx.doi.org/10.1177/0002764294037004008.

Stone, Deborah. 1994. "Helter Shelter." *New Republic* 210 (26): 29–34.

Sutherland, Edwin H. [1937] 1956. *The Professional Thief, By a Professional Thief.* Chicago: The University of Chicago Press.

Takahashi, Lois M. 1996. "A Decade of Understanding Homelessness in the USA: From Characterization to Representation." *Progress in Human Geography* 20 (3): 291–310. http://dx.doi.org/10.1177/030913259602000301.

Teubner, Gunther. 1989. "How Law Thinks: Toward a Constructivist Epistemology of Law." *Law & Society Review* 23 (5): 727–57. http://dx.doi.org/10.2307/3053760.

Thomas, Carol. 1993. "De-Constructing Concepts of Care." *Sociology* 27 (4): 649–69. http://dx.doi.org/10.1177/0038038593027004006.

Tracy, Elizabeth, and Randy Stoecker. 1993. "Homelessness: The Service Providers' Perspective on Blaming the Victim." *Journal of Sociology and Social Welfare* 20 (1): 43–59.

Tyler, Kimberly A., and Morgan R. Beal. 2010. "The High Risk Environment of Homeless Young Adults: Consequences for Physical and Sexual Victimization." *Violence and Victims* 25 (1): 101–15. http://dx.doi.org/10.1891/0886-6708.25.1.101.

Valverde, Marianna. 1996. "Social Facticity and the Law: A Social Expert's Eyewitness Account of Law." *Social & Legal Studies* 5 (2): 201–17. http://dx.doi.org/10.1177/096466399600500204.

–. 2001. "Governing Security, Governing through Security." In *The Security of Freedom: Essays on Canada's Anti-Terrorism Bill.* Edited by Ronald J. Daniels, Patrick Macklem, and Kent Roach, 83–92. Toronto: University of Toronto Press.

–. 2011. "Questions of Security: A Framework for Research." *Theoretical Criminology* 15 (1): 3–22. http://dx.doi.org/10.1177/1362480610382569.

Wacquant, Loic. 1987. "Symbolic Violence and the Making of the French Agriculturalist: An Inquiry into Pierre Bourdieu's Sociology." *Australian and New Zealand Journal of Sociology* 23 (1): 65–88. http://dx.doi.org/10.1177/144078338702300105.

Walby, Kevin, and Randy Lippert. 2012. "Spatial Regulation, Dispersal, and the Aesthetics of the City: Conservation Officer Policing of Homeless People in Ottawa, Canada." *Antipode* 44 (3): 1015–33. http://dx.doi.org/10.1111/j.1467-8330.2011.00923.x.

Waldron, Jeremy. 2006. "Safety and Security." *Nebraska Law Review* 85 (2): 454–507.

West, Candace, and Sarah Fenstermaker. 1995. "Doing Difference." *Gender & Society* 9 (1): 8–37. http://dx.doi.org/10.1177/089124395009001002.

West, Candace, and Don H. Zimmerman. 1987. "Doing Gender." *Gender & Society* 1 (2): 125–51. http://dx.doi.org/10.1177/0891243287001002002.

West, Candace, and Don H. Zimmerman. 2009. "Accounting for Doing Gender." *Gender & Society* 23 (1): 112–22. http://dx.doi.org/10.1177/08912432083 26529.

Wharton, Carol S. 1989. "Splintered Visions: Staff/Client Disjunctions and their Consequences for Human Service Organizations." *Journal of Contemporary Ethnography* 18 (1): 50–71. http://dx.doi.org/10.1177/089124189 018001003.

Whyte, William F. [1943] 1967. *Street Corner Society: The Social Structure of an Italian Slum.* Chicago: University of Chicago Press.

Williams, Jean C. 2003. *"A Roof over My Head": Homeless Women and the Shelter Industry.* Boulder, CO: University Press of Colorado.

Wilson, James Q., and George L. Kelling. 1982. "Broken Windows: The Police and Neighborhood Safety." *Atlantic Monthly* 249 (3): 29–38.

–. 1989. "Making Neighborhoods Safe." *Atlantic Monthly* 263 (2): 46–52.

Wittig, Monique. 1985. "The Mark of Gender." *Feminist Issues* 5 (2): 3–12. http://dx.doi.org/10.1007/BF02685575.

Yngvesson, Barbara. 1993. *Virtuous Citizens, Disruptive Subjects: Order and Complaint in a New England Court.* New York: Routledge.

Zedner, Lucia. 2003a. "The Concept of Security: An Agenda for Comparative Analysis." *Legal Studies* 23 (1): 153–75. http://dx.doi.org/10.1111/j.1748-121X. 2003.tb00209.x.

–, 2003b. "Too Much Security?" *International Journal of the Sociology of Law* 31 (3): 155–84. http://dx.doi.org/10.1016/j.ijsl.2003.09.002.

–. 2009. *Security.* New York: Routledge.

Zukin, Sharon. 2004. *Point of Purchase: How Shopping Changed American Culture.* New York: Routledge.

# Index

Aboriginal clientele, 85
addiction, 85, 216–17. *See also* drugs;
  zero-tolerance policy
administrative chaos: approach
  to, 16; bed-booking procedure
  example, 205–9; The Bubble
  example, 183; definition, 12;
  from differing interpretations of
  care, 204–5, 209, 211; employee
  preference for, 209–10, 229; from
  humdrum, 12–13, 81, 211, 224;
  from legality, 12, 122, 123, 183–4,
  189–90, 224, 226; as norm, 12, 13,
  224, 226; as response to informal
  chaos, 182; zero-tolerance policy
  example, 222, 224
aestheticism, of ethic of care, 41–2,
  49, 80. *See also* physical space, of
  shelter
afternoon shift, 102–4, 205–6
age, 90–1, 172
aid: effectiveness concerns, 195. *See
  also* deservedness, of aid
air quality: The Bubble, 95, 138, 142.
  *See also* odour
alcohol addiction, 85. *See also* drugs;
  zero-tolerance policy
Alliance to End Homelessness, 49

Anderson, Leon, 22
Anderson, Nels, 18

Bachelard, Gaston, 34, 42, 157–8
basement, 61–70; access and
  entrance to, 61–2; kitchen and
  dining hall, 62–7; lighting, 68;
  overflow sleeping quarters, 17,
  67–8; quietness of, 68–9; reasons
  for client appreciation, 68–9; as
  symbolic of inconspicuous care,
  69–70; temperature, 68; washroom,
  69. *See also* kitchen and dining hall
bathrooms. *See* washrooms
Bauman, Zygmunt, 22
bed bugs, 143–51; as common
  part of shelters, 144; employee
  concerns, 78, 144–5, 147–8, 149;
  as health concern, 78, 144–5; and
  locker-emptying policy, 47–8, 146;
  management rejection as security
  concern, 148–9, 150; as nuisance,
  149; response to finding, 143–4,
  145–6; as security concern, 144,
  145, 147–8
bed number, 63–4, 135
bed-booking procedure, 205–9;
  management attempt to enforce

communication problems,
119–21; discretionary rights and,
116–17, 121, 190–1, 228, 244n3;
front-line employee perspective,
109–11; hierarchy and power
struggle between, 112; impact
of management on, 115–17;
impact on care, 58, 121; lack of
professionalism, 113; pay issue,
113–15; value of work and, 58,
117–19
employees, male: fears for female
staff safety, 162–63; relationship
with clients, 171–2, 173–4, 174–5,
176, 179–80; security and violence
fears, 160–2, 163–4, 242n1
employees, young female: Elizabeth
on, 91; impact on client-male
employee relationships, 171–2,
179–80; lack of violence fears, 157,
158, 167–71, 242n1; male fears for
safety of, 162–3
—RELATIONSHIP WITH CLIENTS,
91–7, 171–82; boundaries, 93–5,
175–6, 196–7; and client-male
employee relationships, 171–2,
179–80; concern about optics, 94;
impact of boundaries on care,
94; intimate, 93; management
concerns, 92–3, 97, 176;
manipulation potential, 83, 120,
174, 177, 178, 180–1; and older
female employees, 180–1; platonic,
91–2, 196–7; problems from, 92–3;
as product of gendered thinking of
care, 174–5; safety concerns, 95–7;
sex appeal aspect, 172–3; women
perceived as compassionate
aspect, 173–4; between young
men and female employees, 91–3.
See also employees, female

entitlement, 30
ethic of care: overview, 225;
ambiguity in, 6; comfort aspect,
26, 35; definition, 7, 25; as focus of
book, 13–14; gendered nature of,
7–8; help/helping, 26–8; impact
of legality and security on, 8,
9, 10–11; inconspicuousness of,
69–70; limitations to, 26–8; moral
dimension, 6–7; open-door policy
from, 82; preconditions aspect, 7;
role of space, 14; as self-evident,
201; substance of care aspect, 7,
25–6
—POLYSEMY OF: from differing
employee backgrounds and
perspectives, 11, 196, 202–3;
disorder from, 40, 204–5, 209,
211, 231; impact on employee
relations, 199, 201; impact on
legality, 190, 226; inevitability
of, 202
ethnography, 236–7, 244n1
Etzioni, Amitai, 72, 192
extra-legal, 14

Fanon, Frantz, 88
favouritism, 181
favours, 176–9, 181–2
Fenstermaker, Sarah, 242n2
Ferrill, Lisa, 5, 114, 231, 240n3
flawed consumers, 22
flu (influenza), 138–9, 142, 143
food, 29–30. See also kitchen and
dining hall
Foucault, Michel, 14, 157
francophone clientele, 85–6
free places, 45
front-line employees. See employees,
front-line
funding, 17, 36–7